EARTH POEMS

Earth Poems

Poems from Around the World
to Honor the Earth

Edited by
Ivo Mosley

HarperSanFrancisco
An Imprint of HarperCollins*Publishers*

FIRST EDITION
Set in Fairfield with Adobe Wood Type Ornaments
Library of Congress Cataloging-in-Publication Data
Earth poems : poems from around the world to honor the earth / edited by Ivo Mosley.
ISBN 0-06-251283-8 (pbk.)
1. Nature—Poetry.   2. Earth—Poetry.   I. Mosley, Ivo.
PN6110.N2E17   1996
808.81'936—dc20   95-38116

96 97 98 99 00 ❖ HAD 10 9 8 7 6 5 4 3 2 1

TO XANTHE

Table of Contents

Acknowledgments

I would like to thank my wife, Xanthe; my mother-in-law, Helen Oppenheimer; and Richard Barnes of Frontier Publishing for the help they gave me in the making of this book. My thanks also go to Nancy Palmer Jones at HarperSanFrancisco for her careful improvements.

The gods are just, and of our pleasant vices
Make instruments to plague us.

WILLIAM SHAKESPEARE
KING LEAR 5.3.172–73

Introduction

End of the twentieth century, the world; rivers stinking of effluent, poison waste diffuse in the air, the rain itself become poison—

Trees dying, the soil a sterile holding bank for chemicals; cities, like giant cankers thriving, their millions mostly poor and hungry, their tendrils stretching to the far corners of the earth, draining the land of life—

The earth's riches are plundered for greed, then turned to garbage. Human domination of the earth is all but complete, and some would say almost over.

In the midst of all this, it's hard to feel good about being human. The bright visions of our ancestors have turned to dust or worse in our hands. The question is not "Is nature worth preserving?" but "Is humanity worth preserving?"

This book is an argument for "yes." It's a record of the human spirit seeking out what is good, railing at what is bad, wanting to find harmony; trying to create something in the image with which we are all born, an image that goes under much-abused names like God, Love, and Truth. The poetry here finds beauty in that image and ugliness in its destruction. *Earth Poems* argues that our exploitation of the planet and our spiritual sickness are aspects of one and the same phenomenon. The earth's welfare depends upon the care that our human society gives it. Humanity is a part of nature; the care we give nature is one aspect of caring for ourselves.

The poems come from most of the world's literatures available in translation, as well as from our own. They speak from that common human voice that is all but lost in what Nadezhda Mandelstam has called "the din of life, the furious drumfire of the demands and aspirations of the moment; the noise such that it drowns out everything else in the world, and amidst which one by one the poets fall silent, because they cannot hear the sound of their own voices."

As we destroy the beauty of the world, we are destroying our human spirit. If we succeed, poems like those included here will become relics of the past, a historical creation best left buried so that it does not kindle a fierce longing in us for something we may never regain. But if, instead, we achieve what now seems impossible—if we cease our poisoning of the earth and our destruction of its other species—we may yet live to feel proud again of our humanity and of our place in creation.

There's no point in pretending that we can flourish on earth without effort; we have to struggle, like all species, for our well-being. But our dominance must be restrained. The concerted destruction of our planet, involving governments, corporations, and all the interlocked economies of the world, is something we as individuals may feel powerless to prevent. But the growth of democracy means that now, more than ever before, individuals are a powerful part of the whole. We live in an age of mass decision. In the democratic world, whatever the vanity of our leaders may lead them to believe, they are no longer leaders but followers; the voters are in charge. If the great majority of people put the long-term welfare of our species before the immediate gratification of their appetites, the wave of destruction will be halted.

A change of mood is needed in the human population of the planet. The successes of science have led us to believe that we can have everything. When devices for saving labor put many out of work, the response was to create employment by waste: goods are now made to deteriorate quickly so that more goods will be needed to replace them. More people with more greed and more ability to exploit the earth have made it a dying place. Our technology has won for us a limited autonomy within nature, but this "power" is as substantial as a mirage. We have replaced the beautiful cruelty of nature with drab and spirit-murdering wastelands of concrete, asphalt, plastic, and plate glass.

Anxieties about our condition are hard to acknowledge. The words "This is the end of living and the beginning of survival" used to be ascribed to Chief Seattle. In fact, they were an addition to his famous speech by Ted Perry,[1] an Anglo-American playwright, for a 1971 TV program. It seems we must attribute our own anxieties to a long-dead victim of relentless "progress." Now, we have to face the fact that even our survival is at risk. *Earth Poems* speaks not just for survival but also for the recovery of some of what we've lost. Day by day, species of the earth are disappearing; what will remain after our orgy is finished no one can tell. We may never recover those species, but we can recover what we have lost inside of us, which is respect for the world and joy in being a part of it.

Most people in industrialized countries now live in cities, and it's hard for them to be aware of the effect their lifestyle is having on the earth. For those who want to know, information is available in nature programs on television, in newspapers, and in books. If lemmings had newspapers, maybe they wouldn't jump. The aims of this book are not so much to celebrate nature and warn of impending catastrophe as to help us understand how we got here and to salvage something from the wreckage of our self-esteem. *Earth Poems* is an argument against the unrestrained pursuit of affluence. It is worth asking what affluence has done for us. Happiness is subjective, so the question can only be asked: has the single-minded pursuit of material goods made us more happy?

C. D. Darlington, plant geneticist and historian of human society, wrote, "The twentieth century has been devoted to submerging impartially nature and civilization, art and individuality, under the festering sores of economic growth."[2] In an attempt to avoid this conclusion, intellectuals have busied themselves trying to redefine nature, civilization, art, and individuality. But a rose by any other name is still a rose, and our knowledge of what these things once meant haunts us. As words (like so many other things) are hacked about and sold to the highest bidder or to the most vociferous lobbying group, poetry is the last stronghold of the sacred word.

The poems in these pages share a passionate concern that life should be lived with love, honor, and a belief in the importance of truth. They speak with awe of that great enterprise that is not of our making, the Creation. Poetry depends on the living word for life; it is the guardian of our integrity, our spirituality, and our language. In Simone Weil's words, it is the "light of eternity" made manifest in living words.

Translations: A Note

There is a saying: "Poetry is what gets lost in translation." I would say rather, "Rhymed verse is what gets lost in translation," or more accurately, translators choose which element—poetry or verse—they favor retaining. I have chosen translations that favor poetry. Successful translations that rhyme are like survivors of a massacre—astonishing mostly for their survival.

Every literate person is familiar with the greatest translation in the English language, the Bible, in its revisions from Tyndale through the King James Version to the New Revised Standard Version. The principle followed in that translation is fidelity to structure, meaning, and beauty of language, and that's the principle most translators have adopted here.

Pushkin wrote, "Translators are the post-horses of enlightenment." This statement is no less true today, when the mail is delivered in trucks.

CHAPTER I

Nature

Yes to the Earth

So radiant in certain mornings' light
With its roses and its cypress trees
Is Earth, or with its grain and olives;

So suddenly it is radiant on the soul,
Which stands then alone and forgetful
Though just a moment earlier the soul
Wept bloody tears or dwelt in bitterness;

So radiant in certain mornings' light
Is Earth, and in its silence so expressive,
This wondrous lump rolling in its skies;
Beautiful, tragic in solitude, yet smiling,

That the soul, unasked, replies,
"Yes," replies, "Yes" to the Earth,
To the indifferent Earth, "Yes!,"

Even though next instant skies
Should darken, roses too, and cypresses,
Or the effort of life grow heavier still,
The act of breathing even more heroic,

"Yes," replies the battered soul to Earth,
So radiant in the light of certain mornings,
Beautiful above all things, and human hope.

Sibilla Aleramo, Italian, 1876–1960, tr. I. M.

Nature is our name for everything except ourselves and our contrivances. As the look of the world is more and more shaped by human interference, the word *nature* is being replaced by the word *environment*—as if the rest of creation only exists for us to live in.

While nature was still healthy, human beings both wondered and cursed at its beautiful tyranny. We lived within its framework, and it punished our mistakes. Its uncounted species competed with us for the resources we all needed in order to prosper. Providing sustenance and wonder, causing us to suffer, watching with indifference while we die—nature was a hard taskmaster.

When I die I don't care how God
Treats the earth; let it parch, let it flood.

The earth doesn't know what it consumes:
Skeletons of sheep, carcasses of lion.

Ma'arri, Syrian, 973–1057, tr. George Wightman and Abdullah al-Udhari

But there was pleasure, too, to be had. The joy of being part of nature is evident in the next five poems, where nature and poet are one in the simple fellowship of coexistence.

Winter

Here's my story; the stag cries,
Winter snarls as summer dies.

The wind bullies the low sun
In poor light; the seas moan.

Shapeless bracken is turning red,
The wild goose raises its desperate head.

Birds' wings freeze where fields are hoary.
The world is ice. That's my story.

Anonymous, Irish, ninth century, tr. Brendan Kennelly

 ## *The Moon*

At dead of night,
The darkness seems to have deepened.
To the call of geese
The sky is listening; across it
Appears the passing moon.

Hitomaro, Japanese, seventh century, tr. I. M.

The Blackbird's Song

The little bird is whistling now
From the tip of its yellow beak;
The blackbird on the yellow bough
Is calling over the lake.

Anonymous, Irish, eighth to ninth century, tr. Brendan Kennelly

*Song of Caribou, Musk Oxen, Women,
and Men Who Would Be Manly*

Glorious it is to see
The caribou flocking down from the forests
And beginning
Their wandering to the north.
Timidly they watch
For the pitfalls of man.
Glorious it is to see
The great herds from the forests
Spreading out over plains of white,
Glorious to see.
      Yayai, ya, yiya.

Glorious it is to see
Early summer's shorthaired caribou
Beginning to wander.
Glorious to see them trot
To and fro
Across the promontories,
Seeking a crossing place.
      Yayai, ya, yiya.

Glorious it is
To see the great musk oxen
Gathering in herds.
The little dogs they watch for
When they gather in herds.

Glorious to see.
>Yayai, ya, yiya.

Glorious it is
To see young women
Gathering in little groups
And paying visits in the houses—
Then all at once the men
Do so want to be manly,
While the girls simply
Think of some little lie.
>Yayai, ya, yiya.

Glorious it is
To see longhaired winter caribou
Returning to the forests.
Fearfully they watch for the little people.
While the herd follows the ebb mark of the sea
With a storm of clattering hooves.
Glorious it is
When wandering time is come.
>Yayai, ya, yiya.

Anonymous, Eskimo, tr. (1921–24) Radmussen and Calvert

Writing is young compared to spoken language: five thousand years compared to perhaps five hundred thousand. Historians of language speculate that poetry is as old as language itself, which may have originated as chants cajoling nature to provide for human wants.

The Rain Man Praises Himself

No house is ever too thick-built
To keep me, the rain, from getting in.
I am well known to huts and roofs,
A grandson of Never-Been-There,
I am mother of the finest grasses,
Father of green fields everywhere.
My arrows do not miss their aim,
They strike the owners of huts.
I am a terror to clay walls and the architecture of termites,
Fear-inspiring above and below.
When I pour in in the morning, people say:
"He has cut off our lips and stopped our mouths,
He is giving us juicy fruits.
He has rained and brought us mushrooms,
White as ivory."

Oral tradition, Aandongan, southern Africa;
written down, 1920s; tr. Pettinen and Trask

The word *poet* comes from the Greek for "maker" or "creator." In the poem that follows, the presence of the poet is as important as the imagery of nature.

 You know the place: then

Leave Crete and come to us
waiting where the grove is
pleasantest, by precincts

sacred to you; incense
smokes on the altar, cold
streams murmur through the

apple branches, a young
rose thicket shades the ground
and quivering leaves pour

down deep sleep; in meadows
where horses have grown sleek
among spring flowers, dill

scents the air. Queen! Cyprian!
Fill our gold cups with love
stirred into clear nectar

Sappho, Greek, sixth century B.C., tr. Mary Barnard

Natural imagery can mirror the mood of the poet or it can provide the most extreme contrast, as in the next poem. Sweeney, a pagan prince of ancient Ireland, was driven mad by the curses of priests and the horrors of war.

✹ *The Cliff of Alteran*

As Sweeney ranged over Connaught
  He came to a lonely glen
Where a stream poured over a cliff
  And many holy men

Were gathered. Trees, heavy with fruit,
  Grew there by the score.

There were sheltering ivy bowers
    And apple trees galore.

Deer, hares, and swine were there.
    On the warm cliff fat seals slept.
Sweeney watched while through his heart
    The raving madness swept.

Anonymous, Irish, twelfth century, tr. Brendan Kennelly

In the three-line haiku of Basho, natural imagery and the poet's observation capture a mood, a moment seized for contemplation.

 By the road,
In the hedgerow, a rose—
My horse ate it.

(Written while looking at the ruins of a great castle)
 Summer grasses—
All that remain
Of warriors' dreams.

 Withered branch
A crow settles on it—
Autumn dusk.

Red, red,
The sun is unrelenting—
Autumn wind.

(Written on a journey)
 Fleas, lice;
My horse pisses, right
By my pillow.

(The most famous of all haiku)
 Old pond—
Frog jumps in,
Sound of the water.

Basho, Japanese, 1644–94, tr. I. M.

We humans seem to combine the characteristics of many other animals. We can be fierce like tigers, sadistic like cats, gentle and playful like lambs, or stolid and peaceful like sheep. We can be cooperative like the social insects, rapacious like great black-backed gulls, or busy inhabitants of filth like the dung beetle. Our characteristics are mirrored in nature all around us, at times literally, at others metaphorically, and this is the source of poetic imagery.

A single natural image—the washing of waves back and forth on the seashore—pervades the next poem, giving it a sense of the relentless and desolate indifference of time.

The Old Woman of Beare

The sea crawls from the shore
Leaving there
The despicable weed,
A corpse's hair.
In me,
The desolate withdrawing sea.

The Old Woman of Beare am I
Who once was beautiful.
Now all I know is how to die.
I'll do it well.

Look at my skin
Stretched tight on the bone.
Where kings have pressed their lips,
The pain, the pain.

I don't hate the men
Who swore truth was in their lies.
One thing alone I hate—
Women's eyes.

The young sun
Gives its youth to everyone,
Touching green with gold.
In me, the cold.

The cold. Yet still a seed
Burns there.
Women love only money now.

But when
I loved, I loved
Young men.

Young men whose horses galloped
On many an open plain
Beating lightning from the ground.
I loved such men.

And still the sea
Rears and plunges into me,
Shoving, rolling through my head
Images of the drifting dead.

A soldier cries
Pitifully about his plight;
A king fades
Into the shivering night.

Does not every season prove
That the acorn hits the ground?
Have I not known enough of love
To know it's lost as soon as found?

I drank my fill of wine with kings,
Their eyes fixed on my hair.
Now among the stinking hags
I chew the cud of prayer.

Time was the sea
Brought kings as slaves to me.

Now I near the face of God
And the crab crawls through my blood.

I loved the wine
That thrilled me to my fingertips;
Now the spinster wind
Stitches salt into my lips.

The coward sea
Slouches away from me.
Fear brings back the tide
That made me stretch at the side
Of him who'd take me briefly for his bride.

The sea grows smaller, smaller now.
Farther, farther it goes
Leaving me here where the foam dries
On the deserted land,
Dry as my shrunken thighs,
As the tongue that presses my lips,
As the veins that break through my hands.

Anonymous, Irish, ninth century, tr. Brendan Kennelly

In the next poem, nature is the setting for love, peace, happiness, rest, and magic.

 I know a bank whereon the wild thyme blows,
Where oxslips and the nodding violet grows;
Quite over-canopied with luscious woodbine,
With sweet musk-roses and with eglantine.

There sleeps Titania sometime of the night,
Lull'd in these flowers with dances and delight;
And there the snake throws her enameled skin,
Weed wide enough to wrap a fairy in.

William Shakespeare, 1564–1616,
A Midsummer Night's Dream 2.1.249–56

The comforts of civilization insulate us from the natural world and allow city dwellers more or less to ignore it. Eighteenth-century Europeans were so infatuated with the achievements of humanity that untamed nature barely featured in their poetry. The romantic movement reacted against this human-centeredness. Poets pointed out that humanity is part of nature, not its master, and that there is pleasure to be had in being a small part of a large whole. Goethe wrote:

> The reason I prefer the society of nature is that nature is always right, and the error, if any, can only be on my side. But if I hold converse with men, they will err, and I will err, and so on forever, and we will never get to see matters clearly.

Wordsworth, like many romantics, was painfully conscious of humanity's failings. Here, he laments what we've made of our world and looks back to an earlier time when the world seemed full of wonders.

The world is too much with us; late and soon,
Getting and spending, we lay waste our powers:
Little we see in Nature that is ours;
We have given our hearts away, a sordid boon!
This sea that bares her bosom to the moon;
The winds that will be howling at all hours,
And are up-gathered now like sleeping flowers;
For this, for everything, we are out of tune;

It moves us not.—Great God! I'd rather be
A Pagan suckled in a creed outworn;
So might I, standing on this pleasant lea,
Have glimpses that would make me less forlorn;
Have sight of Proteus rising from the sea;
Or hear old Triton blow his wreathed horn.

William Wordsworth, English, 1770–1850

Friedrich Hölderlin, a German romantic, set himself the heroic task of fusing German "rationality" with the "holy fire" of ancient Greece—and he went mad trying to accomplish it. The poem that follows was written during his years of madness, which may explain the signature and date appended. In this poem, he seems to have thrown off the trappings of intellectual life.

 Summer

Still the time of year is here to see, and fields
Of summer stand in lovely glow and mildness.
The green of fields is gloriously laid out,
To where the brook glides down with little waves.

So strolls the day outside through hills and valleys
Unstoppable, and with its fiery beams,
And clouds stroll peacefully in high-up spaces;
The year seems self-restraining in its glory.

March 9, 1940   Your humble servant, Scardanelli

Friedrich Hölderlin, 1770–1843, German, tr. I. M.

Wang Wei, who was a painter as well as a poet, hears human talk as one of the natural sounds of the forest.

Empty mountains, no one to be seen.
Only the sound of voices, people talking.
Returning shadows penetrate the forest,
Bouncing off the colored moss above.

Wang Wei, 699–761, Chinese, version by I. M. from various translations

Cutting down trees has provided people with room to make fields and put up houses, with fuel to keep warm, and with wood for use. But when few trees are left, when the landscape is impoverished, when the wind holds sway over all, then an intelligent human realizes we have gone too far.

Unfortunately, dollars—or even sheer pigheadedness—often hold precedence over intelligence.

 Letter from the Bird Community to the Mayor

Lord Mayor,
we the bird community called a meeting
one fine clear morning
on the roof of the deserted Parliament building.

All sent their intellectuals to represent them,
all but the crows, for they were too busy
mourning their loved ones, shot dead
and drifting down the River Klang.

Special guests came as observers,
a delegation of butterflies,
involved in the issue.

Lord Mayor,
though we had no hand in electing you
since franchise is not for the feathered,
still we honored you for your promise
of a Green City.

Alas, they have desecrated the Green of nature
to worship the Green of dollars.
Since Kuala Lumpur's mud turned to concrete,
we birds have been the silent sufferers;
the late Woodpecker was crushed under a felled tree,
Turtle-dove was given a fancy name
while he and his kind were cooped up in cages.

The Sparrow delegation is protesting
against the insult in your proverb
"Deaf sparrows feed in the rain";
Sparrow and Titmouse both feel
it's most improper of you to call
certain parts of your anatomy
by their names, when you well know
your "pecker" and your "tit" can't fly
(you have deflated our egos
in the process of inflating yours).

Lord Mayor,
this letter requests that in your wisdom
you will protect each branch, each root,
each leaf, each petal, each bower,
for these have been our homes through the centuries,
and it would also be for the good of man,

his health and happiness, his peace of mind,
to let nature and its myriad beauties bloom
in the brilliant sun.

Usman Awang, Malaysian, born 1929, tr. Adibah Amin

The prime concern of people must obviously be the welfare of people. But how can people thrive in a world depleted of beauty and diversity?

The next poem mourns the destruction that took place in Russia during its years under Stalin. Many in the West imagined that technological ineptitude would preserve Communist countries from the kind of destruction we were seeing in our own countries. But this hope turned out to be grievously wrong; what Communist rulers lacked in technology they more than made up for in carelessness.

The following poem was written before 1934. The poet was a religious mystic, and he was troubled by violence against the land at a time when other poets were understandably more preoccupied with violence against humans. He was shot by a firing squad in October 1937. This poem was discovered among the notes of the secret police, appended as evidence of his crime.

The news received was bitter:
the rippling waves of the Aral Sea in dead ooze,
the storks rare in the Ukraine,
the feather grass drooping in Mozdok,
and in the bright Sarov desert
the wheels of machines squealing underground.
Black clouds brought us further news;
the blue Volga is getting shallow,
evil men in Kerzhents are burning
the green pine fortresses,

the Suzhdal wheat fields bring forth
lichen and stubble.
The cranes call to us
as they're forced to fly in for remains.
The nesting finches' feathers fall out
and they're plagued by ravening aphids,
the furry bees have only
the big veteran mushrooms to buzz at.
The news was black:
that there was no home land left,
as if there were no cherries in October,
when the darkness outside
decides the heart is an ax
that will heat the shivering house,
but the logs don't obey the ax
and howl at the moon.
It's painful when the heart sinks,
but your gray-haired mother is a friend.
How terrifying, to crucify a poem!
The news burned into our souls,
there is no home land left,[1]
the rippling waves of the Aral Sea in dead ooze,
Gritsko is silent in the Ukraine,
and the North, that frozen swan,
has flowed out onto the shelterless waves,
notifying the ships
that there is no home land left.

Nikolai Kluyev, Russian, 1887–1937, tr. Richard McKane

As the world is more and more affected by what we do, we can no longer know whether storms, droughts, floods, plagues, and other natural disasters are acts of God or acts of humans.

The Sun Parrots Are Late This Year

FOR CHICO MENDEZ, MURDERED
BRAZILIAN ENVIRONMENTALIST

The great forests of the world are burning down,
Far away in Amazon they burn,
Far beyond our eyes the trees are cut
And cleared and heaped and fired:
Ashes fill the rivers for miles and miles,
The rivers are stained with blood of mighty trees.
Great rivers are brothers of great forests
And immense clouds shadowing the rose-lit waters
Are cousins of this tribe of the earth-gods
Under the ancient watch of the stars:
All should be secure and beautiful forever,
Dwarfing man generation after generation,
Inspiring man, feeding him with dreams and strength.
But over there it is not so; man is giant
And the forest dwindles; it will soon be nothing,
Shrubs sprouting untidily in scorched black earth.
The sun will burn the earth, before now shadowed
For a hundred thousand years, dark and dripping,
Hiding jeweled insects and thick-veined plants,
Blue-black orchids and white hearts, red macaws,
The green lace of ferns, gold butterflies, opal snakes.
Everything shrivels and dust begins to blow:
It is as if acid was poured on the silken land.

It is far from here now, but it is coming nearer,
Those who love forests are also cut down.
This month, this year, we may not suffer:
The brutal way things are, it will come.
Already the cloud patterns are different each year,
The winds blow from new directions,
The rain comes earlier, beats down harder,
Or it is dry when the pastures thirst.
In this dark, overarching Essequibo forest
I walk near the shining river in the green paths
Cool and green as melons laid in running streams.
I cannot imagine all the forests going down,
The great black hogs not snouting for the pulp of fruit,
All this beauty and power and shining life gone.
But in far, once-emerald Amazon the forest dies
By fire, fiercer than bright axes.
The roar of the wind in trees is sweet,
Reassuring, the heavens stretch far and bright
Above the loneliness of mist-shrouded forest trails,
And there is such a feel of softness in the evening air.
Can it be that all of this will go, leaving the clean-boned
    land?
I wonder if my children, come this way,
Will see the great forest spread green and tall and far
As it spreads now far and green for me.
Is it my imagination that the days are furnace-hot,
The sun-parrots late or not come at all this year?

Ian McDonald, born Trinidad, 1933

Can we really live without loving the land, the sky, the trees? It seems so, but for how long? We have nature in our power now, just as a peasant has his donkey, but a wise peasant loves his donkey and looks after it. Dead donkeys do no more work. It's an old story—that those with power must learn restraint in using it.

In the next poem, a busy Roman official looks with envy on an old man who, he imagines, has had a life of carefree toil.

✳ *The Old Man of Verona*

This man has lived his life in his own fields.
The house that saw him as a little lad
Sees him an old man: leaning on his staff,
On the same earth he crawled on, he will tell you
The centuries that one low roof has seen.
Fate has not dragged him through the brawling crowds,
Nor ever, as a restless traveler,
Has he drunk at unknown springs; no greed of gain
Kept him a-quaking on the perilous seas.
No trumpet sounded for him the attack,
No lawsuit brought him to the raucous courts.
In politics unskilled, knowing naught of the neighboring
    town,
His eye takes pleasure in a wider sky.
The years he'll reckon by alternate crops
And not by parliaments: spring has her flowers,
Autumn her apples: so the year goes by.
The same wide field that hides the setting sun
Sees him return again;
His light the measure of this plain man's day.
That massive oak he remembers a sapling once,
Yon grove of trees grew old along with him.

Verona further seems than India,
Lake Garda is remote as the Red Sea.
Yet, strength indomitable and sinews firm,
The old man stands, a rock among his grandsons.
Let you go gadding, gape at furthest Spain:
You'll have seen life; but this old man has lived.

Claudian, Roman, circa 370–405, tr. Helen Waddell

Nature's laws do not favor humanity over other species. We make our own laws to do that, and we need new man-made laws to protect us from destroying nature.

In Chinese poetry, nature provides a retreat from the disappointments of living with one's fellow human beings. Han Shan took to the mountains as a recluse when his efforts to conform with family expectations failed. His poems were said to have been collected by an admiring local bureaucrat from scribbles on rocks and trees. Han Shan means "cold mountain"; he called himself after the place where he chose to live.

Life on Cold Mountain

My house is at the foot of the green cliff,
My garden, a jumble of weeds I no longer bother to mow.
New vines dangle in twisted strands
Over old rocks rising steep and high.
Monkeys make off with the mountain fruits,
The white heron crams his bill with fish from the pond,
While I, with a book or two of the immortals,
Read under the trees—mumble, mumble.

Han Shan, Chinese, circa 800, tr. Burton Watson

Li Po was so venerated during his life that the emperor would personally season his soup. But he too needed the company of nature, and he spent most of his life wandering. If poetry is wine, his poems are distilled spirit.

 ## Summer in the Mountains

Too lazy to shift my white feather fan
I lie naked in the green woods.
Hanging my hat on a rock,
I bare my head to the breeze in the pines.

Silent Night

Moonlight floods the end of my bed.
I wonder, has frost fallen?
Sitting up, I look at the moon.
Lying back, I think of home.

Talk in the Mountains

You ask me, "Why dwell among green mountains?"
I laugh in silence; my soul is quiet.
Peach blossom follows the moving water;
Here is a heaven and earth, beyond the world of men.

Li Po, Chinese, 701–62, versions by I. M.

CHAPTER 2

Love

The Reign of Love

The world, with steady trust,
Changes in regular seasons.
Seeds that struggle out of earth
Keep to predetermined bounds.
Daily the golden sun
Leads with his chariot the rosy dawn,
And nightly the evening star
Leads out the moon to rule the sky.
The greedy surging sea
Is kept to certain limits
Lest our uncertain world
Be swamped within its flood.

The sequence of these things is tied—
Seas ruled, lands overseen—
By Love which rules in heaven.
Should Love let go the reins,
All things which now are linked
Would move straightway to war;
Things which are beautiful and live in trust
Would fight, and tear apart the scheme of things.

Love, in sacred treaty,
Holds peoples fast in friendship;
Love, in sacred marriage,
Binds lovers fast in innocence;
Love makes laws also for those
Who wish to stay faithful in friendship.

O happy humankind,
If Love, by which heaven is ruled,
Could rule your minds, too!

Boethius, Roman, circa 475–524, tr. I. M.

Love is the force that binds us together and the motive for making good of our lives. When love goes wrong or is denied, then hatred, greed, and envy take over, bringing with them a welter of destruction.

Love between the sexes is the most obvious kind of love that we need for our survival. But no less indispensable are the kinds of love between parents and children, between friends, between companions, between us and the world around us, and the greater love that—it sometimes seems—inspires material substance with life.

Poetry is born of love. It plunders the universe for its imagery, not harming but praising as it goes. Love of the world around us is perhaps the most important kind of all right now, when the world lies at our mercy.

As we destroy the loveliness of the world, are we killing love itself?

 The man
who does not love his children
cannot enjoy spring flowers.

Basho, Japanese, 1644–94, tr. I. M.

In the next poem, love is seen as the one thing left to hang on to in a world where all else of value is being lost.

Dover Beach

The sea is calm tonight.
The tide is full, the moon lies fair
Upon the straits;—on the French coast the light
Gleams and is gone; the cliffs of England stand,
Glimmering and vast, out in the tranquil bay.
Come to the window, sweet is the night-air!
Only, from the long line of spray
Where the sea meets the moon-blanch'd land,
Listen! You hear the grating roar
Of pebbles which the waves draw back, and fling,
At their return, up the high strand,
Begin, and cease, and then again begin,
With tremulous cadence slow, and bring
The eternal note of sadness in.

Sophocles long ago
Heard it on the Aegean, and it brought
Into his mind the turbid ebb and flow
Of human misery; we
Find also in the sound a thought,
Hearing it by this distant northern sea.

The Sea of Faith
Was once, too, at the full, and round earth's shore
Lay like the folds of a bright girdle furl'd.
But now I only hear
Its melancholy, long, withdrawing roar,
Retreating, to the breath

Of the night-wind, down the vast edges drear
And naked shingles of the world.

Ah, love, let us be true
To one another! for the world, which seems
To lie before us like a land of dreams,
So various, so beautiful, so new,
Hath really neither joy, nor love, nor light,
Nor certitude, nor peace, nor help for pain;
And we are here as on a darkling plain
Swept with confused alarms of struggle and flight,
Where ignorant armies clash by night.

Matthew Arnold, English, 1822–88

Love has to contend with all the violence within and without us, and it gets little help from the culture of our times. Friendship especially suffers when everyone's goal is simply to satisfy their wants.

 ## To a Friend

When the moon's splendor shines in a clear sky,
Stand outside and gaze at heaven's brightness,
Marveling how the pure lamp of the moon
Embraces in its beauty two dear friends
In body separate, but bound in mind by love.
Though face to loving face we may not look,
Yet let this light assure us of our love.
Your faithful friend sends you these small verses,

And if on your part friendship's bond stays firm,
May strength and joy be with you all your days!

Walafrid Strabo, German, 809–49, tr. from Latin by I. M.

In the next poem, Tu Fu dreams he is visited by Li Po, his great—and senior—contemporary. Li Po once had the world at his feet but is now in exile, lonely and poor.

Dreaming of Li Po

When death's the cause of parting, tears are finite;
When life's the cause, then grief goes on and on.
The land you're traveling to is full of plague;
I wait in vain for news of you in exile.

Last night, old friend, I saw you in a dream;
I realize now how much you're on my mind.
Caught like a bird, snared in a net of trouble,
Have you found feather wings to visit me?

I fear you may no longer be alive.
No living soul could travel a road so far,
Starting out when maple woods were green,
Returning through mountain passes in the dark.

The moon, sinking low, now fills the roof beams;
I half expect to see it light your face;
The water's deep, the waves are wide and rolling;
Take care, don't let the river dragons get you!

Tu Fu, Chinese, 713–70, version by I. M. from notes and tr. by Hawkes

A laconic poem by Li Po survives, requital for the one just given.

 ## *To Tu Fu*

> On the Mountain of Boiled Rice I met Tu Fu,
> Wearing a bamboo hat in the hot midday;
> Pray, how is it that you have grown so thin?
> Is it because you suffer from poetry?

Li Po, Chinese, 701–62, tr. David Payne

The next poem is a classic poem of friendship between two poets of ancient Greece.

Heraclitus

> They told me, Heraclitus, they told me you were dead,
> They brought me bitter news to hear and bitter tears to shed.
> I wept as I remembered how often you and I
> Had tired the sun with talking and sent him down the sky.
>
> And now that you are lying, my dear old Carian guest,
> A handful of gray ashes, cold and long ago at rest,
> Your pleasant voices are not dead, your nightingales[1] yet wake;
> For Death, though he takes all away, yet these he cannot take.

Callimachus, Greek, circa 305–240 B.C., after tr. by William Cory

Sappho's poetry, once filling nine volumes, is preserved now only in fragments, mostly as short examples of grammar or meter in the work of later writers. But even these fragments have a quality that no other poet can match. The following fragments describe a love that—like the love in Shakespeare's sonnets—seems to straddle the boundary between friendship and eroticism.

 Without warning

As a whirlwind
swoops on an oak
Love shakes my heart

Sappho, Greek, sixth century B.C., tr. Mary Barnard

 I have had not one word from her

Frankly I wish I were dead.
When she left, she wept

a great deal; she said to
me, "This parting must be
endured, Sappho. I go unwillingly."

I said, "Go, and be happy
but remember (you know
well) whom you leave shackled by love

"If you forget me, think
of our gifts to Aphrodite
and all the loveliness that we shared

"all the violet tiaras,
braided rosebuds, dill and
crocus twined around your young neck

"myrrh poured on your head
and on soft mats girls with
all that they most wished for beside them

"while no voices chanted
choruses without ours,
no woodlot bloomed in spring without song. . . ."

Sappho, Greek, sixth century B.C., tr. Mary Barnard

 I confess

I love that
which caresses
me. I believe

Love has his
share in the
Sun's brilliance
and virtue

Sappho, Greek, sixth century B.C., tr. Mary Barnard

Friendship gone wrong is the subject of the next poem, written by a soldier-poet
of ancient Greece. Love let down is the origin of bitterness and hatred.

 Shipwreck

Slammed by the surf on the beach
naked at Salmydessos, where the screw-haired men
of Thrace, taking him in

will entertain him (he will have much to undergo,
chewing on slavery's bread),
stiffened with cold, and loops of seaweed from the slime
tangling his body about,
teeth chattering as he lies in abject helplessness
flat on his face like a dog
beside the beach-break where the waves come shattering in.
And let me be there to watch;
for he did me wrong and set his heel on our good faith,
he who had once been my friend.

Archilochus, Greek, seventh century B.C., tr. Richard Lattimore

When poets write of sexual love, it's not surprising that they look to nature for their imagery. In spring, nature seethes with such love: trees and flowers dangle out their organs for airborne copulation on a massive scale, birds meet midair in a tangle of feathers, and dogs have to be kept inside so that their matings don't stop traffic. Only humankind, lustful all the year round, seems to find this kind of love complicated, with sex a jumble of different desires and motives: inclination, procreation, conjugation, dissipation.

The next poem is uncomplicated enough; its subject is mutual erotic attraction.

Moving fast, a girl came to me one night,
      Hurrying to abscond from innocence.

When she walked, her body said to the wind,
      If you're serious, this is the way you should stir

The branches.

Mu'tazz, Iraqi, 861–908, tr. George Wightman and Abdullah al-Udhari

A strong sexual urge is favored in an obvious way by evolution; the stronger it is, the more likely it'll result in an act that passes it on. But continual promiscuous copulation doesn't favor the successful rearing of children, so evolution has made us choosy as to time, place, and partner and has given us a strong desire to be faithful, to make a union that will be lifelong.

While both sexes share these urges, they seem unequally distributed, and a lot of poetry by men has been devoted to getting women to say yes when they have already said no.

To His Coy Mistress

Had we but world enough, and time,
This coyness, Lady, were no crime.
We would sit down and think which way
To walk, and pass our long love's day.
Thou by the Indian Ganges' side
Should'st rubies find: I by the tide
Of Humber would complain. I would
Love you ten years before the Flood,
And you should, if you please, refuse
Till the Conversion of the Jews.
My vegetable love should grow
Vaster than empires, and more slow;
An hundred years should go to praise
Thine eyes and on thy forehead gaze;
Two hundred to adore each breast;
But thirty thousand to the rest.
An age at least to every part,
And the last age should show your heart:
For, Lady, you deserve this state;
Nor would I love at lesser rate.

But at my back I always hear
Time's wingéd chariot hurrying near:
And yonder all before us lie
Deserts of vast eternity.
Thy beauty shall no more be found;
Nor, in thy marble vault, shall sound
My echoing song: then worms shall try
That long-preserved virginity,
And your quaint honor turn to dust;
And into ashes all my lust.
The grave's a fine and private place,
But none, I think, do there embrace.
Now, therefore, while the youthful glue
Sits on thy skin like morning dew,
And while thy willing soul transpires
At every pore with instant fires,
Now let us sport us while we may;
And now, like amorous birds of prey,
Rather at once our time devour,
Than languish in his slow-chapped power.
Let us roll our strength, and all
Our sweetness up into one ball:
And tear our pleasures with rough strife,
Through the iron gates of life.
Thus though we cannot make our sun
Stand still, yet we will make him run.

Andrew Marvell, English, 1621–78

40   The next poem celebrates the erotic as a pledge of trust.

    The swallow calls to me. It says:
"Day is here! Why aren't you leaving?"
"Stop it, bird, don't be a pest!
I've found my lover in his bed!

"My heart is happy, more than happy!"
Then he wakes: "I'll be close by!
My hand in yours, I'll wander about,
Through all the pleasant places."

For him, I'm the best of the beautiful;
He'll do no harm to my heart.

Anonymous, Egyptian, thirteenth century B.C., version by I. M.

Why be faithful to one another? Is it just human weakness that makes us jealous, needy, unsatisfied? If so, it seems to be a weakness built in, a weakness we must accept; once accepted, it is a weakness from which come trust and love and strength. A violation of this trust is made worse because trust makes us so vulnerable.

But love, being creative, is also messy. It finds its beginnings not just in what's given; it also seeks out the new, driving people into licit and illicit couplings.

    Don't meet with your lover, except by night.
The sun's a scandalmonger, but night's a pimp.
Many's the lover who, wrapped in the cloak of night,
Meets a beloved while gossips are fast asleep.

Mu'tazz, Iraqi, 861–908, version by I. M.

The night was unbeatable—except it was too short.
I made it, I killed it, I folded it away like clothes.
But sun and moon were meeting on the horizon
—Like two glass bowls, of water and of wine.

Mu'tazz, Iraqi, 861–908, version by I. M.

When love is messy, women have been apt to lose out.

I trusted
someone who tired of me.
I am desolate—
unharvested grain
for the autumn wind.

Ono no Komachi, Japanese, ninth century, version by I. M.

Poets sometimes make love affairs into a lifelong occupation. In the next poem, a poet laments that he's no longer in fashion between the sheets.

Vixi Puellis Nuper Idoneus . . .[2]

They flee from me that sometime did me seek,
    With naked foot stalking in my chamber:
I have seen them gentle, tame, and meek,
        That now are wild, and do not once remember
        That sometime they have put themselves in danger
To take bread at my hand; and now they range,
Busily seeking with a continual change.

Thanked be fortune, it hath been otherwise
    Twenty times better; but once, in special,
In thin array, after a pleasant guise,
    When her loose gown from her shoulders did fall,
    And she caught me in her arms long and small,
Therewith all sweetly did me kiss,
And softly said, *"Dear heart, how like you this?"*

It was no dream; I lay broad waking:
    But all is turned, through my gentleness,
Into a strange fashion of forsaking;
    And I have leave to go, of her goodness;
    And she also to use new-fangleness.
But since that I unkindly so am served,
"How like you this?"—what hath she now deserved?

Sir Thomas Wyatt, English, 1503–42

Dante and Petrarch fell in love with unobtainable beloveds. Dante never even met the love of his life; just one glimpse of her in the distance was enough to inspire a lifetime's devotion. Perhaps it is easier to maintain a pure love when you are not also having arguments about bills or irritating personal habits. But the poetry of Dante and Petrarch reminds us that love need not have possession as its object. In an age when women were more or less the property of men, this was a civilizing idea.

 The stars, the heavens, the elements all applied
Their various arts and every extreme care
To make of her a living light, in which
Nature's reflected, and the peerless sun.

So high is their creation, graceful and fresh,
That mortals may not gaze on her for long;
It seems that from her eyes, beyond all measure
Love allows sweet gracefulness to flow.

The air, beaten by her soft rays,
Ignites in virtuous fire and soon is such
That speech and thought are utterly overwhelmed.

No base desire arises, but desire
Of honor, virtue. Tell me now, when
Was ever lust assuaged by highest beauty?

Petrarch, Italian, 1304–74, tr. I. M.

The Persian poet Hafiz observes that the beloved can never finally give the lover what he or she wants. Both the ecstasy and the pain of love arise from this unobtainability. We are in thrall to natural law, the "wheel of heaven" that grants no favors and that therefore seems flawed.

I went into the garden at dawn to gather roses,
When suddenly I heard the voice of the nightingale.

Poor thing, he was stricken in anguish for the love of the
    rose,
And sprinkled the meadows round with his sobs, as he
    looked for help.

Lost then in thought, slowly I paced in the garden,
Considering this affair of the rose and the nightingale.

The rose is become the image of Beauty, and the
    nightingale of Love:
The one will grant no favors, yet the other still remains
    constant.

When the voice of the nightingale prevailed upon my heart,
It seemed I had no power of endurance left.
For many roses have blossomed here in this garden,
But no one has plucked the rose without the stab of a
    thorn.

Hafiz, expect no relief from the turning heavens—
That wheel has a thousand flaws, and grants no favors.

Hafiz, Persian, circa 1320–89, tr. Peter Avery and John Heath-Stubbs

In the next poem, the pain of unrequited love comes close to overwhelming love's
ecstasy.

 ## *Give Me Your Eyes*

Give me your eyes.
I do not ask to touch
The hands of you, the mouth of you,
Soft and sweet and fragrant though they be.
No, lift your eyes to mine;
Give me but one last look
Before I step forth forever;
Even though within that moment's crashing space,
I shall know all of life and death heaven and hell.

Angelina Weld Grimke, American, 1880–1958

Many, if not most, poems of romantic love are about its difficulties. Good poetry is often born of pain. The subject of the next two poems is separation: in the first, by distance; in the second, by death.

 In Kumano Bay
The crinums grow,
Their leaves piled up in hundreds;
My thoughts of you are the same,
And yet we never meet . . .

Hitomaro, Japanese, seventh century, tr. I. M.

 Nocturnal

The sky, the earth, the wind subdued and quiet.
The waves that ripple shoreward from the deep.
The fishes in the sea becalmed in sleep.
The soft reposeful silence of the night.

The fisherman of Helicon who, sprawled
Where in the wind the water ebbs and bobs,
Calls the beloved name in vain, and sobs
For it cannot be any more than called;

"O waves," he says, "before I'm killed by love
Restore to me my nymph, whom you have taken
So early from me and enslaved to death."

Nobody speaks to him. The sea far off
Slaps. In the wind the grove is gently shaken.
His voice is lifted, borne off on its breath.

Luis de Camoens, Portuguese, 1524–80, tr. Keith Bosley

Another troubled poem shows how difficult it is for us to live without love. A Victorian poet lies with a prostitute, lamenting that he cannot be with his true love. The attempt to drown love in dissipation has failed.

 ## *Non sum qualis eram bonae sub regno Cynarae*[3]

Last night, ah, yesternight, betwixt her lips and mine
There fell thy shadow, Cynara! thy breath was shed
Upon my soul between the kisses and the wine;
And I was desolate and sick of an old passion,
Yea, I was desolate and bow'd my head:
I have been faithful to thee, Cynara! in my fashion.

All night upon mine heart I felt her warm heart beat,
Night-long within mine arms in love and sleep she lay;
Surely the kisses of her bought red mouth were sweet;
But I was desolate and sick of an old passion,
When I awoke and found the dawn was gray;
I have been faithful to thee, Cynara! in my fashion.

I have forgot much, Cynara! gone with the wind,
Flung roses, roses, riotously with the throng,
Dancing, to put thy pale lost lilies out of mind:

But I was desolate and sick of an old passion,
Yea, all the time, because the dance was long:
I have been faithful to thee, Cynara! in my fashion.

I cried for madder music and for stronger wine,
But when the feast is finish'd and the lamps expire,
Then falls thy shadow, Cynara! the night is thine;
And I am desolate and sick of an old passion,
Yea, hungry for the lips of my desire:
I have been faithful to thee, Cynara! in my fashion.

Ernest Dowson, English, 1867–1900

Even when the beloved is attained, emotions like jealousy are apt to spoil things.

This evening when I spake with thee, beloved,
as in thy face and in thy mien I saw
that I could not persuade thee with my words,
the longing came for thee to see my heart,

and love, abettor of my purposes,
accomplished that which seemed impossible,
for issuing with the tears which sorrow shed
my heart dissolved in misery distilled.

Enough of cruelty, beloved, enough:
let my harsh jealousy torment thee not
nor vile suspicion violate thy virtue

with foolish shadows, vain appearances,
since now in aqueous humor thou hast seen
and held between thy hands my broken heart.

Juana de Asbaje, Mexican, 1651–95, tr. Samuel Beckett

In the next poem, the poet has a premonition that a love affair is doomed even
before it begins.

 After the wind and the frost,
It was pleasant to toast myself at the fire.
But I didn't look after my heart
And it was stolen from me.

New Year's Day stretches out luxuriantly,
The stems of the New Year's roses are moist,
And in my breast I no longer feel
The trembling of dragonflies.

Ah, it's not hard for me to guess the thief,
I recognized him by his eyes.
But it's frightening that soon, soon,
He himself will return his prize.

Anna Akhmatova, Russian, 1889–1966, tr. Judith Hemschemeyer

Here is a poem in which love, separated from nature by man-made walls, dies.

 Rooms

> I remember rooms that have had their part
> In the steady slowing down of the heart.
> The room in Paris, the room at Geneva,
> The little damp room with the seaweed smell,
> And that ceaseless maddening sound of the tide—
> Rooms where for good or ill—things died.
> But there is the room where we (two) lie dead,
> Though every morning we seem to wake and might just as
> well seem to sleep again
> As we shall somewhere in the other quieter, dustier bed
> Out there in the sun—in the rain.

Charlotte Mew, English, 1869–1928

The celebrations of love that follow were written twenty-four centuries ago. There is disagreement over many aspects of the Song of Solomon. Is it one poem or many? Is there a story, or several stories, buried there? If so, what is that story? The first extract is a declaration of love from boy to girl.

 My beloved speaks and says to me:
> "Arise my love, my fair one,
> and come away;
> for lo, the winter is past,
> the rain is over and gone.
> The flowers appear on the earth,
> the time of singing has come,

and the voice of the turtledove
    is heard in our land.
The fig tree puts forth its figs,
    and the vines are in blossom;
    they give forth fragrance.
Arise my love, my fair one,
    and come away.
O my dove, in the clefts of the rock,
    in the covert of the cliff,
let me see your face,
    let me hear your voice,
for your voice is sweet,
    and your face is comely.
Catch us the foxes,
    the little foxes
that spoil the vineyards,
    for our vineyards are in blossom."

Anonymous, Hebrew, fourth century B.C.,
Song of Solomon 2:10–15, Bible, Revised Standard Version

In the next extract from the Song of Solomon, love and desire throw a girl into confusion. Torn between accepting and rejecting her lover, she roams the city and is beaten by night watchmen, perhaps because they think she's a whore.

     I slumbered, but my heart was alert.
        Listen! My beloved is entreating:

(he speaks)   "Open to me, my sister, my darling,
            my dove, my perfect one,

for my forehead is drenched with dew,
    my locks with the mist of the night."

(she answers)   "I have slipped off my robe.
        How can I put it on?
    I have bathed my feet.
        How can I get them soiled?"

My beloved stretched his hand in through the hole,
    and my insides moaned for him.
I arose to open to my beloved,
    and my hands dripped myrrh,
my fingers—liquid myrrh,
    on the handles of the lock.
I opened to my beloved,
    but my beloved had turned away and gone.
Because of him my soul went forth:
    I sought him but did not find him,
        I called him but he did not answer me.
The night watchmen who roam the city found me—
    they beat me and bruised me,
took my shawl away from me—
    those who watch the walls.
I ask you to promise, girls of Jerusalem:
    if you find my beloved
do not tell him
    that I am sick with love.

Anonymous, Hebrew, fourth century B.C.,
Song of Solomon 5:3–8, tr. Michael V. Fox

52

The next poem playfully asks the simple question, "Why can't we have sex whenever we want?"

 Comin' Thro' the Rye

O gin[4] a body meet a body,
    Comin' thro' the rye;
Gin a body fuck a body,
    Need a body cry?

      Comin' thro' the rye, my jo,
        An' comin' thro' the rye;
      She fand a staun o' staunin' graith[5]
        Comin' thro' the rye.

Gin a body meet a body,
    Comin' thro' the glen;
Gin a body fuck a body,
    Need the warld ken?[6]

Gin a body meet a body
    Comin' thro' the grain;
Gin a body fuck a body
    Cunt's a body's ain.[7]

Gin a body meet a body,
    By a body's sel,[8]
What na[9] body fucks a body,
    Wad a body tell?

Mony a body meets a body
    They darena weel avow;[10]

Mony a body fucks a body,
    Ye wadna think it true.

    Comin' thro' the rye, my jo,
        An' comin' thro' the rye,
    She fand a staun o' staunin' graith
        Comin' thro' the rye.

Robert Burns, Scottish, 1759–96

Lots of great literature has been devoted to answering the question posed in the last song. Burns himself supplied his own answer, which is an expert one, as he had a great deal of experience in both "well-placed" and "illicit" love.

The sacred lowe[11] o' well-placed love,
    Luxuriantly indulge it;
But never tempt the illicit rove,
    Though nothing should divulge it;
I waive the quantum of the sin,
    The hazard of concealing;
But och! it hardens a' within,
    And petrifies the feeling!

Robert Burns, Scottish, 1759–96, stanza 6 of "Epistle to a Young Friend"

Aleksandr Pushkin seems to have suffered a "petrification of feeling"—or at least a jaded appetite—after a dozen or so years of passionate physical affairs with different girls. In the next poem he describes how he needed the coldness of the girl he married to stimulate him. Later he found his wife's flirtations with other men unbearable. He challenged one of them to a duel and was killed.

 No, I don't miss the dissipated nights,
The moans and cries of a young bacchante
Writhing like a serpent in my arms
When, with fierce caresses and love-bites,
She hastens the moment of final spasm.

Dearer to me are you, my quiet friend,
How tormentingly happier I am with you,
When at long last you condescend
To yield to my pleas, tenderly, without rapture,
Cold, ashamed, scarcely responding to
My transports, avoiding them with your lips, your eyes,
More and more coming to life, until
At last you share my pleasure against your will.

Aleksandr Pushkin, Russian, 1799–1837, tr. D. M. Thomas

Ono no Komachi had many lovers; one of them is said to have died of exposure while he waited under her window a hundred nights for her to admit him. She wrote the following two poems of disillusion, both using the image of a fading flower; one is about men's hearts, the other about her own life.

 A flower which fades
With no outward sign
Is the heart
Of man
In this world.

The color of the flowers
Has faded;
Fruitlessly
I have spent my life,
As the long rains fall. . . .

Ono no Komachi, Japanese, ninth century, tr. I. M.

In the interests of monogamy, argues Maruyama in the next poem, we must be prepared to make some sacrifices.

 Snares

There are men, there are women,
attracting each other, being attracted.
They wander near sites lush with grass,
exchange love poems, write and enjoy verse, stories—
    whatever.
Once you accidentally saunter into a thicket,
you aggravate your agonies, your grudges, your tears.
In the end, you kill your partner and snuff out your life.

Listen to their cries of grief, to their screams!
Doesn't every conceivable ploy
exist in snares set up by God
(whom I've not yet had the pleasure of meeting)?

Let's move ahead, eyes alert.
It's best to step lightheartedly over snares.
If by chance your foot gets caught in one,

you're not to shout and thrash fecklessly about.
I'd rather you imitate the courage and determination of the
     hyena.
It escapes by chewing off its paw.
True love starts there.

Maruyama Kaoru, Japanese, 1899–1974, tr. Robert Epp

If sexual love without fidelity may prove unsatisfactory in the end, sex without
love is unattractive from the very start.

 The window-frame shakes. What is below?
A bevy of damp-crotched young pricks
in the street, on the hunt for sex,
none of your old-style love. They go

in their powerful cars anywhere.
Duty? Down the drain. It is not
their concern. Nobody has taught
them anything. And they prefer

noise to music. Amplified bleats,
wails and howls, after their disco-
theques shut, they blare among the streets.

They have houses, women, snappy
cars, and that is all they have; no
wonder they are so unhappy.

George Faludy, Hungarian, born 1910, tr. George Johnston

When love is absent, what we like to call humanity dies. The next poem sees this death lurking even where new life is being born. The new life in question doesn't seem to have much of a chance of flourishing.

 The Distinct Impression

"I was delivering a child
In this kip of a bedroom in Keogh Square.
The woman jerked and groaned in the bed
Sweat wetting her hair.

"Six children lumped and stared at me
As I worked on her.
In the bed with the woman was her man,
Face to the wall, an occasional snore.

"'Is it out yet?' he asked of a sudden.
If I'd a bucket o' boilin' water then
I'd have emptied it over his skin.

"I had the distinct impression
That the moment the child was out of the woman
The bastard would be back in."

Brendan Kennelly, Irish, born 1936, from The Book of Judas

Two of Shakespeare's sonnets differentiate between lust and love.

 Th' expense of spirit in a waste of shame
Is lust in action; and till action, lust
Is perjured, murd'rous, bloody, full of blame,

Savage, extreme, rude, cruel, not to trust;
Enjoy'd no sooner but despiséd straight;
Past reason hunted, and, no sooner had,
Past reason hated, as a swallowed bait
On purpose laid to make the taker mad;
Mad in pursuit, and in possession so;
Had, having, and in quest to have, extreme;
A bliss in proof, and proved, a very woe;
Before, a joy proposed; behind, a dream.
All this the world well knows; yet none knows well
To shun the heaven that leads men to this hell.

Let me not to the marriage of true minds
Admit impediments; love is not love
Which alters when it alteration finds,
Or bends with the remover to remove.
O, no! it is an ever-fixed mark
That looks on tempests and is never shaken;
It is the star to every wand'ring bark,
Whose worth's unknown, although his height be taken.
Love's not Time's fool, though rosy lips and cheeks
Within his bending sickle's compass come;
Love alters not with his brief hours and weeks,
But bears it out even to the edge of doom.
If this be error and upon me proved,
I never writ, nor no man ever loved.

William Shakespeare, English, 1546–1616, sonnets 129 and 116

Love within families is the subject of the next dozen poems.

   The oddest event in life;
(God is neither forgetful,
Nor does he break his promises),
Two in bed become three.

Ma'arri, Syrian, 973–1057, tr. George Wightman and Abdullah al-Udhari

Primitive

I have heard about the civilized,
the marriages that run on talk, elegant and
honest, rational. But you and I
are savages. You come in with a bag,
hold it out to me in silence.
I know Moo Shu Pork when I smell it
and understand the message: I have
pleased you greatly last night. We sit
quietly, side by side, to eat,
the long pancakes dangling and spilling,
fragrant sauce dripping out,
and glance at each other askance, wordless,
the corners of our eyes clear as spear points
laid along the sill to show
a friend sits with a friend here.

Sharon Olds, American, born 1942

This short glimpse of a marriage was written by a religious man.

 If she believes or wears a cross,
Always be kind to your tired wife

Though she knocks religion and says:
"Friends, don't give a fig for old creeds,

People commit huge crimes having learned
Only petty acts earn hellfire."

> *Ma'arri, Syrian, 973–1057,*
> *tr. George Wightman and*
> *Abdullah al-Udhari*

Not all poets are so committed to their marriages. This comment on his marriage comes from Li Po, the most celebrated poet of ancient China.

 To His Wife

Three hundred and sixty-five days
And every day I'm drunk as mud.
What difference in being Li Po's wife
Or married to old Commissioner Flask?

> *Li Po, Chinese, 701–62,*
> *tr. John Scott*

The glorious flowering of a tree after many years is an image of magnificence and sadness in the next poem.

The Flame-Tree Blooms

It was you planted it;
and it grew high and put on crops of leaves,
extravagant fans; sheltered in it the spider weaves
and birds move through it.

For all it grew so well
it never bloomed, though we watched patiently,
having chosen its place where we could see
it from our windowsill.

Now, in its eighteenth spring,
suddenly, wholly, ceremoniously
it puts off every leaf and stands up nakedly,
calling and gathering

every capacity in it, every power,
drawing up from the very roots of being
this pulse of total red that shocks my seeing
into an agony of flower.

It was you planted it;
and I lean on the sill to see it stand
in its dry shuffle of leaves, just as we planned,
these past years feeding it.

Judith Wright, Australian, born 1915

The next poem also has an image of the profuse abundance of trees.

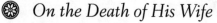 *On the Death of His Wife*

When in this world
You were still alive
Hand in hand
We two would watch
In front of the house
Where, on a bank, stood
The elm trees,
Their branches spreading here and there.
Though like the spring leaves
Thick and numerous
I loved you,
You who were my wife;
Though I leaned on you,
You who were my love,
The laws of this world
You could not disobey.
Like shimmer rising
From burning desolate fields
In a white cloth
Heavenly robe, hidden from my sight
As a bird does
You made a morning journey;
Like the sun going in
You were lost to my sight.
A keepsake for my eyes you left me—
A small child;

When he cries and asks for something,
To give him I have nothing, but,
As a man does, clumsily
I hold him to my side.
Where with my love
I used to sleep,
Our pillows side by side,
In our wedding room,
Through the day now
I'm sad till dark;
Through the night
I sigh until dawn.
Though I weep and moan
I don't know what to do;
Though I love her
I don't know how to meet her.
Then, "On Birdlike
Hagai Mountain
Your wife is living,"
Someone told me; so,
Forcing my way across mountain peaks
I went there with great hardship.
But no good came of it:
For, of my love
As someone living in this world,
Even as a jewel-glow, faintly,
I realize now
No sign will evermore be seen.

Just as last year we saw it
The autumn moonlit night
Once more is bright; but
My love who watched it with me
Grows ever distant on departing time.

Near the road to Fusuma
Among the hills of Hikide
I left my love;
As I came down the mountain road
I felt as one not living.

Hitomaro, Japanese, seventh century, tr. I. M.

This next song, though written down 2,500 years ago, could well be entitled "Song of the Divorce Courts."

 Zip, zip the valley wind!
Nothing but wind and rain.
In days of peril, in days of dread
It was always "I and you."
Now in time of peace, of happiness,
You have cast me aside.

Zip, zip the valley wind!
Nothing but wind and dust storms!
In days of peril, in days of dread
You put me in your bosom.
Now in time of peace, of happiness
You throw me away like slop-water.

Zip, zip the valley wind
Across the rocky hills.
No grass but is dying,
No tree but is wilting.
You forget my great merits,
Remembering only my small faults.

Anonymous, Chinese, seventh century B.C.,
Book of Songs *109, tr. Arthur Waley*

In the next poem, a father, a civil servant, is miserable at having to leave his family to meet the demands of his job.

 Children

Children don't know what worry means!
I stand up to go and they hang on my clothes.
I'm about to scold them
But my wife eggs them on in their silliness:
"The children are silly but you're much worse!
What good does all this worrying do?"
Stung by her words, I go back to my seat.
She rinses a wine cup to put before me.
How much better than Liu Ling's[12] wife,
Grumbling at the cost of her husband's drinking!

Su T'ung Po, Chinese, 1037–1101, tr. Burton Watson

Here is a poem by a daughter remembering her father.

 ## *Father*

They say, his strange, large eyes,
Opal-like, odd, Nordic eyes,
Always looked far-off. He could
Fuss half a day with a flower's root.
He'd lean over it—and its fragile
Refined petal's belligerent fragrance.
In women, too, he sought the soul.
He collected pictures, books, old embroidery;
He also grappled with men.
The table glittered at his opulent feasts.
Servants moved silently, and the wines'
Crystal fire shimmered deep, flaming.
He savored it, as long as the tablecloth
And flowers were unsplotched. But later
When the word became more and more shrill,
Heated, the smoke more stifling,
The country elite railed at the government.
Ten spoke at once—and roared bent over
Gross, crude jokes—and slumping,
They stammered in brotherly kisses, while
Some started snoring, thick-lipped.
Then he became upset, pensive,
He stared at them with clouded, sad eyes,
And felt that just he was the lonely one there.
Then he whistled for his dog.
The vizsla came padding, nuzzled up against him,

And put his smart, pedigreed head in his lap.
In the graying wine-vapor morning
Petting him, they looked at each other.

They say: later I became the light of his eye.
For me, he forgot his celebrated flowers,
He leaned over my lacy, ribboned cradle,
And guarded me like a costly porcelain,
How often he kept watch at my small sickbed!
And when one day, untutored,
I could draw my first two letters, he drew me close,
And whispered, "That's the way, little one!
When you grow up, the world will be different!"
And then came the disease, and he lingered,
For a long time, knowing his end.
And he wasn't much older than I am today! . . .
They say, he suffered nights because of me,
If he looked at me he clenched his hands in his lap.
"You'll be a beggar!" he said, and his words choked.
"Why couldn't I have been stingy, for your sake!"
Oh, my father, if you could know, that's nothing!
If only I never had a greater worry!
But you see, the world hasn't changed since then;
You were so wrong, Father.
Now I hear the news—your grave is so grassy.
The marble bows and the gold letters
Are all washed away, I was there so long ago,
And every year there are downpours.
How many storms! How many have I survived,
And life, Father, what chaos!

. . . If you could see, now you have a grandchild,
Bright-eyed, loud, lively small thing,
But his eyes are different from yours or mine!
Good! Because storms will come!—But maybe
The world will be different when he grows up?
It's been so long that you've slept below!
You weren't much older than I am today,
And time has washed away your golden letters,
And I hear the news, your grave is grassy.
Can I bring my flowers once more?
Who knows? Life is such chaos,
And I am so tired—Father.

Margit Kaffka, Hungarian, 1880–1918, tr. Laura Schiff

A more difficult father-daughter love is the subject of the next poem.

 ## My Father Still Sleeping After Surgery

In spite of himself,
my father loved me. In spite
of the hands that beat me, in spite
of the mouth that kept silent, in spite
of the face that turned cruel
as a gold Chinese king,
he could not control the love
that came out of him.
The body is monumental, a colossus
through which he breathes.

His hands crawl over his stomach
jerkily as sand crabs on five legs;
he makes a fist
like the fist of a newborn.

Toi Derricote, American, born 1941

Love between parents and children is crucial for survival. But children must also change with the times. What growing son has not felt about his father what the poet expresses in the next poem?

 father and son
minds apart
face to face
in awkward silence
why—?

Takuboku, Japanese, 1885–1912, tr. Carl Sesar

By the same poet, about his mother:

 kidding around
carried my mother
piggyback
I stopped dead, and cried.
she's so light . . .

Takuboku, Japanese, 1885–1912, tr. Carl Sesar

A poem of a mother's love for her child:

 Sleep Close to Me

Fold of my flesh
I carried in my womb,
tender trembling flesh,
sleep close to me!

The partridge sleeps in the wheat
listening to its heartbeat.
Let not my breath disturb you;
sleep close to me!

Little tender grass
afraid to live,
don't move from my arms;
sleep close to me!

I have lost everything,
and tremble until I sleep.
Don't move from my breast;
sleep close to me!

Gabriella Mistral, 1889–1957, Chilean, tr. D. M. Pettinella

Osip Mandelstam, who had no children of his own, reminds us that no duty stands higher than to do our best for children. The next poem—written when Mandelstam was facing certain extermination by the Soviet system under Stalin —celebrates pleasure, unity with nature, the integrity of poetry, the defense of freedom, and the continuation of the human species.

I sing when my throat is wet, my soul is dry,
and when my eye is moist enough and thinking does not lie.
Is it good, the wine? The furs, are they not fine?
And the swaying dance of Colchis in the blood?
But my breast grows taut, quiet without a tongue:
it is not I who sing, it is my breathing sings,
the mountains' scabbards hold my hearing, and my head is
    deaf.

The song that has no profit is its own praise,
delight for friends and burning coals for enemies.

The one-eyed song, growing out of moss,
the one-voiced gift of hunters' lives
sung on horseback and in the heights,
the breath held free and open,
caring only in honor and anger
to get the young ones to their wedding without a fall . . .

Osip Mandelstam, Russian, 1891–1938, tr. David McDuff

Love, in the heart that values it, survives until death. The next poem was written
not long before the writer committed suicide. We can even love the earth that
claims us as our grave.

 Moorland Night

My face is against the grass—the moorland grass is wet—
    My eyes are shut against the grass, against my lips
    there are the little blades,

Over my head the curlews call,
And now there is the night wind in my hair;
My heart is against the grass and the sweet earth;—it has
gone still, at last.
It does not want to beat anymore,
And why should it beat?
This is the end of the journey
The Thing is found.

This is the end of all the roads—
Over the grass there is the night-dew
And the wind that drives up from the sea along the
moorland road;
I hear a curlew start out from the heath
And fly off, calling through the dusk,
The wild, long, rippling call.
The Thing is found and I am quiet with the earth.
Perhaps the earth will hold it, or the wind, or that bird's cry,
But it is not for long in any life I know. This cannot stay,
Not now, not yet, not in a dying world, with me, for very
long.
I leave it here:
And one day the wet grass may give it
back—
One day the quiet earth may give it
back—
The calling birds may give it as they go by—
To someone walking on the moor who starves for love and
will not know

Who gave it to all these to give away;
Or, if I come and ask for it again,
Oh! then, to me!

Charlotte Mew, English, 1869–1928

Rumi argues that our physical mortality—the same for us all, as individuals and as species—makes it imperative that we seek out love.

 One handful of dust shouts, "I was hair!"
One handful of dust shouts, "I am a bone!"
Confusion reigns, until Love appears:
"Draw close to me, for I am life eternal!"

*Rumi, Persian, 1207–73, adapted by I. M.
from tr. by Anne-Marie Schimmel*

CHAPTER 3

Religion

Man, living in the dust,
Is like a bug trapped in a bowl.
All day he scrabbles round and round,
But never escapes from the bowl that holds him.
The immortals are beyond his reach,
His cravings have no end,
While months and years flow by like a river
Until, in an instant, he has grown old.

Han Shan, Chinese, circa 800 A.D., tr. Burton Watson

Hard work was created for everyone,
    and a heavy yoke is laid on the children of Adam,
from the day they come forth from their mother's womb
    until the day they return to the mother of all the living.
Perplexities and fear of heart are theirs,
    and anxious thought of the day of their death.
From the one who sits on a splendid throne
    to the one who grovels in dust and ashes,
from the one who wears purple and a crown
    to the one who is clothed in burlap,
there is anger and envy and trouble and unrest,
    and fear of death, and fury and strife.
And when one rests upon his bed,
    his sleep at night confuses his mind.
He gets little or no rest;
    he struggles in his sleep as he did by day.
He is troubled by the visions of his mind

like one who has escaped from the battlefield.
At the moment he reaches safety he wakes up,
   astonished that his fears were groundless.
To all creatures, human and animal,
   but to sinners seven times more,
come death and bloodshed and strife and sword,
   calamities and famine and ruin and plague.

Jesus Ben Sira, Jewish Egyptian, circa 180 B.C., Sirach 40:1–9,
Bible, New Revised Standard Version

The grimness of life leads humanity to look for a higher purpose behind what appears to be the arbitrary cruelty of nature. God, love, truth, purpose, goodness, and justice are alive for us as long as we believe in them, and disappear from us when we deny them. By giving them our loyalty, we discover their fruits. By making certain sacrifices in their favor, we create our own limited justice and well-being within the limits set down for us by nature.

We are also able to feel a delight in being one part, not the master, of a continually changing creation.

 O God,
Whenever I listen to the voice of anything you have
   made—
The rustling of the trees,
The trickling of water,
The cries of birds,
The flickering of shadow,
The roar of the wind,
The song of the thunder,

I hear it saying:
God is One!
Nothing can be compared with God!

Rabi'a, Iraqi, eighth century,
tr. Charles Upton

Religion assumes that behind nature there is a deity whose purpose we cannot fully comprehend. This assumption is not unreasonable, since our understanding is limited by the terms of our existence.

I see mankind under two lights,
Past and future; and in two states,
Time and place. If we want to know
How God accounts for this oddness
We'll get an evasive answer.

Ma'arri, Syrian, 973–1057,
tr. George Wightman and Abdullah al-Udhari

Religion is often blamed for causing wars, persecution, and civil strife. But who knows how history would have gone without religion? From the examples of recent societies that rejected religion—those led by Hitler, Stalin, and Pol Pot, for instance—history would have been an extremely short and bloody affair.

It seems the first human ideas of God were centered around female fertility. Whatever poems were chanted to this Mother Goddess have been lost. Poems to goddesses that survive are from thousands of years later, by which time the Father God had become supreme.

The poem that follows addresses Gaia, Greek goddess of the earth.

✸ *Hymn to Earth, Mother of All*

Gaia, mother of all, hard, splendid as rock,
Eldest of all beings; I sing the greatness of Earth!
She feeds the world's creatures; those on the sacred land,
Those in the paths of the sea, and those that fly in air;
All are hers; she feeds them, from her sacred store.
Fair children and fair harvests depend on her blessing;
She provides for us to live, and when she withholds we die.
Happy the man she delights to honor! Abundance is his,
His trees grow heavy with fruit, his land heavy with corn.
His pastures teem with cattle, his house is full of good
   things.
Such men rule with just laws in cities of fair women;
Beauty, wealth and fortune follow them in plenty.
Their sons exult in ever-fresh delight; and, garlanded,
Their daughters skip merrily on the soft flowers of the field.
Such are those you honor, holy goddess, generous spirit.
Mother of gods, bride of the starry sky, farewell!
To cheer my heart, please give me things for making you
   this song;
In this and other songs, I'll keep your memory alive.

*Anonymous, Greek, sixth century B.C., version by I. M. from existing tr.
by Shelley, Evelyn-White, Boer, and Cashford*

The next poem tells of the goddess Aphrodite—called "the Cyprian" because she was born in Cyprus—goddess of love in all its manifestations.

 Aphrodite

Listen, my children; Love is not only Love,
But many are the names whereby she is called.
She is Death; she is indomitable Force;
She is wild Frenzy, and vehement Desire;
She is Lamentation. All things meet in her,
Virtue, Tranquillity, and Violence.
Into all living hearts she instills herself.
Of this goddess, what creature is not the prey?
Into the shoals of fish that swim the sea
She enters, and within the four-foot tribes
On land she harbors; and among the birds
On divine wing she flits. What deity
Who wrestles with her is not overthrown?
If I may tell—and the truth may be told—
She rules the heart of Zeus. Without a spear,
Without sword, all the purposes of mortals
And gods the Cyprian has power to confound.

Sophocles, Greek, 495–406 B.C., tr. R. C. Trevelyan

The next excerpt is from a hymn addressed to Inanna, goddess of the moon and of war. The poet (a high priestess) curries Inanna's favor by describing the goddess's ability to destroy those who don't worship her. It was written during a time of war, and goddesses had to be fierce to maintain their place in the pecking order.

✸ *from The Adoration of Inanna in Ur*

My Queen; the Anunna, the great gods,
Fled before you like fluttering bats,
Could not stand before your awesome face,
Could not approach your awesome forehead.
Who can soothe your angry heart!
Your baleful heart is beyond soothing!
Queen, happy of liver, joyful of heart,
But whose anger cannot be soothed; daughter of Nanna,
Queen, first in the land, who has ever paid you enough
      homage!

The mountain which did not pay you homage—
Vegetation was accursed on it,
You burned down its great gates,
Its rivers ran with blood because of you, its people had
      nothing to drink,
Its troops were led off willingly before you.
Its forces disbanded willingly before you.
The amusement places of its cities were filled with
      turbulence.
Its adult males were driven off as captives before you.

Against the city that said not "Yours is the land,"
That said not "It belongs to the father that begot you,"
You spoke your holy word, turned away from it,
Kept your distance from its womb.
Its woman spoke not of love with her husband,

In the deep night she whispered not tenderly with him,
Revealed not to him the holiness of her heart.

Rampant wild cow, elder daughter of Nanna,
Queen greater than An, who has ever paid you enough
    homage!

Enheduanna, Sumerian, born circa 2300 B.C., tr. Samuel N. Kramer

Though it would seem that female deities are more protective of the earth and vengeful of transgressions against nature, religions overseen by male gods haven't entirely neglected the values of conservation. Human beings are seen as God's stewards, and it's their duty to look after nature. The trouble is, prosperity brings with it a belief that we can do without God's laws. The consequences of this are described in the next two extracts, the first of which could hardly be more like a description of the present day.

Hear the word of the Lord,
        O people of Israel;
for the Lord has an indictment
        against the inhabitants of the land.
There is no faithfulness or loyalty,
        and no knowledge of God in the land.
Swearing, lying and murder,
        and stealing and adultery break out;
        bloodshed follows bloodshed.
Therefore the land mourns,
        and all who live in it languish;
together with the wild animals

and the birds of the air,
even the fish of the sea are perishing.

Hosea, Hebrew, eighth century B.C., Hosea 4:1–3,
Bible, New Revised Standard Version

A later stage in the desecration of law and the land is described in the Book of
Isaiah:

The earth mourns and withers,
the world languishes and withers;
the heavens languish together with the earth.
The earth lies polluted under its inhabitants;
for they have transgressed the laws,
violated the statutes,
broken the everlasting covenant.
Therefore a curse devours the earth,
and its inhabitants suffer for their guilt;
therefore the inhabitants of the earth are scorched,
and few men are left.
The wine mourns,
the vine languishes,
all the merry-hearted sigh.
The mirth of the timbrels is stilled,
the noise of the jubilant has ceased,
the mirth of the lyre is stilled.
No more do they drink wine with singing;
strong drink is bitter to those who drink it.

The city of chaos is broken down,
     every house is shut up so that none can enter.
There is an outcry in the streets for lack of wine;
     all joy has reached its eventide;
     the gladness of the earth is banished.
Desolation is left in the city,
     the gates are battered into ruins.

Isaiah, Hebrew, circa 700 B.C., Isaiah 24:4–12,
Bible, Revised Standard Version

Religions differ greatly, but they have in common the notion that in order to flourish we must live in accordance with rules not of our making.

In the following poem, the poet rants against his servitude to God, entertaining all sorts of ideas of indulging himself until he is interrupted by a voice to which he cannot help but respond.

 The Collar

I struck the board and cried, "No more.
     I will abroad.
    What? shall I ever sigh and pine?
My lines and life are free; free as the rode,[1]
    Loose as the wind, as large as store.
      Shall I still be in suit?
    Have I no harvest but a thorn
    To let me blood,[2] and not restore
What I have lost with cordial fruit?
      Sure there was wine

Before my sighs did dry it: there was corn
                    Before my tears did drown it.
              Is the year only lost to me?
                    Have I no bays to crown it?
No flowers, no garlands gay? All blasted?
                    All wasted?
Not so, my heart; but there is fruit,
              And thou hast hands.
                    Recover all thy sigh-blown age
On double pleasures: leave thy cold dispute
Of what is fit, and not. Forsake thy cage,
                    Thy rope of sands,
Which petty thoughts have made, and made to thee
Good cable, to enforce and draw,
                    And be thy law,
While thou didst wink and wouldst not see.
                    Away, take heed:
                    I will abroad.
Call in thy death's head there: tie up thy fears.
                    He that forbears
              To suit and serve his need,
                    Deserves his load."
But as I raved and grew more fierce and wild
                    At every word,
Methought I heard one calling, "Child!"
                    And I replied, "My Lord!"

George Herbert, English, 1593–1633

In Taoism, "the Way" has the primacy that other religions give to God. The Way represents the order of spontaneous change that governs the universe. If we live in conformity with the Way, we flourish; if we go against it, we don't.

There is a thing confusedly formed,
Born before heaven and earth.
Silent and void
It stands alone and does not change,
Goes round and does not weary.
It is capable of being the mother of the world.
I know not its name
So I style it "the Way."
I give it the makeshift name of "the great."
Being great, it is further described as receding,
Receding, it is described as far away,
Being far away, it is described as turning back.

Hence the Way is great; heaven is great; earth is great; and man is also great. Within the realm there are four things that are great, and man counts as one.

Man follows earth,
Earth follows heaven,
Heaven follows the Way,
The Way follows itself.

Lao Tzu, Chinese, fourth to third century B.C., from the Tao Te Ching, compiled from translations by D. C. Lau and R. Payne

The theme that God is everywhere is common to most religions. The next poem is by Kabir, a poet loved by both Hindus and Muslims.

 I laugh when I hear the fish in the water is thirsty.
Don't you know, God's in your own house,
That you wander the forests so listlessly?
In your home is the truth; go where you will,
To Benares or Mathura;[3]
If your soul is a stranger to you, the whole world is
   unhomely.

*Kabir, Hindi, 1440–1518, tr. Rabindranath Tagore
and Robert Bridges, modernized*

Kabir used imagery from nature to describe the love between God and himself.

 How could the love between You and me sever?
As the leaf of the lotus lies on the water,
      so You are my Lord and I am your servant.
As the moon-bird "chakor" gazes all night at the moon,
      so You are my Lord and I am your servant.
From the beginning until the end of time there is
                  love between You and me;
   and how shall such love be extinguished?

Kabir says, As a river arriving at the ocean,
   so my heart touches You.

*Kabir, Hindi, 1440–1518, tr. Rabindranath Tagore
and Robert Bridges, modernized*

The next poem goes deeper into the same subject. It is a mystical poem—that is, the language of metaphor overwhelms the rationality that we need for everyday life.

 Gaze on the cheeks of love, that you may gain the
    attributes of true men; sit not with the cold ones so you
    will not be chilled by their breath.
From the cheeks of love seek something other than the
    form; your business is to be a fellow sufferer with love.
If you have the attributes of a clod, you will never fly in the
    air; you will fly in the air if you break to pieces and
    become dust.
If you do not break to pieces, he who composed you will
    break you; when death breaks you, how will you become
    a unique pearl?
When a leaf becomes yellow, the fresh root makes it green;
    why are you content with a love from which you turn
    yellow?

Rumi, Persian, 1207–73, tr. A. J. Arberry

Most religions see humility as appropriate to our station, and pride as coming before a fall.

 He is walking in the road
As proud as any king.
He looks down on everyone,
For his house is full of riches.

If you don't bow down to someone,
God himself will humble you.

Anonymous song, Gond (India),
oral tradition written down and translated
circa 1930 by V. Elwin and S. Hivale

The intoxication of religious ecstasy is compared to drunkenness in the next poem. Hafiz was by profession a lecturer on the Koran, in which wine is forbidden. Poets have often got into trouble for not being earnest enough concerning religion, but Shiraz, where Hafiz lived, was governed with relative tolerance.

 The dawn is breaking, cup-bearer; fill up with wine:
The revolving heavens will not delay, so hurry!

Let us get drunk with a cup of the rose-red wine—
Before this transient world has itself passed out.

The sun of wine has risen upon the east of the bowl:
If pleasure is what you aim at, waste no time in sleep.

Since one day we'll be clay for Fate to make pitchers of,
Let my skull be a cup kept sweet, being filled with wine.

We are not bigots or puritans; we need no penance:
Preach to us only with a cup of unmixed wine.

This worship of wine, Hafiz, is a virtuous business,
So be resolute in pursuit of righteous works!

Hafiz, Persian, circa 1320–89,
tr. John Heath-Stubbs and Peter Avery

In the next poem, the beauty of nature inspires the poet to praise God. Marbod writes of spring with one eye on the fruits of harvest—he was a medieval monk and not forgetful of his belly. For him, the edible is evidence of the credible.

A Description of the Beauty of Spring

Now I must mend my manners
    And lay my gruffness by.
The earth is making merry,
    And so, I think, must I.
The flowers are out in thousands,
    Each in a different dress.
The woods are green and like to fruit,
    The earth has donned her grassy fleece,
And blackbirds, jackdaws, magpies, nightingales
Are shouting each other down in equal praise.

There's a nest in the tree with young ones in it
    And lurking in the branches are the unfledged birds.
The bearded grain is whitening to harvest,
    Lovely are the gardens with the half-blown rose;
Add to these the vines, and the grapes, and the hazel nuts,
The young girls dancing, and their mothers dancing too,
And the young men at play, and the good feast toward,
    And the quiet shining day.

So many lovely things, and if a man looks on them,
And his mood is not softened, nor a smile on his face,
An intractable clod is he, at odds with his heart is he,
For who can behold earth's beauty without praising it

Has a grudge against earth's Maker, whose honor all these
    serve,
Cold winter, summer, autumn, comely spring.

Marbod of Rennes, French, circa 1035–1123,
tr. from Latin by Helen Waddell

The next poem concerns the search for wisdom, which is as different from knowl-
edge as life is from matter.

 Silver has its mines,
    and gold a place for refining.
Iron is extracted from the earth,
    the smelted rocks yield copper.
Man makes an end of darkness,
    to the utmost limit he digs
    the black rock in shadow dark as death.
Foreigners bore into ravines
    in unfrequented places,
    swinging suspended far from human beings.
That earth from which bread comes
    is ravaged underground by fire.
There, the rocks have veins of sapphire
    and their dust contains gold.
That is a path unknown to birds of prey,
    unseen by the eye of any vulture;
a path not trodden by the lordly beasts,
    where no lion ever walked.

Man attacks the flint,
>   upturning mountains by their roots.
He cuts canals through the rock,
>   on the watch for anything precious.
He explores the sources of rivers,
>   bringing hidden things to light.
But where does Wisdom come from?
>   Where is Intelligence to be found?

No human being knows the way to her,
>   she is not to be found on earth where they live.
>   "She is not in me," says the Abyss;
>   "Nor here," replies the Sea.
She cannot be bought with solid gold,
>   nor paid for with any weight of silver,
nor valued against gold of Ophir,
>   precious agate or sapphire.
Neither gold nor glass compares with her,
>   for her, a vase of fine gold would be no exchange,
let alone coral or crystal:
>   better go fishing for Wisdom than for pearls!
Topaz from Cush is worthless in comparison,
>   and gold, even refined, is valueless.
But where does Wisdom come from?
>   Where is Intelligence to be found?

She cannot be seen by any living creature,
>   she is hidden from the birds of the sky.
Perdition and Death both say,
>   "We have heard only rumors of her."

God alone understands her path
    and knows where she is to be found.
(For he sees to the remotest parts of the earth,
    and observes all that lies under heaven.)
When he willed to give weight to the wind
    and measured out the waters with a gauge,
when he imposed a law on the rain
    and mapped a route for thunderclaps to follow,
then he saw and evaluated her,
    looked her through and through, assessing her.
Then he said to human beings,
    "Wisdom?—that is fear of the Lord;
Intelligence?—avoidance of evil."

Anonymous, Hebrew, fifth century B.C.,
Book of Job 28, New Jerusalem Bible

Sacrifice is an ancient and important part of religion. The idea is to give up one thing in order to gain something better. Even without religion, we make sacrifices—for instance, we may suppress the desire to be rude to someone, in the interests of peace and harmony. If the gain is more long term—the welfare of the planet, for example—voices of short-term self-interest grow loud in opposition to change. How much do we have to sacrifice to allow the planet to regain its health?

It's doubtful whether law can replace religion in enforcing such large-scale sacrifice.

In the next poem, George Eliot wants to make a sacrifice of her life, not by destroying it but by living for a higher ideal. By being "to other souls the cup of strength in some great agony," she will experience the heaven of joining the "choir invisible whose music is the gladness of the world."

O May I Join the Choir Invisible

Longum illud tempus, quum non ero,
magis me movet, quam hoc exiguum.[4]
CICERO, *AD ATTICUM* 12.18

O may I join the choir invisible
Of those immortal dead who live again
In minds made better by their presence: live
In pulses stirred to generosity,
In deeds of daring rectitude, in scorn
For miserable aims that end with self,
In thoughts sublime that pierce the night like stars,
And with their mild persistence urge man's search
To vaster issues.
       So to live is heaven:
To make undying music in the world,
Breathing as beauteous order that controls
With growing sway the growing life of man.
So we inherit that sweet purity
For which we struggled, failed, and agonized
With widening retrospect that bred despair.
Rebellious flesh that would not be subdued,
A vicious parent shaming still its child
Poor anxious penitence, is quick dissolved;
Its discords, quenched by meeting harmonies,
Die in the large and charitable air.
And all our rarer, better, truer self,
That sobbed religiously in yearning song,
That watched to ease the burthen of the world,

Laboriously tracing what must be
And what might yet be better—saw within
A worthier image for the sanctuary,
And shaped it forth before the multitude
Divinely human, raising worship so
To higher reverence more mixed with love—
That better self shall live till human Time
Shall fold its eyelids, and the human sky
Be gathered like a scroll within the tomb
Unread for ever.
                    This is life to come,
Which martyred men have made more glorious
For us who strive to follow. May I reach
That purest heaven, be to other souls
The cup of strength in some great agony,
Enkindle generous ardor, feed pure love,
Beget the smiles that have no cruelty—
Be the sweet presence of a good diffused,
And in diffusion ever more intense.
So shall I join the choir invisible
Whose music is the gladness of the world.

George Eliot, English, 1819–80

The why and how of leading a good life have preoccupied Judeo-Christian religious thinking. The simple answer to why—in order to feel good—is offset in many people's minds by the prosperity of some who lead bad lives and also by the short-term pleasures that can be had from behaving badly. But life would be a very simple affair if good behavior were rewarded with prosperity.

The subject of good and bad behavior is tackled at length in the Book of Wisdom, chapters two and three, from which the following is extracted. ("They" in the first line refers to "the unrighteous.")

For they reasoned unsoundly, saying to themselves,
"Short and sorrowful is our life,
and there is no remedy when a life comes to its end,
and no one has been known to return from Hades.
For we were born by mere chance,
and hereafter we shall be as though we had never been,
for the breath in our nostrils is smoke,
and reason is a spark kindled by the beating of our hearts;
when it is extinguished, the body will turn to ashes,
and the spirit will dissolve like empty air.
Our name will be forgotten in time,
and no one will remember our works;
our life will pass away like the traces of a cloud,
and be scattered like mist
that is chased by the rays of the sun
and overcome by its heat. . . .

"Come, therefore, let us enjoy the good things that exist,
and make use of the creation to the full as in youth.
Let us take our fill of costly wine and perfumes,
and let no flower of spring pass us by.
Let us crown ourselves with rosebuds before they wither.
Let none of us fail to share in our revelry;
everywhere let us leave signs of our enjoyment,
because this is our portion, and this our lot.
Let us oppress the righteous poor man;

let us not spare the widow
or regard the gray hairs of the aged.
But let our might be our law of right,
for what is weak proves itself to be useless.

"Let us lie in wait for the righteous man,
Because he is inconvenient to us and opposes our actions;
he reproaches us for sins against the law,
and accuses us of sins against our training. . . .
Let us test him with insult and torture,
so that we may find out how gentle he is,
and make trial of his forbearance.
Let us condemn him to a shameful death,
for, according to what he says, he will be protected."

But the souls of the righteous are in the hand of God,
and no torment will ever touch them.
In the eyes of the foolish they seemed to have died,
and their departure was thought to be a disaster,
and their going from us to be their destruction;
but they are at peace.
For though in the sight of others they were punished,
their hope is full of immortality. . . .

But the ungodly will be punished as their reasoning
    deserves,
those who disregarded the righteous
and rebelled against the Lord;
for those who despise wisdom and instruction are
    miserable.

Their hope is vain, their labors are unprofitable,
and their works are useless.
Their wives are foolish, and their children evil;
their offspring are accursed.

Anonymous, Jewish Greek, circa 50 B.C.,
The Wisdom of Solomon 2–3, Bible, New Revised Standard Version

Why is there so much suffering in the world? In the Book of Job, Job asks this question, adding, "In particular, why me?" None of the replies he gets satisfies him, and eventually he calls on God himself to answer. God breaks his usual silence and tells Job that the mysteries of creation are not Job's to comprehend. Here is how God begins.

Then the Lord answered Job out of the whirlwind:
　　　"Who is this that darkens counsel
　　　　by words without knowledge?
Gird up your loins like a man,
　　　　I will question you, and you shall declare to me.
Where were you when I laid the foundations of the earth?
　　　　Tell me, if you have understanding.
Who determines its measurements—surely you know!
　　　　Or who stretched the line upon it?
On what were its bases sunk,
　　　　or who laid its cornerstone
when all the morning stars sang together
　　　　and all the heavenly beings shouted for joy?"

Anonymous, Hebrew, fifth century B.C.,
Book of Job 38:1–7, Bible, New Revised Standard Version

In the Book of Job, God is challenged by Satan, who wishes to test the endurance of Job's love for God. God allows Job to suffer at Satan's hand. Job "persists in his integrity" and demonstrates that his loyalty to God is not dependent on good fortune. Job's fortunes are restored, but it may be that his true reward lies in his dialogue with God.

In a more recent poem, Edwin Muir notices that the finer qualities of hope, faith, charity, love, and pity are inconceivable without "shapes of terror and grief." In this light, materialism—which avoids any sort of pain, let alone "terror and grief"—seems a futile philosophy.

 ## *One Foot in Eden*

One foot in Eden still, I stand
And look across the other land.
The world's great day is growing late,
Yet strange these fields that we have planted
So long with crops of love and hate.
Time's handiworks by time are haunted,
And nothing now can separate
The corn and tares[5] compactly grown.
The armorial weed in stillness bound
About the stalk; these are our own.
Evil and good stand thick around
In the fields of charity and sin
Where we shall lead our harvest in.

Yet still from Eden springs the root
As clean as on the starting day.
Time takes the foliage and the fruit
And burns the archetypal leaf
To shapes of terror and of grief

Scattered along the winter way.
But famished field and blackened tree
Bear flowers in Eden never known.
Blossoms of grief and charity
Bloom in these darkened fields alone.
What had Eden ever to say
Of hope and faith and pity and love
Until was buried all its day
And memory found its treasure trove?
Strange blessings never in Paradise
Fall from these beclouded skies.

Edwin Muir, Scottish, 1887–1959

Under the protection of organized religions, ways of life grow up that are comfortable and fruitful. Four poems follow that express the comforts and consolations of a religious way of life in a difficult or hostile world.

In the first, Mahadevi explains that her love for the god Krishna fulfills her desire for perfection.

Other men are thorn
under the smooth leaf.
I cannot touch them,
go near them, nor trust them,
nor speak to them confidences.

Mother,
because they all have thorns
in their chests,

I cannot take
any man in my arms but my lord

white as jasmine.

Mahadevi, Dravidian (India), twelfth century,
tr. A. K. Ramanujan

Milton, incapacitated by blindness, reassures himself that there is a place for him in God's creation even though he is unable to work. God's mercy does not demand of us more than we can give.

 When I consider how my light is spent,
Ere half my days in this dark world and wide,
And that one talent which is death to hide,
Lodg'd with me useless, though my soul more bent
To serve therewith my Maker, and present
My true account, lest he returning chide;
Doth God exact day-labor, light deny'd?
I fondly ask; but Patience to prevent
That murmur, soon replies, God doth not need
Either man's work or his own gifts; who best
Bear his mild yoke, they serve him best, his state
Is kingly. Thousands at his bidding speed
And post o'er land and ocean without rest:
They also serve who only stand and wait.

John Milton, English, 1608–74

The poet of the next piece lives in a ghetto. Outside are people who hate him. Brought up on hatred of Jews, they value nothing but the "swill and guzzle" that democracy is happy to encourage.

Good Night, Wide World

Good night, wide world
Big stinking world!
Not you but I slam shut the door.
With my long gabardine,
My fiery, yellow patch,
With head erect,
And at my sole command,
I go back into the ghetto.
Wipe off all markings of apostasy!
I roll my body in your grime;
Glory, glory, glory to you,
Crippled Jewish life!
I cast out all your unclean cultures, world!
Though all has been laid waste,
I burrow in your dust,
Sorrowing Jewish life.

Swinish German, hostile Polack,
Thievish Amalekite—land of swill and guzzle,
Slobbering democracy,
With your cold compress of sympathy,
Good night, brash world with your electric glare.

Back to my kerosene, my shadowed tallow candles,
Endless October and faint stars,

To my twisting streets and crooked lantern,
To my sacred scrolls and holy books,
To tough Talmudic riddles and lucid Yiddish speech,
To law, to duty, and to justice,
To what is deeply mine.
World, joyously I stride
Toward the quiet ghetto lights.

Good night, I give you in good measure
All my redeemers;
Take your Jesus Marxes; choke on their daring
Burst with each drop of our baptized blood.

And still I trust that though He tarry,
My waiting will spring newly day by day.
Green leaves again will rustle
On our withered tree.
I need no comforting.
I walk again my straight and narrow way;
From Wagner's heathen blare to Hebrew chant
And the hummed melody.
I kiss you, cankered Jewish life,
The joy of homecoming weeps in me.

Jacob Glatstein, Yiddish, 1896–1971, tr. Marie Syrkin

Religious storytelling is an attempt to approach the deepest truths by metaphor. Only a fanatic claims that he or she has arrived at absolute and literal truth, and such claims are made with one intent: to gain power.

Insisting that dogma is literal truth may result in social cohesiveness, but it also requires the oppression of dissidents and a stifling of scientific, intellectual, and cultural creativity. It can lead to a kind of general social sclerosis.

In the next poem, Ma'arri warns us not to believe all we're told. In the first couplet he's referring to the doctrine of reincarnation.

> They say the soul's ferried corpse to infant
> Till, cleaned by each crossing, it's fit for God.
>
> Don't believe what you're told unless your mind
> Confirms its truth: palm trunks, lofty as clouds,
>
> Stay wood. Be calm, take care and bear in mind
> The Indian sword is worn thin as it's honed.

Ma'arri, Syrian, 973–1057, tr. George Wightman and Abdullah al-Udhari

Religion gets a bad name when its representatives behave badly. However, it would be odd if they didn't behave badly sometimes, since they're only human.

Anything with as much influence over human affairs as religion is bound to be a source of conflict. The subject of the next poem is a man hijacking religion in the cause of factional hatred and a lust for power.

Calvin described in his journals certain inappropriate sexual arousals, ascribing them to the devil's influence. In this poem, these arousals are seen as pathological.

John Calvin

> His forehead was unlined but moist, and shone
> above his long French nose. He didn't care
> to touch his wife, so he caressed his beard
> into smooth waves as he proclaimed the Lord

thrust sin into men's souls so he could hurl
them latterly to Hell. It was so vile,
so horrible, it had to be believed.
In dreams he loved to hone castrating knives
and in Geneva did away with lust,
jailed loving couples, poets, all who smiled
with happiness, or laughed, or studied books,
and well-dressed men that danced, especially if
their pants were bulging with distended pricks.
He himself had rarely such ill luck,
though thirty years or so ago, in Paris,
when a student, he once watched a colleague
being soundly caned in the College yard
and saw the victim shaking on his bunk,
blood welling from his wealed and naked arse,
and did get an erection. Poor Servetus,
whom he had first denounced to the Inquisition,
like a fool sought sanctuary in Geneva,
and Calvin had him burned on a slow fire,
his followers herding all the people there
to watch the blaze as, at his window, sniffing
that rank smoke, he licked his swollen lips,
himself remote from lechery—yet how come
his prick swelled stiff and jutted its bald head?
The ways of God are mysteries indeed!

George Faludy, Hungarian, born 1910, tr. Robin Skelton

When will mankind realize it is one?
Will it ever bridge the gulfs that divide it?
The white tramples the black,
The Jew is proud that he is chosen of the Lord,
Another thinks he's best because he came from Brahma's
    mouth.

When shall we give up rotting in fancied poses by the grace
    of the Lord?

Like a bunch of puppies, some with eyes just open,
Some with just one eye open, others yet to open their eyes,
Engaged in unseemly scrabble for the mother's breast,
Alas! we are all absorbed in wrangling and recrimination.

Srinivasa, Dravidian (India), born 1891, tr. unknown

But without God, "anything goes." As Christianity began to lose its grip on European civilization under the onslaught of "enlightened" thinking, Christians found little to prevent them from behaving as brutally as they wished. As democracy gained ground, the will of the people replaced Christian authority—and the will of the people was not always benevolent.

The next poem expresses the outrage of a Jewish poet watching Jews everywhere being threatened and violated by those who still called themselves Christians, inheritors of the Jewish God, worshipers of the Jew Jesus.

Pluck, O prophet, the firebrand from your altar,
And cast it to the villains—
Let it serve them for roasting, to set their kettles on,
And to warm their palms.
Fling the ember from your heart
And let it light their pipes,
Let it illume the stealthy smirk on their lips
And the evil cunning in their eyes.
Lo, they come, these villains,
Mouthing the prayers you've taught them,
Feeling your pain and sharing your hope,
Their souls straining toward your ruined shrine,
So as to pounce on the wreckage,
Burrow in its rubble heap,
And cart away its scattered stones
To pave their floors and fence their gardens,
To mount as tombstones over graves.
And when they find your scorched heart in the rummage,
They'll throw it to their dogs.

Trample upon your altar, stamp it with contempt
And scatter its fire and smoke.
Sever with one sweep of the hand the spiderweb
Strung like harp strings in your heart,
Whence you wove a song of life
And a dream of salvation—
Vain oracles beguiling the ear.
Disperse them to the winds,

Frayed and shimmering let them drift
On a sunny day at summer's end,
So that no soul will find its mate,
No filament match its comrade,
But all melt away in a first downpour of rain.
Smash your hammer, your iron hammer,
Fractured by many vain poundings against stony hearts,
And mold it into a spade
To dig a grave for us.

Speak the curse God's wrath sets on your tongue,
Let not your lips falter;
Though your word be bitter as death,
Yea, death itself,
We'll hear and know it.

Lo, the bloated night has hemmed us in,
Darkness has overwhelmed us,
And we reel like the blind.
Something has happened,
We know not what,
There is none to see and none to tell
Whether the sun rose for us or set—
Set forever.
Boundless, frightful is the encompassing void,
And there is no refuge;
If we pray or wail in the dark,
Who will give ear?
If we voice God's harrowing malediction,
On whose head will it fall?

And if we gnash our teeth and clench our fist,
On whose skull will it descend?
Chaos will swallow them all,
The wind carry them off,
Doom lies in wait for them,
No stay, no strength, no road.
And the heavens are silent,
They know their iniquity against us,
They have sinned to hell,
And bear their guilt in silence.

Open now your lips, O prophet of the end.
If you have a word, speak out!
Though it be bitter as death,
Yea, death itself,
Speak out!
Wherefore shall we fear death,
His angel already astride upon our shoulders
And his bridle in our mouth?
With shouts of resurrection on our lips,
And with frolickers' mirth
We gambol to the grave.

H. N. Bialik, Hebrew, 1873–1934, tr. A. A. Steinbach

Temporarily horrified at crimes against humanity, the West nevertheless proceeds at full speed with crimes against the planet.

Meanwhile, banality invades religion to numb the pain of thought.

Open Your Hearts

Open your hearts to the Holy Spirit
For Christ's sake.
We'll be back to you in a moment
After this commercial break.

Brendan Kennelly, Irish, born 1936, from The Book of Judas

It's an old story that when people desert religion, they adopt the criterion of profit to decide whether something is good. In the next poem, Gautama, the first Buddha, argues that wealth is an unreliable provider of happiness.

The man whose heart's desires are gratified,
is glad indeed to see success secured.

But, if his heart's desires and aims are foiled,
he smarts as if a dart had wounded him.

Yet, should he shun desires as he would shun
a snake's head underfoot, by vigilance
he overcomes the world's seductive lures.

Whoso with boundless appetite desires
fields, lands, or gold, herds, horses, women, serfs,
and kinsfolk—him tumultuous desires

(weak tho' they seem) o'ercome at last; they crush
their victim. Here on, ills come surging in
like waves that flood some wrecked ship's crazy hold.

Therefore by watchfulness discard desires;
expel them: bale your ship: and cross the Flood
to safety's haven on the further shore.

Gautama, Indian, sixth century B.C.,
tr. from Pali by Lord Chalmers

Han Shan takes up this theme, looking to peace and beauty to give him happiness and mocking those obsessed with possessions.

In a tangle of cliffs I chose a place—
Bird-paths, but no trails for men.
What's beyond the yard?
White clouds clinging to vague rocks.
Now I've lived here—how many years—
Again and again, spring and winter pass.
Go tell families with silverware and cars,
"What's the use of all that noise and money?"

Han Shan, Chinese, circa 800,
modern tr. by Gary Snyder

Our age of materialism fosters the notion that we have no need of God or religion. Under these circumstances, we human beings become the most important, intelligent, and godlike creatures in the universe. Unfortunately, when we have such a high opinion of ourselves, we are apt to make a terrible mess.

The next two poems attack the notion that scientific knowledge does away with the existence of God.

The rose has come into the garden, from
Nothingness into Being.

Once I did not know the birds were described,
classified, observed, fixed in their proper localities.
Each bird that sprang from the tree, passed overhead,
    hawked from the bough,
was sole, new, dressed as no other was dressed.
Any leaf might hide the paradise-bird.

Once I believed any poem might follow my pen,
any road might beckon my feet to mapless horizons,
any eyes that I met, any hand that I took, any word that I
    heard,
might pierce to my heart, stay forever in mine, open worlds
    on its hinge.
All then seemed possible; time and world were my own.

Now that I know that each star has its path, each bird
is finally feathered and grown in the unbroken shell,
each tree in the seed, each song in the life laid down—
is the night sky any less strange; should my glance less
    follow the flight;
should the pen shake less in my hand?

No, more and more like a birth looks the scheduled rising
    of Venus:
the turn of a wing in the wind more startles my blood.
Every path and life leads one way only,

out of continual miracle, through creation's fable,
over and over repeated but never yet understood,
as every word leads back to the blinding original Word.

Judith Wright, Australian, born 1915

In the next poem, Auden celebrates the god Terminus, who in the ancient world was responsible for boundaries. Here, Terminus is given new life. He is called on to distinguish between the tall stories of science and the world we really live in, to temper our outlandish extravagance, and to provide limits within which we may be intimate and play.

 ## *Ode to Terminus*

The High Priests of telescopes and cyclotrons
keep making pronouncements about happenings
    on scales too gigantic or dwarfish
    to be noticed by our native senses,

discoveries which, couched in the elegant
euphemisms of algebra, look innocent,
    harmless enough but, when translated
    into the vulgar anthropomorphic

tongue, will give no cause for hilarity
to gardeners or housewives: if galaxies
    bolt like panicking mobs, if mesons
    riot like fish in a feeding-frenzy,

it sounds too like Political History
to boost civil morale, too symbolic of

the crimes and strikes and demonstrations
we are supposed to gloat on at breakfast.

How trite, though, our fears beside the miracle
that we're here to shiver, that a Thingummy
  so addicted to lethal violence
  should somehow have secreted a placid

tump with exactly the right ingredients
to start and cocker Life, that heavenly
  freak for whose manage we shall have to
  give account at the Judgment, our Middle-

Earth, where Sun-Father to all appearances
moves by day from orient to occident,
  and his light is felt as a friendly
  presence not a photonic bombardment,

where all visibles do have a definite
outline they stick to, and are undoubtedly
  at rest or in motion, where lovers
  recognize each other by their surface,

where to all species except the talkative
have been allotted the niche and diet that
  become them. This, whatever micro-
  biology might think, is the world we

really live in and that saves our sanity,
who know all too well how the most erudite
  mind behaves in the dark without a
  surround it is called on to interpret,

how, discarding rhythm, punctuation, metaphor,
it sinks into a driveling monologue,
 too literal to see a joke or
 distinguish a penis from a pencil.

Venus and Mars are powers too natural
to temper our outlandish extravagance:
 You alone, Terminus the Mentor,
 can teach us to alter our gestures.

God of walls, doors and reticence, nemesis
overtakes the sacrilegious technocrat,
 but blessed is the City that thanks you
 for giving us games and grammars and meters.

By whose grace, also, every gathering
of two or three in confident amity
 repeats the pentecostal marvel,
 as each in each finds his right translator.

In this world our colossal immodesty
has plundered and poisoned, it is possible
 You still might save us, who by now have
 learned this: that scientists, to be truthful,

must remind us to take all they say as a
tall story, that abhorred in the Heav'ns are all
 self-proclaimed poets who, to wow an
 audience, utter some resonant lie.

W. H. Auden, English, 1907–73

In a "rational" society, morality is abandoned in favor of making decisions based strictly on knowledge. The trouble is, we never know enough to be sure that we are deciding correctly. Even the knowledge we have may be ignored if it impinges on our comfort.

Compared to a moral climate created by religion, laws are ineffectual at restraining undesirable behavior. But established religions seem more keen on the management of illusions than on working out how we may restrain our behavior and safeguard our future.

The final poem, written by a Japanese Buddhist monk, asks a question normally asked by children. Later it may be forgotten, not because it's been answered but because a literal answer is impossible.

❋ *To Inscribe on a Picture of a Skull I Painted*

All things born of causes end when causes run out;
but causes, what are they born of?
That very first cause—where did it come from?
At this point words fail me, workings of my mind go dead.
I took these words to the old woman in the house to the
    east;
the old woman in the house to the east was not pleased.
I questioned the old man in the house to the west;
the old man in the house to the west puckered his brow
    and walked away.
I tried writing the question on a biscuit, fed it to the dogs,
but even the dogs refused to bite.
Concluding that these must be unlucky words, a mere
    jumble of a query,
I rolled life and death into a pill, kneading them together,
and gave it to the skull in the meadowside.
Suddenly the skull came leaping up,

began to sing and dance for me,
a long song, ballad of the Three Ages,
a wonderful dance, postures of the Three Worlds.
Three worlds, three ages, three times danced over—
"the moon sets on Chang-an and its midnight bells."[6]

Ryokan, Japanese, 1758–1831, tr. Burton Watson

CHAPTER 4

War

The existence of nuclear weapons and the proliferation of nuclear material present the threat of massive destruction. Even without nuclear weapons, war wreaks human misery and environmental havoc, but the habit of war seems hard to give up.

War has played a major role in human history. Conquest of territory and migrations of people have contributed to the flourishing of our species, as different cultures have come together to make civilizations. Nowadays, more peaceful methods are available to accomplish the ends that war has served, and war is now seen only as a sickness and a scourge, the most obvious of "those facts of filth and violence that we're too dumb to prevent."[1]

War in early patriarchal civilization was starkly described in the fifth century B.C. by Heraclitus of Ephesus: "War is father and king of all; some he shows to be gods, others men; some he makes slaves, others free." The first poem is an insight into war as it was waged by early human peoples in order to increase their living space and to attract glory. It is also eloquent on war's destruction of the natural environment.

❀ *Where the Lilies Were in Flower*

Fish leaping
in fields of cattle;

easy unplowed sowing
where the wild boar has rooted;

big-eyed buffalo herds
stopped by fields of lilies
flowering in sugarcane beds;

ancient cows bending their heads
over water flowers
scattered by the busy dancers
swaying with lifted hands;

queen's-flower trees full of bird cries,
the rustle of coconut trees,
canals from flowering pools
in countries
with cities sung in song;

　　　but your anger
　　　touched them, brought them terror,
　　　left their beauty in ruins,
　　　bodies consumed by Death.

The districts are empty, parched;
the waves of sugarcane blossom,
stalks of dry grass.
The thorny babul of the twisted fruit
neck to neck with the giant black babul.

The she-devil with the branching crest
roams
astraddle on her demon,
and the small persistent thorn
is spread in the moving dust
of ashen battlefields.

Not a sound, nothing animal,
not even dung,
in the ruins of public places
that kill the hearts of eager men,
chill all courage,
and shake those who remember.

But here,
the sages have sought your woods.
In your open spaces, the fighters play
with bright-jeweled women.
The traveler is safe on the highway.
Sellers of grain shelter their kin
who shelter, in turn, their kin.

The silver star will not go near
the place of the red planet: so it rains
on the thirsty fields.
Hunger has fled
and taken disease with her.

Great one,
your land blossoms
everywhere.

Kumattur Kannanar, Tamil, first century A.D.(?), tr. A. K. Ramanujan

As we become more civilized, we accept as "kin" a wider circle of people, and religious or tribal wars then seem not glorious but obscene. We recognize that humanity is all one species, and as humans we value all our different races. Our governments are asked to direct their efforts more toward avoiding war than toward planning the next one.

Li Po wrote eloquently against war.

✳ *Fighting South of the Ramparts*

Last year we were fighting at the source of the Sang-kan;
This year we are fighting on the Onion River road.
We have washed our swords in the surf of Parthian seas;
We have pastured our horses among the snows of the T'ien
    Shan.
The King's armies have grown gray and old
Fighting ten thousand leagues away from home.
The Huns have no trade but battle and carnage;
They have no fields or plowlands,
But only wastes where white bones lie among yellow sands.
Where the House of Chi'n built the Great Wall that was to
    keep away the Tartars,
There, in its turn, the House of Han lit beacons of war.
The beacons are always alight, fighting and marching never
    stop.
Men die in the field, slashing sword to sword;
The horses of the conquered neigh piteously to Heaven.
Crows and hawks peck for human guts,
Carry them in their beaks and hang them on the branches
    of withered trees.
Captains and soldiers are smeared on the bushes and grass;
The General schemed in vain.
Know therefore that the sword is a cursed thing,
Which the wise man uses only if he must.

Li Po, Chinese, 701–62, tr. Arthur Waley

Although European civilization has held war in high esteem, the greatest long poem of Western civilization, *The Iliad,* is antiwar. It was performed regularly and with the utmost veneration during the war-filled years of ancient Greece and has been held in the highest regard ever since.

In this extract, the Danaans (Achaeans, Greeks) are losing the day's fighting against the Trojans. Achilles is sulking and won't fight. His friend Patroclus is begging Achilles's permission to lead his Myrmidons and fight and to put on Achilles's armor to frighten the Trojans. We see in this extract the allure of war as well as its folly.

✸ *from The Iliad*

". . . send me forth now at the head of the Myrmidon host,
That I may be a light of hope to the Danaans.
And let me strap on my shoulders that armor of yours,
That the zealous Trojans may take me for you and quickly
Withdraw from the fighting. Then the battling, war-worn
    sons
Of Achaeans may have a chance to catch their breath—
Such chances in battle are few—and we who are fresh
May easily drive, with little more than our war-screams,
The exhausted Trojans away from the ships and the
    shelters
And back toward the city."
Such was his plea, poor childish
Fool that he was, for it was his own hard death
And doom for which he pleaded.

Homer, Greek, ninth to sixth century B.C.(?),
from book 16, tr. Ennis Rees

For European civilization, the First World War was a watershed. The idea of war as a good thing grew dim in the face of the slaughter of most of the males of an entire generation. From then on, the poetry of war would be represented not so much by this:

The naked earth is warm with spring,
    And with green grass and bursting trees
Leans to the sun's gaze glorying,
    And quivers in the sunny breeze;
And life is color and warmth and light,
    And a striving evermore for these;
And he is dead who will not fight;
    And who dies fighting has increase.

Julian Grenfell, English, 1888–1915, first stanza of "Into Battle"

as by this:

Dulce et Decorum Est[2]

Bent double, like old beggars under sacks,
Knock-kneed, coughing like hags, we cursed through sludge,
Till on the haunting flares we turned our backs
And towards our distant rest began to trudge.
Men marched asleep. Many had lost their boots
But limped on, blood-shod. All went lame; all blind;
Drunk with fatigue; deaf even to the hoots
Of gas shells dropping softly that dropped behind.

Gas! Gas! Quick, boys!—An ecstasy of fumbling,
Fitting the helmets just in time;
But someone still was yelling out and stumbling,
And flound'ring like a man in fire or lime.
Dim, through the misty panes and thick green light,
As under a green sea, I saw him drowning.

In all my dreams, before my helpless sight,
He plunges at me, guttering, choking, drowning.

If in some smothering dreams you too could pace
Behind the wagon that we flung him in,
And watch the white eyes writhing in his face,
His hanging face, like a devil's sick of sin;
If you could hear, at every jolt, the blood
Come gargling from the froth-corrupted lungs,
Obscene as cancer, bitter as the cud
Of vile, incurable sores on innocent tongues,—
My friend, you would not tell with such high zest
To children ardent for some desperate glory,
The old Lie: Dulce et decorum est
Pro patria mori.[3]

Wilfred Owen, English, 1893–1918

Grenfell and Owen were both killed in the First World War. Keith Douglas was killed in the Second World War. In the next poem, Douglas feels for the girlfriend of a dead enemy.

✲ *Vergissmeinnicht*[4]

Three weeks gone and the combatants gone
returning over the nightmare ground
we found the place again, and found
the soldier sprawling in the sun.

The frowning barrel of his gun
overshadowing. As we came on
that day, he hit my tank with one
like the entry of a demon.

Look. Here in the gunpit spoil
the dishonored picture of his girl
who has put: *Steffi. Vergissmeinnicht*
in a copybook gothic script.

We see him almost with content,
abased, and seeming to have paid,
and mocked at by his own equipment
that's hard and good when he's decayed.

But she would weep to see today
how on his skin the swart flies move;
the dust upon the paper eye
and the burst stomach like a cave.

For here the lover and killer are mingled
who had one body and one heart.
And death who had the soldier singled
has done the lover mortal hurt.

Keith Douglas, English, 1920–44

The act of killing a fellow human being is described by the same poet. Empathy for the enemy and a horror of war's horrors make war more difficult to wage.

 ## How to Kill

Under the parabola of a ball,
a child turning into a man,
I looked into the air too long.
The ball fell into my hand, it sang
in the closed fist: *Open Open
Behold a gift designed to kill.*

Now in my dial of glass appears
the soldier who is going to die.
He smiles, and moves about in ways
his mother knows, habits of his.
The wires touch his face; I cry
NOW. Death, like a familiar, hears

and look, has made a man of dust
of a man of flesh. This sorcery
I do. Being damned, I am amused
to see the center of love diffused
and the waves of love travel into vacancy.
How easy it is to make a ghost.

The weightless mosquito touches
her tiny shadow on the stone,
and with how like, how infinite
a lightness, man and shadow meet.

They fuse. A shadow is a man
When the mosquito death approaches.

Keith Douglas, English, 1920–44

The poems that Owen and Douglas wrote before they experienced war had a youthful and conventional tone. There is a terrible sense of war forging their versifying metal into hardened poetic steel—and then, with a final blow, destroying it.

The strange exhilaration of war and the enlivening proximity of death are described in the next poem.

A whole night,
Thrown down near a friend
Already butchered
With his mouth
Baring its teeth
Toward the full moon:
With the congestion
Of his hands
Penetrating my silence,
I've written letters
Full of love.

Never have I been
So
Attached to life.

Giuseppe Ungaretti, Italian, 1888–1970, tr. I. M.

War, though it involves women's cooperation, is waged largely by men. But there's no doubt that women are capable of being warlike—as women political leaders of our time have demonstrated. The next poem describes such a woman, and is by a woman poet.

The old woman's shoulders
were dry, unfleshed,
with outstanding veins;
her low belly
was like a lotus pad.

When people said
her son had taken fright,
had turned his back on battle
and died,

she raged
and shouted,

> "If he really broke down
> in the thick of battle,
> I'll slash these breasts
> that gave him suck,"

and went there,
sword in hand.

Turning over body after fallen body,
she rummaged through the blood-red field
till she found her son,
quartered, in pieces,

and she rejoiced
more than on the day
she gave him birth.

Kakkaipatiniyar Naccellaiyar,
Tamil, first century A.D.(?),
tr. A. K. Ramanujan

The next two poems express more familiar sentiments of those left behind when
men go to war.

 I climb that wooded hill
And look toward where my father is.
My father is saying, "Alas, my son is on service;
Day and night he knows no rest.
Grant that he is being careful of himself,
So that he may come back and not be left behind!"

I climb that bare hill
And look to where my mother is.
My mother is saying, "Alas, my young one is on service;
Day and night he gets no sleep.
Grant that he is being careful of himself,
So that he may come back, and not be cast away."

I climb that ridge
And look toward where my elder brother is.
My brother is saying, "Alas, my younger brother is on
    service;

Day and night he toils.
Grant that he is being careful of himself,
So that he may come back and not die."

> *Anonymous, Chinese,*
> *seventh century B.C.,*
> Book of Songs *124, tr. Arthur Waley*

✹ *May 1915*

Let us remember Spring will come again
To the scorched, blackened woods, where the
    wounded trees
Wait, with their old wise patience for the heavenly
    rain,
Sure of the sky: sure of the sea to send its healing breeze,
    Sure of the sun. And even as to these
      Surely the Spring, when God shall please,
    Will come again like a divine surprise
To those who sit today with their great Dead, hands in their
    hands, eyes in their eyes,
At one with love, at one with Grief: blind to the scattered
    things and changing skies.

> *Charlotte Mew, English, 1869–1928*

Separation forced on a poet by war sets him to thinking of his old home.

 ## *Thinking of My Brothers on a Moonlit Night*

Drums on the watchtower have emptied the roads—
At the frontier it's autumn; a wild goose cries.
This is a night in which dew becomes frost;
The moon is bright like it used to be at home.

I have brothers, but they're scattered;
My home's broken up; are they dead or alive?
If letters are sent, they never arrive;
This war that separates us seems unending.

Tu Fu, Chinese, 712–70, version by I. M. after tr. by David Hawkes

The millions of lives thrown into ruin by war are represented here by an extract from a poem written 1,800 years ago by a Chinese noblewoman. She was captured by nomadic tribesmen during one of their periodic rampages in China. She was forced to marry a chief, by whom she had two children. When he died, tribal custom forced her to marry his son. After twelve years she was ransomed. She had to return to China and leave her children behind. Back in China, she was scorned for her two marriages to barbarians, the second of which was, in their minds, incestuous. She remarried a Chinese, but the translator speculates that her new husband was ordered to marry her by the emperor who had ransomed her.

 ## *from Poem of Sorrow*

Cho's company came down upon the east,
Their metal armor glinting in the sun.
The men of the plains were weak and cowardly,

The invading soldiers were all Hu and Chi'ang.
Trampling across the fields, they surrounded the cities;
In the towns they attacked, everything was destroyed.
Heads were lopped off till no one was left to kill,
Just bones and corpses propping each other up.
On their horses' flanks they hung the heads of men,
On their horses' backs they carried off women and girls.
We galloped for days westward into the passes,
The endless road was dangerous and steep.
When I looked back, into the mist-hung distance,
I felt as though my very heart was breaking.
In all they captured over ten thousand women,
Our captors would not let us keep together.
Sometimes when sisters found themselves side by side,
Longing to speak, they dared not utter a word.
If by some trivial fault we angered the soldiers,
At once they'd bawl out, "Kill these prisoners!
We'd better take knives and finish them off,
Why waste our time on keeping them alive?"
I had no desire to go on living longer,
I could not bear their cursing and reviling.
Sometimes they flogged us with rods as well,
And the pain we felt was mingled with our hatred.
During the day we trudged on weeping and crying,
At night we sat there, groaning to ourselves.
We longed to die, but could not get the chance,
We longed to live, with nothing left to live for.
How could the Blue Above be so unjust
To pour on us such anger and misfortune?

The border wilds are different from China,
And men know little of Righteousness and Truth.
It is a place where frost and snow abound,
And the northern wind blows spring and summer long.
It sent my clothes flapping about as it blew,
And whistled shrilly all around my ears.
Moved by the seasons, I thought of my father and mother,
My grief and sighing never came to an end.
When a stranger arrived from the world outside,
I was always overjoyed to hear of it,
I would welcome him, ask what news he had,
Only to find his district was not mine.
By luck my constant wish was gratified,
My relatives sent someone to rescue me.
But now when I was able to escape,
I found I had to leave my children there.
Natural bonds tie children to a woman's heart,
I thought of our parting, never to meet again,
In life and death eternally separated—
I could not bring myself to say good-bye.
My children came and clung around my neck,
Asking their mother where she was going to.
"They say that you have got to go away,
How can you ever come back to us again?
Mother, you were always so loving and so kind,
Why have you now become so harsh to us?
We have not even grown into men,
How can you not look back and think of us?"
The sight of them destroyed me utterly,

I grew confused, behaved like one run mad.
Weeping and wailing, I fondled and caressed them,
When I had to set out, I turned back time and again.
The women who were taken captive with me
Came to bid me farewell and see me off.
They were glad that I could go back, though alone;
The sound of their crying hurt me grievously.
Because of this the horses stood hesitating,
Because of this the carriage did not move.
All the lookers-on were crying and wailing,
Even the passersby were crying too.
But I had to go, I had to harden my heart.
Daily our caravan hurried me further away.
On and on we went, three thousand leagues,
When would I ever see those I had left behind?
I brooded on the children of my womb,
The heart in my breast was broken evermore.
I got home to find my family was wiped out,
Nor had I any kin at all alive.
My hometown had become a mountain forest,
In its ruined courts the thorns and mugworts grew,
And all around, white bones of unknown men
Lay scattered with no one to bury them.
Outside the gates I heard no human voices,
Only wolves were howling, barking all around.
I stood alone, facing my lonely shadow,
My cry of anguish battered at my heart.
I climbed a hill and gazed into the distance,
And soul and spirit suddenly fled from me.

A bystander encouraged me to patience,
Kept urging me to try and go on living.
Though I went on living, what had life left for me?
I entrusted my fate to yet another man,
Exhausted my heart to summon strength to go on.
My wanderings have made all men despise me,
I live in fear of being cast aside once more.
How long can a woman's life go dragging on?
I shall know sorrow till the very end of my days.

Tsai Yen, Chinese, circa 190 A.D., tr. J. D. Frodsham and Cheng Hsi

Displaced victims of war are the subjects of the next poem. The poet notes with irony how the victims' presence illuminates the limitations of a more normal way of life; conventional people who live protected lives are unable to cope with the extremities of feeling and experience.

 ## *Victims*

They are aging now, some dead.
In the third-class suburbs of exile
their foreign accents
continue to condemn them. They should
not have expected more.

They had their time
of blazing across headlines,
welcomes, interviews, placings
in jobs that could not fit,
of being walked round carefully.

One averts the eyes
from horror or miracle equally.

Their faces, common to humankind,
had eyes, lips, noses.
That in itself was grave,
seen through such a flame.

The Czech boy, talking,
posturing, desperate to please,
restless as a spastic trying
to confine his twitches
into the normal straitjacket—
what could we do with him?

The neighbors asked him
to children's parties,
being at sixteen a child;
gave him small jobs
having no niche to hold him
whether as icon, inhabitant
or memento mori.
He could not be a person
having once been forced to carry
other children's corpses
to the place of burning.

But when we saw him walk
beside our own children
darkness rose from that pit.
Quickly but carefully

(he must not notice)
we put our bodies
between our children and the Victim.

Absit omen,[5] you gods—
avert the doom,
the future's beckoning flame.

Perhaps he did not notice. At last
he went away.

In what backstreet of what city
does he keep silence, unreadable
fading graffito of half-
forgotten obscenity?

Think: such are not to be pitied.
They wear already
a coat of ash seared in.
But our children and their children
have put on, over the years,
a delicate cloak of fat.

Judith Wright, Australian, born 1915

The theme of ash continues in the most famous poem about the Holocaust. Celan's parents died in an internment camp, his father of typhus, his mother murdered. He himself survived but with a legacy of mental torment. He committed suicide in 1970.

Margarete is a German girl, Shulamith a Jewish girl. Shulamith is the name traditionally given to the girl in the Song of Songs. In concentration camps, some inmates were forced to play "civilized" music while others were burned. The poem is not so much about war itself as about the madness that war unleashes.

 Death Fugue

Black milk of daybreak we drink it at sundown
we drink it at noon in the morning we drink it at night
we drink and we drink it
we dig a grave in the breezes there one lies unconfined
A man lives in the house he plays with the serpents he writes
he writes when dusk falls to Germany your golden hair
    Margarete
he writes it and steps out of doors and the stars are flashing
he whistles his pack out
he whistles his Jews out in earth has them dig for a grave
he commands us strike up for the dance

Black milk of daybreak we drink you at night
we drink in the morning at noon we drink you at sundown
we drink and we drink you
A man lives in the house he plays with the serpents he writes
he writes when dusk falls to Germany your golden hair
    Margarete
your ashen hair Shulamith we dig a grave in the breezes
    there one lies unconfined.

He calls out jab deeper into the earth you lot you others
    sing now and play
he grabs the iron in his belt he waves it his eyes are blue

jab deeper you lot with your spades you others play on for
   the dance

Black milk of daybreak we drink you at night
we drink you at noon in the morning we drink you at
   sundown
we drink and we drink you
a man lives in the house your golden hair Margarete
your ashen hair Shulamith he plays with the serpents

He calls out more sweetly play death death is a master from
   Germany
he calls out more darkly now stroke your strings then as
   smoke you will
rise into air
then a grave you will have in the clouds there one lies
   unconfined

Black milk of daybreak we drink you at night
we drink you at noon death is a master from Germany
we drink you at sundown and in the morning we drink and
   we drink you
death is a master from Germany his eyes are blue
he strikes you with leaden bullets his aim is true
a man lives in the house your golden hair Margarete
he sets his pack on to us he grants us a grave in the air
he plays with the serpents and daydreams death is a master
   from Germany

your golden hair Margarete
your ashen hair Shulamith

Paul Celan, German, 1920–70, tr. Michael Hamburger

Technology allows war to be waged from a distance. Arms industries profit from wars in remote parts of the world. Western governments use arms as bargaining chips in their race to strip the assets of the Third World. In this, it seems that governments are nastier than their electorates, for much of this trade has to be conducted in secret.

Long ago there was a saying, "The god of war is just, killing only those who kill." It was never wholly accurate, but now those who kill are remote from those who are killed. The killed are for the most part poor and uneducated, conscripts or civilians, the least privileged and least influential of the populations involved.

✸ *The Sound of Leaves*

War, only war, all twelve
months of the year. Our eyes
are cactus plants,
the thorns growing inward
to pierce our
tenderest nerves.

War, only war.
The orchids on the wall,
the ceiling fan's whirl overhead,
all suffocate me.
Man sheds civilization
like a snakeskin

and bares the horror
of his naked face.

North, south, east, west—
no white-horsed hero
from the legends
will come to rescue us.

Each corner of the sky
is pushed down into darkness,
into the mush of rotting corpses
working their poison
on the air. Breath drowns
in this blind sea named time.

Still, sometimes the sound of leaves
makes me open my eyes to the sky.
Again, the mind begins to build its nest
among quiet wings,
the shadow of the shal tree
falls green
over my house
over the smell
of this warm, wet earth.

*Razia Hussain, Bangladeshi, born 1938,
tr. Chitra Divakarumi*

The proliferation of armaments is described in the next poem, first published in
1953. Great powers, too frightened of each others' armaments to go to war with

each other (especially when the leaders themselves would be incinerated in such a conflict), busy themselves with wars that are sporadic and far from home, while the threat of mass destruction hangs over us all.

 Every Day

> War will no more be declared,
> just continued. The unheard-of
> has become the commonplace. The hero
> stays far from the fighting. The weakling
> is moved to the zone of fire.
> The uniform of the day is patience;
> its decoration, the shabby star
> of hope above the heart.
>
> It will be awarded
> when nothing more is happening,
> when the barrage falls silent,
> when the enemy has become invisible,
> and the shadow of eternal armament
> fills the sky.
>
> It will be awarded
> for flight from banners
> for bravery in face of friends
> for the treachery of unworthy secrets,
> and the nonaction
> of every briefing.

Ingeborg Bachmann, Austrian, 1926–73, tr. I. M.

Environmental disasters in one country increasingly affect the welfare of neighboring states. As environmental degradation becomes more acute and living standards increasingly hard to maintain, war over such issues is an ugly possibility.

If international laws were based on a recognition of actual human nature and needs rather than on the rights of whoever has political power, they might help prevent disputes from becoming wars.

However, most of us consider that slavery, extermination, and the yoke of foreign domination are things worth fighting against, and the final poem honors the sacrifices made in war.

Behold, O Earth, how wasteful we have been,
Spreading our seed in your secret sacred lap;
Not shining barley seed, not heavy wheat
Not gold-streaked grain of rye, nor tasseled corn;
Behold, O Earth, how wasteful we have been!
The fairest of our flowers in your dust,
Flowers that hardly saw the morning sun,
Some half in bud, some full in fragrant bloom,
Before life's noon, their innocence our grief;
Their dew not dry, they met a light that was new.
Accept these best, youth of the purest dream,
Whole in heart, not stained by guilt of the world,
The weave of their days to be finished in life yet to be.
These are our best: what better have you seen?
Cover them over; the corn will soon be green,
Strong with their strength; the sanctity of earth
Increased by sacrifice; in death's mystery
May they make splendid amends for us that live.
Behold, O Earth, how wasteful we have been!

Saul Tchernikhovsky, 1875–1943, Hebrew,
version by I. M. from tr. by H. Auerbach

CHAPTER 5

Civilization

REPORTER:
*Mr. Gandhi, what do you think of
modern civilization?*

MAHATMA GANDHI:
That would be a good idea!

There are two meanings to the word *civilization*. One refers to the accumulation of material and organizational strengths with which people win for themselves some respite from the harsh conditions of primitive life. The other refers more to a state of mind in which people behave toward each other with decency and consideration. Gandhi's remark points out that the two don't necessarily go together.

As Europeans explored and conquered territory from the sixteenth century onward, they came across the remains of many collapsed civilizations. Unable to accept the implication that their own civilization, too, would one day collapse, they developed theories of lost races who built the civilizations, then mysteriously disappeared. The thought that the peasants tilling the ground among the ruins could be descendants of those who had built and enjoyed the civilizations was unbearable to them.

It is said, "Forests precede civilizations; deserts follow."

Ozymandias

I met a traveler from an antique land
Who said: Two vast and trunkless legs of stone
Stand in the desert . . . Near them, on the sand,
Half sunk, a shattered visage lies, whose frown,
And wrinkled lip, and sneer of cold command,
Tell that its sculptor well those passions read
Which yet survive, stamped on these lifeless things,
The hand that mocked them, and the heart that fed:
And on the pedestal these words appear:
"My name is Ozymandias, king of kings:
Look on my works, ye Mighty, and despair!"
Nothing beside remains. Round the decay
Of that colossal wreck, boundless and bare
The lone and level sands stretch far away.

Percy Bysshe Shelley, English, 1792–1822

Damage to the land is a classic prelude to the collapse of civilization. Trees attract rainfall. If too many trees are cut down, other vegetation also suffers. Overintensive farming methods, developed to support large city populations, impoverish the soil. Warfare is destructive of land, people, and resources. Pollution is a relative newcomer to the list, though today it's perhaps the most threatening item of all. Here is an early short poem about pollution:

 Saucepan soot
Drifts ashamed
Among the irises

Kagu no Chiyo, Japanese, 1701–55, tr. I. M.

In the next poem the poet asks, where does responsibility lie for the system that tyrannizes our lives and poisons our world?

 ## *A Voiced Lament*

Who's sprinkled salt on our children's milk?
Who's muddied our waters?
Hey, who goes there?

Are we living a fairy tale, which century is this?
Whence can the poison have seeped
Into our apple, onto our comb?

The light of day comes to our room unbidden,
Wakes us and takes us away, forces
A pickax, a pen into our hands.
The wagonloads go past, go past.
Pushed into harness, we climb the slope;

We pluck night from the forty thieves,
Sing it a lullaby in our arms.
Should not its arms enfold our sleep?
Who is rocking whom?

They are walking the dead away,
Mindful of proper ceremony.
Is that the wind, is someone blowing?
The living are in their lockers:
Then who is it whose breath
Ruffles these well-kept files?
Hey, who goes there?

Gulten Akin, Turkish, born 1933, tr. Nermin Menemencioglu

A more recent poem concerns the defilement of Lake Erie. Pollution on this scale is like a nightmare become real.

In My Black Book

I.

The freshwater goddess, Lake Erie,
is dead.

Every day now, more and more of her putrid corpse
washes up on the sand.

Fish that silvered in her veins, upturned and bloated.
Underwater plants she patiently tended,
mutant and withered.

Her foaming brains are deposited in Cleveland.
In banks. In Coke bottles.

2.

I hate to say "I remember when" but I do.
I remember when swimming in her was like crystal-
    gazing.
I remember the autumn afternoon I made my first
deep dive as a child

and lost my bathing suit. Down, down in slow-motion
descent, naked, wide-eyed in the wavering
light, ringing in my ears . . .

I could see clear through
the shimmer of her blue-white veils down to the bottom,
her glowing shells, her lake stones like jewels.

And I was held, suspended, in the dance of a goddess.

3.

Erie, it's no use.
You slump in thick and listless, like goulash soup.
Scientists say it will take at least
500,000 years before you regenerate, if you do.

O Erie, what are we going to do with you?

We have roped off our old approaches and posted
    warnings:
SEVERE POLLUTION ZONE, NO BATHING PERMITTED,
KEEP AT A SAFE DISTANCE

We have dismantled our carousels and prancing horses.

And all along your shores
lanterns burn down to a low uneven glow
and go out.

In darkness, in silence
you lay out there a great snake goddess
dying, dead.

And each dawn, you coil the oily slime of our horizon.

4.

Look, I still keep your address here
in my black book:

Lake Goddess Erie
c/o U.S.A.
Western Hemisphere

Frank Polite, American, born 1936

All these thoughts seem a long way from the high hopes with which Western civ-
ilization began.

 Numberless are the world's wonders, but none
More wonderful than man; the storm-gray sea
Yields to his prows, the huge crests bear him high;
Earth, holy and inexhaustible, is graven
With shining furrows where his plows have gone
Year after year, the timeless labor of stallions.

The light-boned birds and beasts that cling to cover,
The lithe fish lighting their reaches of dim water,
All are taken, tamed in the net of his mind;
The lion on the hill, the wild horse windy-maned,
Resign to him; and his blunt yoke has broken
The sultry shoulders of the mountain bull.

Words also, and thoughts as rapid as air,
He fashions to his good use; statecraft is his,
And his the skill that deflects the arrows of snow,
The spears of winter rain: from every wind
He has made himself secure—from all but one:
In the late wind of death he cannot stand.

O clear intelligence, force beyond all measure!
O fate of man, working both good and evil!
When the laws are kept, how proudly his city stands!
When the laws are broken, what of his city then?
Never may the anarchic man find rest at my hearth,
Never let it be said that my thoughts are his thoughts!

Sophocles, Greek, 495–406 B.C.,
from Antigone, *tr. Dudley Fitts*

Three centuries later, Greek civilization was in ruins, destroyed by its love of war. But out of the ruins of Greek civilization grew the Roman, and out of the ruins of Roman civilization grew modern Europe.

Today, poets are no longer full of such praise for our species, nor are they themselves held in such high esteem. There is mutual contempt between the destroyers and the impotent guardians of our human spirit.

Our neighbor's forty, an engineer, Swiss,
but could be anything—French, Belgian, German.
The policeman slaps his back. The whore squeals bliss.
He is a treasured guest of King Hassan.
Prospecting for oil in the desert and long gone,
his faucets are still running, his TV on.

On his bedside table are rings of cognac,
as on the year-old book he borrowed from Lily.
He only reads machines, writes only checks.
We visited, we drank, the boredom deadly.
Cretinous technocrat, our century's pet—
Just seeing him, the Princess ached to vomit.

In his brand-new Rolls he barreled out
the other morning, glancing up to check
the balconies for admirers, at the gate

ran down a puppy, didn't turn a hair.
Kill him? No point. We can't escape his like;
our very air is thick with murderers' sperm.

George Faludy, Hungarian, born 1910,
tr. Robin Skelton

Today's dream is that everyone will be able to share in the fruits of civilization.
For those who know poverty, escaping from hardship is a potent dream.

Shantytown

She sees a husband in her dream;
a swell with a salary of one hundred liras.
She marries, and moves to the city.
Letters arrive at their address,
The Happy Nest Apartments, basement floor.
They live in a flat neat as a box.
No more laundry, no more washing windows,
if she washes dishes, they are her own.
She has children, like angels, like drops of light.
She buys a second-hand pram,
mornings she goes to the Red Crescent Gardens,
so that little Yilmaz may play in the sand,
like the children of swells.

The sewage worker's best dream
is of the Turkish bath.
He stretches out on a marble platform,
a row of masseurs line up at his head.
One pours water,
one soaps him,
another waits his turn with a loofah.
As new customers enter,
the snow-white sewage worker leaves the bath.

Orhan Veli Kanik, Turkish, 1914–50,
tr. Nermin Menemencioglu

After a while, the magic of material comfort wears off, and once again we are left with the age-old unanswerable puzzle of why we are here. The materialist solution to this puzzle—"to acquire as much as we can"—leads to endless hard work, guilt at achieving our aims at the expense of others, the collapse of a family life that is starved of love and attention, and damage to the planet.

I work, work
and still
no joy in my life
I stare
at my hands

Ishikawa Takuboku, Japanese, 1885–1912, tr. Carl Sesar

Machines have multiplied the productivity of human labor many times. But machines also give us the power to destroy the world and ourselves along with it.

The Secret of the Machines

We were taken from the ore-bed and the mine,
  We were melted in the furnace and the pit—
We were cast and wrought and hammered to design,
  We were cut and filed and tooled and gauged to fit.
Some water, coal, and oil is all we ask,
  And a thousandth of an inch to give us play:
And now, if you will set us to our task,
  We will serve you four and twenty hours a day!

  We can pull and haul and push and lift and drive,
  We can print and plow and weave and heat and light,

We can run and race and swim and fly and dive,
    We can see and hear and count and read and write!

Would you call a friend from half across the world?
    If you'll let us have his name and town and state,
You shall see and hear your crackling question hurled
    Across the arch of heaven while you wait.
Has he answered? Does he need you at his side?
    You can start this very evening if you choose,
And take the Western Ocean in the stride
    Of seventy thousand horses and some screws!

    The boat express is waiting your command!
    You will find the *Mauretania* at the quay,
    Till her captain turns the lever 'neath his hand,
    And the monstrous nine-decked city goes to sea.

Do you wish to make the mountains bare their head
    And lay their new-cut forests at your feet?
Do you want to turn a river in its bed,
    Or plant a barren wilderness with wheat?
Shall we pipe aloft and bring you water down
    From the never-failing cisterns of the snows,
To work the mills and tramways in your town,
    And irrigate the orchards as it flows?

    It is easy! Give us dynamite and drills!
    Watch the iron-shouldered rocks lie down and quake,
    As the thirsty desert-level floods and fills,
    And the valley we have dammed becomes a lake.

But remember, please, the Law by which we live,
    We are not built to comprehend a lie,
We can neither love nor pity nor forgive.
    If you make a slip in handling us you die!
We are greater than the Peoples or the Kings—
    Be humble, as you crawl beneath our rods!—
Our touch can alter all created things,
    We are everything on earth except—The Gods!

Though our smoke may hide the Heavens from your eyes,
It will vanish and the stars will shine again,
Because, for all our power and weight and size,
We are nothing more than children of your brain!

Rudyard Kipling, English, 1865–1936

In countries where machines do much of the work, employment for humans has become something of a scarcity. It might be sensible to share work out, but no: like all scarcities, work has become something to compete for. Being in work has become what divides the affluent from the poor.

Being busy, then, has become a status symbol. The affluent are rarely at rest; when they are not working, they are enjoying a leisure pursuit. Contemplation has become the preserve of the unemployed, who are powerless to influence human affairs.

To stimulate demand for human labor, we must want goods more than anything. Our sense of wonder is directed away from the wonders of nature and toward the wonders of human creation.

The Motoka[1]

You see that Benz sitting at the rich's end?
Ha! That motoka is motoka
It belongs to the Minister for Fairness
Who yesterday was loaded with a doctorate
At Makerere with whiskey and I don't know what
Plus I hear the literate thighs of an undergraduate.

You see those market women gaping their mouths?
The glory of its inside has robbed them of words,
I tell you the feather seats the gold steering
The TV the radio station the gear!
He can converse with all the world presidents
While driving in the backseat with his darly
Between his legs without the driver seeing a thing! ha!
    ha! ha!
Look at the driver chasing the children away
They want to see the pistol in the door pocket
Or the button that lets out bullets from the machine
Through the eyes of the car—sshhhhhhhhhhhhhhhhhh!
Let's not talk about it.

But I tell you that motoka can run
It sails like a lyato, speeds like a swallow
And doesn't know anyone stupid on its way.
The other day I heard—
But look at its behind, that mother of twins!
A-ah! That motoka is motoka

You just wait, I'll tell you more
But let me first sell my tomatoes.

Theo Luzuka, African, contemporary

Lost in wonder at our own creations, we lose our sense of wonder at the world—
at what used to be called God's creation. The voice in the next poem is that of
Judas, spirit of betrayal through the ages.

✿ *Whenever That Happened*

Hell is the familiar all stripped of wonder.
Was there a moment
When wonder at the world died in my eyes?
Had I a friend I could recognize?
When did I take friendship for granted?
When did I get used to the thought of murder?
When did my flesh cease to astonish me?
When did my mind become gray-familiar?
Whenever that happened is when I knew
I could do anything.
When wonder died in me power was born.
I can change the world because I no longer dream of blue,
I can betray a god because I never heard a girl sing
Of steps in the street or sunlight blessing a field of corn.

Brendan Kennelly, Irish, born 1936

As democracy gained precedence in the nineteenth century, education was taken under state control. Though the original intention was perhaps to enlighten, education soon became another battleground for politicians. Some said education should be used to make us more economically effective, others said it should be used to make us all equal. The original aims of education—to develop our individual talents, to make us more understanding, and to equip us with civilized values—went adrift.

 ## *In an Urban School*

The guard picks dead leaves from plants.
The sign over the table reads:
Do not take or *touch* anything on this table!
In the lunchroom the cook picks up in her dishcloth
what she refers to as "a little friend,"
shakes it out,
and puts the dishcloth back on the drain.
The teacher says she needs stronger tranquilizers.
Sweat rises on the bone of her nose,
on the plates of her skull under unpressed hair.
"First graders, put your heads down. I'm taking names
so I can tell your parents
which children do not obey their teacher."
Raheim's father was stabbed last week.
Germaine's mother, a junkie,
was found dead in an empty lot.

Toi Derricote, American, born 1941

Recently, in terror of favoring one system of values over another, educators have favored giving children freedom to explore their own paths, as if children are innately decent and civilized. This freedom has produced a generation even keener on consumer pleasures than their parents are.

 ## To a Young Man Driving His Own Car

So you're already driving your own car
I'll bet your friends are jealous
As you were learning to drive
I thought how splendid for you
to go speeding everywhere
Getting any kind of license is good
I often said
Now you speed about in your car
you can't see the roadside trees changing
with the seasons
you can't see the merchants selling fruit
or fish at the roadside
you can't see the woman running along
with a sick child slung on her back
Always on the lookout for traffic patrols
and red lights
your eyes fixed straight ahead
you speed about
your eyes have grown sharper
your mind has grown busier
and though the price of fuel
may go up even more
and exhaust fumes block your view

you drive around
and do not intend to walk anywhere I'm sure
and those years of youth that people spend
walking or running
getting about by bus or subway
you are spending at over 40 mph
When I see you speeding along in your car
I feel you have isolated yourself
too lightly
and my heart grows heavy

Kwang-kyu Kim, Korean, born 1941, tr. Brother Anthony of Taize

Today, young people have to face the fact that the generations preceding them have made the world into a place that is poisoned, sick, and dying. Even to exist as a consuming human being in the way they have been brought up is to contribute to the poisoning of the world. Getting a job—"if they are lucky"—will only add to the waste and pollution, because a high turnover of goods is the principal way of stimulating growth in employment.

Meanwhile, the yearning of young people for a decent world is exploited by the entertainment and music industries. These industries, along with fashion, drugs, and the lure of powerful comforts like owning a car, redirect the energies and good intentions of young people toward getting and spending. Stupefied, they are incapable of working toward or even thinking about a better society.

In the next poem, the character speaking is again Judas the betrayer.

 ## Money in Love

My good friend, the Pinstripe Pig, says
There's money in love
Especially in shining teenage eyes.

Pinstripe's mind, all bonny-bladed edge,
Hires me to write songs
That shiver their little fannies
While they pour out tears and screams
And tidal monies.

Pinstripe sits in his office all day
Breaking record after record.
"Thanks be to God," he sighs, "for the fucking young,
The fucking young."
　　　　　　Child, if you're lucky,
Pinstripe will blow you a kiss, he's music-lord
Thrilling your days with love's old sweet song.

Listen to Pinstripe, child, and you can't go wrong.

Brendan Kennelly, Irish, born 1936

Along with affluence comes the illusion that we can do without moral restraint. We forget that we owe our survival as a species to morality, which enables us to trust each other and cooperate. Such cooperation, as Charles Darwin noted, gives us an edge over other species.

The curse Timon uttered on the citizens of Athens describes a state of affairs in many ways similar to how we live today. Timon speaks as he leaves the city, whose citizens loved him while he was rich but deserted him once he was poor. The curse he utters invites their extinction. Much of what he wishes on them, we have embraced voluntarily.

❀ Let me look back on thee. O thou wall,
That girdles in those wolves, dive in the earth,
And fence not Athens! Matrons, turn incontinent!

Obedience fail in children! Slaves and fools,
Pluck the grave wrinkled senate from the bench,
And minister in their steads! To general filths
Convert o' th' instant, green virginity!
Do 't in your parents' eyes! Bankrupts, hold fast:
Rather than render back, out with your knives,
And cut your trusters' throats! Bound servants, steal!
Large-handed robbers your grave masters are
And pill[2] by law. Maid, to thy master's bed!
Thy mistress is o' the brothel. Son of sixteen,
Pluck the lined crutch from thy old limping sire,
With it beat out his brains! Piety and fear,
Religion to the gods, peace, justice, truth,
Domestic awe, night-rest and neighborhood,
Instruction, manners, mysteries and trades,
Degrees, observances, customs and laws,
Decline to your confounding contraries,
And yet confusion live! Plagues incident to men,
Your potent and infectious fevers heap
On Athens, ripe for stroke! Thou cold sciatica,
Cripple our senators, that their limbs may halt
As lamely as their manners! Lust and liberty
Creep in the minds and marrows of our youth,
That 'gainst the stream of virtue they may strive,
And drown themselves in riot! Itches, blains,
Sow all th' Athenian bosoms, and their crop
Be general leprosy! Breath infect breath,
That their society, as their friendship, may
Be merely poison! Nothing I'll bear from thee

But nakedness, thou detestable town!
Take thou that too, with multiplying bans!
Timon will to the woods, where he shall find
The unkindest beast more kinder than mankind.
The gods confound—hear me, you good gods all!—
Th'Athenians both within and out that wall!
And grant, as Timon grows, his hate may grow
To the whole race of mankind, high and low!
Amen.

William Shakespeare, English, 1564–1616,
The Life of Timon of Athens 4.1

The "green" movement comes not from governments, not from those who should know and be responsible, but from individuals who see and hate what our civilization is doing to the world. In democracies, politicians must follow the will of the voters. For the majority of voters, a politician's job is to sniff the direction in which affluence lies. Our future depends on the voters getting wise.

To make things worse, politicians say to voters, "The more you consume, the better"—partly because politicians don't want to derail the gravy train, partly because the change we need is so alarmingly radical. The next poem adopts the semiliterate voice of a well-known Australian politician.

God Gave Us Trees to Cut Down

My Goodness;
if I was to have a say in the way things should be done in
    Victoria:
like we run them and have them here in Queensland,
then by crikey;

those forests—rain forests and what have they—in
  Gippsland there;
and let me tell you,
we have been down this road with the conservationists too:
and, by golly, we gave them what for.

And why should they cut down their trees?
What use are they? well I'll tell you:
the Japanese—I know they're a funny mob of people—
but they make paper out of trees, see,
and we all need paper.
You know this—what a stupid question to ask.
What would you do without paper and cardboard and—
  goodness, I ask you.
Of course we must cut down trees;
golly, what did God give them to us for.

And look at the other States, and all of them and what have
  you;
they have taken a leaf out of our Queensland way of doing
  things.
Just look at Mr. Grey in Tasmania; he cuts down many
  trees,
now; unfortunately they don't seem to have the courage
to stand up to the Federal Government and sit firmly on
  their position
—but let me tell you, they cut down many trees in
  Tasmania.
And in Western Australia
—just look at them—well—

they cut down their Jarra, and all their other sorts there.
And in New South Wales previous governments,
and even the present government sells their trees to the
    Japanese,

and my goodness, so they should.
Don't worry about South Australia, they don't have any
    trees.
Unfortunately the Northern Territory has been given to the
    Aboriginals,
and we all know they worship trees and sticks and plants
    and things
and what have you
and all sorts of things so we all know where that place is
    going;
and what a pity;
minerals and the Casino and Ayers Rock
—as they now call it: Uluru; and what a shame—don't you
    think it a shame?
And you see? they worship rocks too. All the minerals will
    go down the drain.

But here in Queensland we don't let the Federal
    Government
down there in Canberra tell us what to do
—and why should we?
If they come up here we soon give them short shrift and
    short change.
We send them running back down south with their tails
    between their legs

and their hats behind their backs like little schoolboys.
That's the way to do it—you've got to show them who's
    boss.
And so I would tell Mr. Cain not to worry about those
    conservationists,
just run right over them:
cut right through the lot of them as if they weren't there.
Golly, that's the way we do it in Queensland.

My goodness, you should know
God gave us those rain forests to cut down . . .

W. Les Russell, Aboriginal Australian, born 1949

The great nightmare of civilization is that the control of it will be given into the wrong hands. The Holocaust did not take place somewhere wild and uncivilized; it occurred right in the heart of civilized and democratic Europe. The next poem is about what happens when power is handed over to extremists, whose promises of order and plenty lead to nightmare.

 ## The Shield of Achilles

    She looked over his shoulder
        For vines and olive trees,
    Marble well-governed cities,
        And ships upon untamed seas,
    But there on the shining metal
        His hands had put instead
    An artificial wilderness
    And a sky like lead.

A plain without a feature, bare and brown,
    No blade of grass, no sign of neighborhood,
Nothing to eat and nowhere to sit down,
    Yet, congregated on its blankness, stood
An unintelligible multitude,
    A million eyes, a million boots in line,
Without expression, waiting for a sign.

Out of the air a voice without a face
    Proved by statistics that some cause was just
In tones as dry and level as the place:
    No one was cheered and nothing was discussed;
    Column by column in a cloud of dust
They marched away enduring a belief
Whose logic brought them, somewhere else, to grief.

    She looked over his shoulder
        For ritual pieties,
    White flower-garlanded heifers,
        Libation and sacrifice,
    But there on the shining metal
        Where the altar should have been,
    She saw by his flickering forge-light
        Quite another scene.

Barbed wire enclosed an arbitrary spot
    Where bored officials lounged (one cracked a joke)
And sentries sweated, for the day was hot:
    A crowd of ordinary decent folk
    Watched from without and neither moved nor spoke

As three pale figures were led forth and bound
To three posts driven upright in the ground.

The mass and majesty of this world, all
    That carries weight and always weighs the same,
Lay in the hands of others; they were small
    And could not hope for help and no help came;
    What their foes liked to do was done, their shame
Was all the worst could wish; they lost their pride
And died as men before their bodies died.

    She looked over his shoulder
        For athletes at their games,
    Men and women in a dance
        Moving their sweet limbs
    Quick, quick, to music,
        But there on the shining shield
    His hands had set no dancing-floor
        But a weed-choked field.

A ragged urchin, aimless and alone,
    Loitered about that vacancy; a bird
Flew up to safety from his well-aimed stone:
    That girls are raped, that two boys knife a third,
    Were axioms to him, who'd never heard
Of any world where promises were kept
Or one could weep because another wept.

    The thin-lipped armorer,
        Hephaestos,[3] hobbled away;

Thetis[4] of the shining breasts
　　Cried out in dismay
At what the god had wrought
To please her son, the strong
Iron-hearted man-slaying Achilles
Who would not live long.

W. H. Auden, English, 1907–73

At the other end of the political scale, common humanity is also denied to a large number of people. For fascists, the enemy is identified by "race"; for Communists, they are identified by "class."

In the next poem, the malice of the leaders seems to go beyond what the people want—but the people are impotent to object.

 Six Years Old

1.

Six years old and all alone
He looks for something to eat.
His father, the village landlord,
Has paid his blood-debt to the peasants;
Abandoning him, his mother had gone
South.

His mother bore him,
He ate, slept on soft bedding,
Wore soft pretty clothes.
He never knew how happy he was.

Then came the storm;
Who could spare a thought for such a tiny pawn?
Yet humans will always care for humans;
There will always be compassion.

A wretched, hungry old man
Trembles and shuffles as he hunts for crabs;
He feels pity for this skinny child
Who has neither mother nor father;
He gives him a handful of rice.

Limbs like sticks,
Swollen stomach but scrawny neck, the orphaned child
Surveys the world through round bloodshot eyes:
"I bow to you, madam, I beg a bowl of gruel;
Please madam, some rice . . . "

2.
A young cadre working outside the village
Looks down the road;
She hears his forlorn cry.
She trembles as she recalls
The hunger years of long ago;
Just five years old and she must lick
Leaves found in the marketplace.

She runs down the lane,
Takes him by the hand and into her house.
From yesterday's supper
She gives him a bowl of rice.

Another girl, of peasant stock,
Aspiring to Party membership,
Turns her back to hide her tears:
"A landlord's child, too young to know his fault;
I gave him a bowl of gruel
And they questioned me for three long days."

The land-reform cadre recoiled
And gazed at the child, searching for a trace
Of the enemy.
She saw only a child.
The child ate its fill,
Lay down on the ground to sleep.
She thought of the husband she would have
And of their pink, milk-fat children.

3.
She lost her job because of it.
In a cold dark room by the light of a lamp
She wrote her confession.

The tongue has no strength
The road is crooked;
The eye is too small
There is no horizon;
The mind is lazy
The color of rusty iron.

Sleeping for years
On the page of a book;

The people are machines,
Muscles but no heart.

4.
"In relationship with reactionaries,"
"Loss of revolutionary vigilance."
Night after night she weeps beside the lamp
And asks herself:
"How could I pity the enemy's child?
How happy I would be if I could have
Hated the child!"

Bui Hoang Cam, Vietnamese, born 1922, tr. David McAree

Civilization has a long reach. If a buyer of cat litter knew that a sacred aboriginal mountain was being disemboweled to produce it, would he or she make the purchase anyway? But though we don't know the price of our petty comforts, we can (if we want to) form a fair impression of the general price of our civilization.

 Time Is Running Out

The miner rapes
The heart of the earth
With his violent spade.
Stealing, bottling her black blood
For the sake of greedy trade.
On his metal throne of destruction,
He labors away with a will,
Piling the mountainous minerals high
With giant tool and iron drill.

In his greedy lust for power,
He destroys old nature's will.
For the sake of the filthy dollar,
He dirties the nest he builds.
Well he knows that violence
Of his destructive kind
Will be violently written
Upon the sands of time.

But time is running out
And time is close at hand,
For the Dreamtime folk are massing
To defend their timeless land.
Come gentle black man
Show your strength;
Time to take a stand.
Make the violent miner feel
Your violent
Love of land.

Oodgeroo Noonuccal, Aboriginal Australian, born 1920

When civilized countries steal land occupied by other people, civilized theory and civilized practice are at their most divergent. Australia was declared *terra nullius* —"the land of no one"—by the explorer Captain James Cook, as if the native population did not exist or were animals. Later, racial contempt enabled colonists to maintain their view of themselves as civilized even while they slaughtered those who had lived there before them.

In the next poem, an Aboriginal Australian poet takes Christian colonists to task for their hypocrisy.

Memo to JC

When you were down here JC and walked this earth,
You were a pretty decent sort of bloke,
Although you never owned nothing, but the clothes on your
     back,
And you were always walking round, broke.
But you could talk to people, and you didn't have to judge,
You didn't mind helping the down and out
But these fellows preaching now in your Holy name,
Just what are they on about?
Didn't you tell these fellows to do other things,
Besides all that preaching and praying?
Well, listen, JC, there's things that ought to be said,
And I might as well get on with the saying.
Didn't you tell them "don't judge your fellow man"
And "love ye one another"
And "not put your faith in worldly goods."
Well, you should see the goods that they got, brother!
They got great big buildings and works of art,
And millions of dollars in real estate,
They got no time to care about human beings,
They forgot what you told 'em, mate;
Things like, "Whatever ye do to the least of my brothers,
This ye do also unto me."
Yeah, well these people who are using your good name,
They're abusing it, JC,
But there's still people living the way you lived,
And still copping the hypocrisy, racism and hate,

Getting crucified by the fat cats, too,
But they don't call us religious, mate.
Tho' we've got the same basic values that you lived by,
Sharin' and carin' about each other,
And the bread and wine that you passed around,
Well, we're still doin' that, brother.
Yeah, we share our food and drink and shelter,
Our grief, our happiness, our hopes and plans,
But they don't call us "Followers of Jesus,"
They call us black fellas, man.
But if you're still offering your hand in forgiveness
To the one who's done wrong, and is sorry,
I reckon we'll meet up later on,
And I got no cause to worry.
Just don't seem right somehow that all the good you did,
That people preach, not practice, what you said,
I wonder, if it all died with you, that day on the cross,
And if it just never got raised from the dead.

Maureen Watson, Aboriginal Australian, contemporary

Europeans went overseas in search of wealth and land for their burgeoning populations. Medicine, increasing longevity, hygiene, and better nutrition all played a part in population growth, as did laws against primitive methods of population control, such as abortion, infanticide, and nonprocreative forms of sex.

Populations in the more civilized countries are now more stable. The old system of colonialism has been replaced by a new one, which is in many ways worse. Corrupt Third World governments are maintained through the use of arms supplied by the West in return for the right to strip Third World lands of their assets.

But our lifestyle doesn't make us happy. What we've done to chickens we've done to ourselves. Factory-farm chickens are cooped up in boxes, their only functions to consume and produce—who would ask them if they're happy? Who would believe them if they answered that they were?

 The Unhappy Race

White fellow, you are the unhappy race.
You alone have left nature and made civilized laws.
You have enslaved yourselves as you enslaved the horse and
   other wild things.
Why, white man?
Your police lock up your tribe in houses with bars,
We see poor women scrubbing floors of richer women.
Why, white man, why?
You laugh at "poor blackfellow," you say we must be like you.
You say we must leave the old freedom and leisure,
We must be civilized and work for you.
Why, white fellow?
Leave us alone, we don't want your collars and ties,
We don't need your routines and compulsions.
We want the old freedom and joy that all things have but
   you,
Poor white man of the unhappy race.

Oodgeroo Noonuccal, Aboriginal Australian, born 1920

A cry of "Leave us alone!" is often heard when civilization invades a tribal land.

 The ever-touring Englishmen have built their bungalows
All over our sweet forest.

They drive their trains with smoke:
O look at them, how they talk on wires to one another,
With their wires they have bound the whole world together
    for themselves.

Anonymous song, Gond (India), 1930s,
tr. V. Elwin and S. Hivale

The further people move away from dirt and physical work, the less they are aware of their dependence on nature. Insulated from the earth by plate glass and concrete, the highly paid occupants of luxury apartments make decisions that devastate the globe, in return for short-term profits.

The next poem contrasts the builders of high-rise buildings with the people who will inhabit them later.

✸ *Builders*

On great Ur-slabs of concrete terraces,
or rust-red bones of girder and cross-member,
they sit, eating their sandwiches
at noon. They look at home there
among the stylized trunks of metal forests,
the unfinished work.
Maybe the half-built is our proper habitat,
manhandling raw material
in basic contact, manipulation, direction
of various substances. Simple . . .

Later, the place changes.
Dressed in plastic wall boards, fitted
with doors and windows, connected

by cables, wires and pipes to the feed-in world,
it becomes part of a circuit.

Coming in later to consult officials,
sign papers, buy, sell, argue over contracts,
they observe the fake marble, the carpets
covering those bare encounters of concrete and steel,
the corridors scurrying with unfamiliar errands:
wondering. Wondering about building.
How whatever we construct gets complicated,
gets out of order and beyond our control.

Judith Wright, Australian, born 1915

In a poem that's a bit unfair to pigs, Brendan Kennelly describes the kind of man
who thrives among the fake marble and carpets.

 ## *The Pig*

You, Heavenly Muse, how will you justify
The pig's ways to men?
How will you sing
Of the pig's origin?
What thighs opened wide
To let out that snout
Rammed on a carcass of timeless slime?
When the old sly juices went to work
What womb
Sheltered our little darling?

What breasts
Gave it suck?

Suck, suck.

And on our treacherous planet
What hearts worry for its welfare?

The pig is everywhere.
He grunts between the lovers in their bed
His hot sperm flooding the girl
His dungeon breath rutting into her skin
Where a man's fingers move in what he thinks
Are patterns of enchantment.
The pig's eyes smile in the dark.

The pig's eyes glow with ambition.
He knows that where his head won't go
His tail will enter,
His little corkscrew tail.

The pig sits on committees,
Hums and haws, grunts yes and no,
Is patient, wise, attentive,
Wary of decision (alternatives are many).
When he hefts his bottom from the chair
The seat is hot.
His head is dull
But, maybe, he's just a little stronger now.

The pig knows how to apologize.
He would hurt nobody.

If he did, he didn't mean it.
His small eyes redden with conviction.
Remorse falls like saliva from his jaws.

The pig is bored
But doesn't know it.
The pig gobbles time
And loves the weekend.
The pig is important
And always says, "It seems to me" and "Yes, let's face it."
The pig chews borrowed words,
Munching conscientiously.
Sometimes he thinks he's a prophet, a seer so elegant
That we should bow down before him.
He is more remote from a sense of the unutterable
Than any words could begin to suggest.

The pig knows he has made the world.
Mention the possibility of something beyond it—
He farts in your face.

The pig's deepest sty is under his skin.
His skin is elegantly clad.
The pig knows might is right.
The pig is polite.
The pig is responsible and subtle.
How can this be so?
I don't know, but I have seen the pig at work
And know the truth of what I see.

The pig has lived in me

And gone his way, snouting the muck
In the wide sty of the world.

His appetite for filth is monstrous
And he knows
There is more sustenance in filth
Than in the sweet feast at the white table
Where friends gather for a night
Talk and laugh
In a room with warm light.

The pig might enter that room
And swallow everything in sight.

But the pig's sense of timing
Is flawless.
His own throat is fat, ready to cut,
But no one will do that.
Instead, the pig will slit
Some other throat.
There will be no blood but a death,
The pig will hump into the future

Huge
Hot
Effective

His eyes darting like blackbirds for the worm
Waiting to be stabbed, plucked, gulped,
Forgotten.

And still our darling lives
As though there were no
Oblivion.

Brendan Kennelly, Irish, born 1936

There is a story in Greek mythology about a giant named Antaeus. He was only strong when standing on his mother Earth. Hercules realized this and managed to kill the giant by holding him up in the air; the giant lost his strength and Hercules squeezed him to death. Hercules himself was an earthy kind of hero.

We have truly come a long way from our natural contact with Mother Earth. Even our farmers traverse their fields in machines, usually with headphones on, substituting pop music or other people's chatter for the grinding mechanical noise. The countryside itself has been transformed into a semi-industrial landscape. Most of the population now lives in towns, and most voters have no experience of life in the countryside. In the next poem, Pan, the god of wildness and fear, moves from the country to the city.

 Panic

Not in deserted meadows Pan wanders
But in the crowded cities where millions live.
Asphalt and concrete are his stamping ground
At noon, during the long hot summers.

From luxury flats in block apartments
He leaps into the latest cars.
He lives with giant banks for background
Surrounded by his minions.

He singles out the silent, the helpless,
Avoiding those who bare their teeth

Near factory walls and muffled fortress gate.
He pounces on the meager joys
Of vanquished men, discouraged women.

Not in the sultry summers alone
But any day, almost, in the big cities
He combs the boulevards with mute malicious laughter.
Seeing him face-to-face the unemployed
Turn giddy as they pace the hard dank pavements.

Where the poor, the sick, the hungry crawl,
In the city's belly, in remote alleyways,
His sense of mischief unassuaged, he vents
More fury in Man's cruel civilization
Of atom bombs and guided missiles.

Tomorrow? If there is a trace of him in the news,
The bread, the water with its taste of hemlock,
Or if his shadow falls on the faces of children,
There is little hope in tomorrow for such as us.

Behcet Necatigil, Turkish, born 1916,
tr. Nermin Menemencioglu

The great effort of building a civilization is its own exhilaration—but what are people to do once it's largely built? Is frustration inevitable? We are living organisms, and the essence of life is struggle. If civilization is so constricting that struggle is done away with, then apathy, boredom, and the desire to knock it all down result.

❁ *Twentieth Century*

I am being consumed by life
Wasting, not doing anything,
Between the four symmetrical
Walls of my house.

Oh, workers! Bring your picks!
Let my walls and roof fall,
Let air move my blood,
Let sun burn my shoulders.

I am a twentieth-century woman.
I spend my day lounging,
Watching, from my room,
How a branch moves.

Europe is burning,
And I'm watching its flames
With the same indifference
With which I contemplate that branch.

You, passerby, don't look me
Up and down; my soul
Shouts its crime aloud, yours
Hides under its words.

Alfonsina Storni, Argentinian, 1892–1938, tr. Marion Freeman

In the next poem, the same feelings of claustrophobia and frustration, voiced by
a young man, lead him to violence.

The Lament of a Discontented Young Man
(At the beginning of a conscripted century)

Paris, Peking . . . London, or Rome?
How desolate is this city, the world!
City or village, it all means the same: Nothing.
To change one's surroundings
is utterly senseless now.
If only something different—
if only a great riot would begin.

For who can still bear this grayness
which lets liars sparkle and gleam?
O clenched fist, come:
let this so worthless life crash down,
then let the great doctor, Death, arrive,
and after death the opening of eyes,
the horrors,
let something different come,
rebellions, why do you hesitate?

Blood, blood, blood.
Man will be much more beautiful
once he is cleaned with blood,
and better too.
Then come with your angels and trumpets,
O Resurrection,
and come with your armies of millions,
drive the vigor of youth into this desolate
globe, the earth,

and let the redeeming rifle come,
Amen.

Endre Ady, Hungarian, 1877–1919,
tr. Fred Marnau and Michael Hamburger

The same poet wrote, a few years later, of the fruits his prayer had borne.

 ## Prayer After the War

Lord, I have come from the war,
all is departed and past:
now reconcile me to yourself, and to myself,
since you are peace.

Look, my heart is a fiery
ulcer, and nothing gives relief.
Then with a kiss overpower my heart
to soften it.

For a long time already
my sad great eyes have been shut
to this world, there's nothing to see, but you:
you they embrace.

These two running legs have been
knee-deep in blood, look, O Lord,
look down, now no feet remain, only knees,
Lord, only knees.

I do not fight now, nor kiss,
My mouth is bloodless, withered,

my devoured arms are crutches, so are
all other parts.

Look at me therefore, O Lord,
all is departed and past,
now reconcile me to yourself, and to myself,
since you are peace.

Endre Ady, Hungarian, 1877–1919,
tr. Fred Marnau and Michael Hamburger

Another pair of contrasting pieces gives impressions of what civilization is trying
to uphold and of the terrible consequences when it breaks down. In Germany,
during the Thirty Years' War, religious bigots joined secular rulers in the struggle
for power. Armed bands looted and robbed; no one was safe. Gryphius describes
the results:

✸ Tears of the Fatherland

So, now we are destroyed; utterly; more than utterly!
The gang of shameless peoples, the maddening music of
     war,
The sword fat with blood, the thundering of the guns
Have consumed our sweat and toil, exhausted our reserves.
Towers are on fire, churches turned upside down;
The town hall is in ruins, the strong cut down, destroyed.
Young girls are raped; wherever we turn our gaze,
Fire, plague, and death pierce heart and spirit through.
Here, town and ramparts run with ever-fresh streams of
     blood.

It's three times six years now, since our mighty river's flow
Was blocked almost by corpses, just barely trickling
    through.
Yet, I pass over in silence something more terrible than
    death,
More desperate even than plague, fire, and famine;
That so many were bereaved of their soul's treasure too.

Andreas Gryphius, German, 1616–64, tr. I. M.

A contemporary of Gryphius, the novelist Hans von Grimmelshausen, described his astonishment at arriving in Switzerland and finding civilized conditions of a kind he had never experienced in his native Germany, so long had the war been going on:

> There I saw people trading and walking about in peace. The stables were full of cattle, the barnyards were full of chickens, geese, and ducks running about, the streets were safely used by travelers. Taverns were full of people, who sat there enjoying themselves. There was no fear of an enemy, no concern of plunder, and no anxiousness about losing property or life. Everyone lived securely beneath his vine or fig tree, and indeed, measured against German countries, they lived in pure voluptuousness and joy. I took the country for an earthly paradise.

This truly sounds like civilization. The next dozen poems are about the pursuit of civilized pleasures that are not destructive, either to humanity or to the planet.

⚘ It's a pleasure
When, rising in the morning,
I go outside and
Find that a flower has bloomed
That was not there yesterday.

It's a pleasure
When, a most infrequent treat,
We've fish for dinner
And my children cry with joy
"Yum-yum!" and gobble it down.

It's a pleasure
When, without receiving help,
I can understand
The meaning of a volume
Reputed most difficult.

Tachibana Akemi, Japanese, 1812–68, tr. Donald Keene

 Sitting in silence
and looking wise
isn't half as good
as drinking wine
and making a riotous shouting!

Otomo no Tabito, Japanese, 665–731, tr. I. M. after tr. by Arthur Waley

 Let me go home now;
The feast can go on without me;
My child may be crying,
And my patient wife
Waiting for me to come home!

Yamanoue Okura, Japanese, circa 660–733, tr. I. M.

The next poem, written by a medieval monk, celebrates the labor as well as the results of horticulture. It is the introduction to a much longer poem, which goes on to celebrate the plants of the medieval garden.

A quiet life has many rewards: not least of these
Is the joy that comes to him who devotes himself to the art
They knew at Paestum, and learns the ancient skill of obscene
Priapus[5]—the joy that comes of devoting himself to a garden.
For whatever the land you possess, whether it be where sand
And gravel lie barren and dead, or where fruits grow heavy
In rich moist ground; whether high on a steep hillside,
Easy ground in the plain or rough among sloping valleys—
Wherever it is, your land cannot fail to produce
Its native plants. If you do not let laziness clog
Your labor, if you do not insult with misguided efforts
The gardener's multifarious wealth, and if you do not
Refuse to harden or dirty your hands in the open air
Or to spread whole baskets of dung on the sun-parched soil—
Then, you may rest assured, your soil will not fail you.
This I have learned not only from common opinion
And searching about in old books, but from experience—
Experience of hard work and sacrifice of many days
When I might have rested, but chose instead to labor.

Walafrid Strabo, German, 808–49, tr. from Latin by Raef Payne

✸ On First Looking into Chapman's Homer

Much have I travel'd in the realms of gold
And many goodly states and kingdoms seen;
Round many western islands have I been
Which bards in fealty to Apollo hold.
Oft of one wide expanse had I been told
That deep-brow'd Homer ruled as his demesne:
Yet did I never breathe its pure serene
Till I heard Chapman speak out loud and bold:

Then felt I like some watcher of the skies
When a new planet swims into his ken;
Or like stout Cortez when with eagle eyes
He stared at the Pacific—and all his men
Look'd at each other with a wild surmise—
Silent, upon a peak in Darien.[6]

John Keats, English, 1795–1821

Elsewhere in this book are the poems "Heraclitus," on the pleasure of talk, and "Pangur Ban," on the pleasure of learning.

The healing, integrating, all-containing power of art is celebrated in the next poem. Its last lines refer to the story of King David's love for Bathsheba, which drove him to plot her husband's death by having him placed in the front line of battle.

Suddenly
color bursts upon us like the sound
of a great symphony   in chords
both luminous and vibrant.
In your tumultuous vision
of angels and clowns, of acrobats
peasants and animals
man is the mediator between God
and His creation.   What is real
and what illusion?

Everything changes, you say
except the heart,
man's love and his striving
to know the divine.   You reconcile
suffering with love,
the individual pain
that each man carries deep within himself.

And so we too are included in your vision:
fly over snow-decked villages,
lie tensely stretched in dark-green poetical grass
or rocked by a blossoming lilac tree,
levitated by love.
Or kneel with David tenderly
before the beautiful Bathsheba
while in the foreground, evilly,

an eagle foreshadows her husband's fate:
death in a battle to which her lover condemns him.

Anne Ranasinghe, German Jewish Sri Lankan
writing in English, born 1925

The next poem concerns the enjoyment of music. Salinas was a blind organist, musical theorist, and collector of folk songs, who lived in Spain from 1513 to 1590. Unfortunately none of his music survives.

Ode to Salinas

The air grows calm, is
Bathed in loveliness and unusual light,
Salinas, when your music sounds
Extreme in its refinement
Under your skilled well-governed hand.

At this divine sound,
My soul, from cowering in oblivion,
Arises to regain
A sense and memory of
The glory of its first exalted state.

And, as it greets itself,
In destiny and thoughts it now grows stronger;
Estranged is the gold
Which the blind crowd adores
So fleeting and so fickle in its beauty.

Through and out of air
It soars, arriving at the highest sphere,
And there it hears another
Mode imperishable,
The music that is origin of all.

There it sees the great
Master, industrious on a zither immense,
Produce with adept motion
The sacred harmony
By which the eternal temple is sustained.

And now my soul, composed
Of numbers that agree, sends in reply
Consonant music;
Both, insistently,
Combine to make the softest harmony.

Here my soul navigates
Upon a sea of gentleness until
At last it drowns,
Its senses deaf
To any outside mishap or occurrence.

O blessed unawareness!
O death that gives us life! O sweet oblivion!
Would it but last, that I
Might never be thrust back
To this base and vile way of being!

To this good I call you,
You glory of Apollo's sacred choir—

My friends, whom I love
And treasure above all—
For everything but this is lamentation.

Play on, play on, Salinas!
Your music sound forever in my ears!
To divine goodness it
Awakens my senses,
Leaving them deaf to all other things.

Luis de León, Spanish, 1527–1591(?), tr. I. M.

The pleasures of living in the country are celebrated in many poems. In the next two, the poet has been disappointed by his reception in the city and is making the best of things in the country.

✸ *Drinking Wine: Two Poems*

In the quiet of the morning I heard a knock at my door;
I threw on my clothes and opened it myself.
I asked who it was who had come so early to see me;
He said he was a peasant, coming with good intent.
He brought with him a full flagon of wine,
Believing my household had fallen on evil days.
"You live in rags under a thatched roof
And seem to have no desire for a better lot.
The rest of mankind have all the same ambitions;
You too must learn to wallow in their mire."
"Old man, I am impressed by what you say,
But my soul is not fashioned like other men's.

200

To drive in their rut I might perhaps learn;
To be untrue to myself could only lead to muddle.
Let us drink and enjoy together the wine you have brought;
For my course is set now and cannot be altered."

 I built my hut in a zone of human habitation,
Yet near me there sounds no noise of horse or coach.
Would you know how that is possible?
A heart that is distant creates a wilderness round it.
I pluck chrysanthemums under the eastern hedge,
Then gaze long at the distant hills.
The mountain air is fresh at dusk of day;
The flying birds two by two return.
In these things there lies a deep meaning;
Yet when we would express it, words suddenly fail us.

Tao Yuan Ming, a.k.a. Tao Ch'ien, Chinese, 372–427, tr. Arthur Waley

A walk was a cure for depression long before shopping sprees were invented.

 ## *Third Day of the Third Month, Rain: Written to Dispel My Depression*

1.

I go out the door; it's raining, but I can't go back now,
so I borrow someone's bamboo hat to wear for a while.
Spring has tinted ten thousand leaves, and I didn't even
  know;

the clouds have taken a thousand mountains and swept
    them away.

2.
I look for flowers in the village
    but they hide from me on purpose;
and even when I find them, they only sadden me.
It would be better to lie down
    and listen to the rain
        in the spring mountains—
a quick downpour, then a few scattered drops.

3.
As spring dies, the scenes grow more beautiful:
the poet will remember them for the rest of his life.
Level fields overflowing with green—
    wheat in every village;
soft waters reflecting red—
    flowers on every bank.

Yang Wan-Li, Chinese, 1127–1206, tr. Jonathan Chaves

The next poem concerns the way in which civilization affects our enjoyment of the world around us. The story behind the poem is this: a Chinese king, feeling guilty at the enormous gap in wealth between himself and his subjects, reflects aloud that at least the delightful breeze he is enjoying can be enjoyed by his subjects. A courtier, the poet Sung Yu, doesn't let the emperor get away with such sloppy thinking. Whether we enjoy the wind, he says, depends on where we are when it's blowing.

"The wind is born from the land
And springs up in the tips of the green duckweed.
It insinuates itself into the valleys
And rages in the canyon mouth,
Skirts the corners of Mount T'ai
And dances beneath the pines and cedars.
Swiftly it flies, whistling and wailing;
Fiercely it splutters its anger.
It crashes with a voice like thunder,
Whirls and tumbles in confusion,
Shaking rocks, striking trees,
Blasting the tangled forest.
Then, when its force is almost spent,
It wavers and disperses,
Thrusting into crevices and rattling door latches.
Clean and clear
It scatters and rolls away.
Thus it is that this cool, fresh hero wind,
Leaping and bounding up and down,
Climbs over the high wall
And enters deep into palace halls.
With a puff of breath it shakes the leaves and flowers,
Wanders among the cassia and pepper trees,
Or soars over the swift waters.
It buffets the mallow flower,
Sweeps the angelica, touches the spikenard,
Glides over the sweet lichens and lights on willow shoots,
Rambling over the hills
And their scattered host of fragrant flowers.

After this, it wanders round the courtyard,
Ascends the jade hall in the north,
Clambers over gauze curtains,
Passes through the inner apartments,
And so becomes Your Majesty's wind.
When this wind blows on a man,
At once he feels a chill run through him,
And he sighs at its cool freshness.
Clear and gentle,
It cures sickness, dispels drunkenness,
Sharpens the eyes and ears,
Relaxes the body and brings benefit to men.
This is what is called the hero wind of Your Majesty."

"How well you have described it," said the king. "But now may I hear about the wind of the common people?" And Sung Yu replied:

"The wind of the common people
Comes whirling from the lanes and alleys,
Poking in the rubbish, stirring up the dust,
Fretting and worrying its way along,
It creeps into holes and knocks on doors,
Scatters sand, blows ashes about,
Muddles in dirt and tosses up bits of filth.
It sidles through hovel windows
And slips into cottage rooms.
When this wind blows on a man,
At once he feels confused and downcast.
Pounded by heat, smothered in dampness,

His heart grows sick and heavy,
And he falls ill and breaks out in a fever.
Where it brushes his lips, sores appear;
It strikes his eyes with blindness:
He stammers and cries out,
Not knowing if he is dead or alive.
That is what is called the lowly wind of the common people."

Sung Yu, Chinese, third century B.C.,
tr. Burton Watson

Too much civilization, however, can insulate us from the intense joy that comes from living close to nature.

 ## *Clearing the Fields*

We clear the grasses and trees,
We plow and carve the land,
Two thousand men and women scrabbling weeds
Along the low wetlands, along the dike walls.
The masters, the eldest sons,
The laborers, the hired servants,
They mark out the fields, they ply their plows,
Overflowing food baskets are brought to them,
They gaze on their fair wives
And press close to them.
They have sharp plowshares,
They have set to work on the south acres,
They sow the many kinds of grain.

Each seed holds a moist germ;
Splendidly, splendidly the young grain shoots forth,
Sleekly, sleekly the young plants rise,
Tenderly, tenderly comes the young grain.
Thousands of weeders scrabbling among the weeds!
Host upon host of reapers!
Close-huddled stooks arranged in due order!
Myriads, many hundred thousands and millions of grains!
From them come wine and sweet liquor,
Offering to the ancestors, the male and the female,
In fulfillment of sacrifices.
So glory shall come to the land.
They will have a sharp smell of pepper,
They will give comfort to the aged.
It is not only here that it is so,
It is not only now that it is so:
But in most ancient times ever and ever.

*Anonymous, Chinese, seventh century B.C.,
from* Book of Songs, *tr. Robert Payne*

The prosperity of tribal peoples depends on their not overusing the land. The myth of Eden is about leaving primitive conditions for the gains and sacrifices of civilization (it's no coincidence that New York is called the Big Apple).

Civilization draws people and resources to its cities. Industry demands a substantial workforce that will do repetitive work for low pay. Then, as technology swallows up jobs, many are put out of work. The next poem tells of the anger that builds up in people whose dream is never realized.

Harlem

What happens to a dream deferred?

Does it dry up
like a raisin in the sun?
Or fester like a sore—
And then run?
Does it stink like rotten meat?
Or crust and sugar over—
like a syrupy sweet?

Maybe it just sags
like a heavy load.

Or does it explode?

Langston Hughes, American, 1902–67

Forugh Farrokhzad took the garden as a metaphor for civilization, which needs care and thought in its cultivation. Her poem of a neglected garden prophesies violence for a society that ceases to look after itself.

 I Pity the Garden

No one cares about the flowers
No one cares about the fish
No one wants
to believe the garden's dying
the garden's heart bloating beneath the sun
the garden's mind slowly slowly

being drained of its green memories
And it's as though the garden's feelings
are a solitary something decaying in the garden's solitude.

The courtyard of our house is lonely
the courtyard of our house
yawns
waiting for some unknown cloud to rain
and the pool of our house is empty
From the treetops, innocent little stars
fall to earth
and the sound of coughing comes at night
through the wan windows of the fishes' house
The courtyard of our house is lonely

Father says
"It's beyond me now
It's beyond me now
I lugged my load
and did my work"
And sits in his room from sunup to sundown
reading either the old epic poems
or the *History of Histories*
Father says to Mother
"To hell with the birds and the fish
What do I care
if there's a garden or not
when I'm dead
My pension's good enough for me"

All her life
Mother's been a prayer rug
spread at the gate of hell's terrors
Mother hunts for sin's footprints
under everything
and believes the garden's been fouled
by some sin's blaspheming
Mother prays all day long
Mother sins naturally
and blows[7] on all the flowers
and blows on all the fish
and blows on herself
Mother awaits the coming of heaven
and the descent of forgiveness

My brother calls the garden a graveyard
My brother laughs at the rioting weeds
and counts the corpses of the fish
rotting away to atoms
beneath the water's turbid skin
My brother's addicted to philosophy
My brother thinks the garden's healed
by its destruction
He gets drunk
and beats his fists on doors and walls
and mumbles
about his aches and tired hopelessness
He takes his pessimism out
to the street and the bazaar

along with his ID and pocket calendar and handkerchief
and lighter and fountain pen
And his pessimism's
so tiny he loses it each night
in the crowd at the bar

And my sister, once a friend to flowers
who used to gather them silently, lovingly
with her heart's simple words
when Mother had punished her
and treat the family of fish
with tidbits and the sun too now and then—
she's in her house across town
She's in her phony house
with her phony goldfish
and in her phony husband's love nest
singing phony songs
beneath the branches of phony apple trees
and making real children
She
showers herself with eau de cologne
whenever she visits us
and smudges the hem of her skirt with the garden's poverty
Every time she visits us she's
pregnant

The courtyard of our house is lonely
The courtyard of our house is lonely
All day long
sounds of shattering

and explosions can be heard
Instead of flowers our neighbors are planting
machine guns and mortars in their garden grounds
Our neighbors are covering
their tiled pools
and the tiled pools
becoming ammunition caches
without ever being asked
And the kids on our street
have loaded their briefcases
with little bombs
The courtyard of our house feels sick
I fear the time
that is heartless
I fear the image of all these futile hands
and the sight of all these strange faces
I'm lonely as a pupil
who's crazy
about her geometry class
I imagine that the garden could be taken to the hospital
I imagine . . .
I imagine . . .
I imagine . . .
And the garden's heart lies bloating beneath the sun
and the garden's mind is slowly slowly
drained of its green memories

Forugh Farrokhzad, Persian, 1934–67,
tr. Jascha Kessler and Amin Banani

We fill our immediate surroundings with roads and ugly architecture, then invade the wildernesses as tourists. If we looked after our own backyards, streets, towns, cities, and countrysides and made sure they were beautiful, we wouldn't have such a relentless appetite for travel.

Human beings and beauty are not incompatible. We lived on the earth for hundreds of thousands of years before we began turning it into a giant cesspool afloat with islands of garbage.

The next two poems are about love of native place.

 Happy is he who, like Ulysses, makes a good journey
(Or like that other who won the golden fleece)
And who then returns, used well by the world and wise,
To live with his kin and thereby end his days!

When will I see again, alas!, my little village,
Smoke rising from its chimneys? In what season
Will I see again the plot round my little house
That's a province to me, and much else besides?

More pleasing to me is the house built by my forebears
Than Roman palaces with their brilliant facades;
More than hard marble, I love the fineness of slate;

Sweeter's my Gallic Loire than the Latin Tiber,
More dear my little Liré than the Palatine Hill;
And more than sea air, I love the softness of Anjou.

Joachim du Bellay, French, 1522–60, tr. I. M.

In the month of June the grass grows high
And round my cottage thick-leaved branches sway.

There is not a bird but delights in the place where it rests:
And I too—love my thatched cottage.
I have done my plowing:
I have sown my seed.
Again I have time to sit and read my books.
In the narrow lane there are no deep ruts:
Often my friends' carriages turn back.
In high spirits I pour out my spring wine
And pluck the lettuce growing in my garden.
A gentle rain comes stealing from the east
And a sweet wind bears it company.
My thoughts float idly over the story of the king of Chou,
My eyes wander over the pictures of Hills and Seas.
At a single glance I survey the whole Universe.
He will never be happy, whom such pleasures fail to please!

Tao Yuan Ming, a.k.a. Tao Ch'ien,
Chinese, 372–427, tr. Arthur Waley

The human spirit can survive poverty and hardship, but can it survive affluence and power?

It's hard not to notice that poems celebrating life, love, and humanity tend to be written by poets who are enduring hardship. Poems of complaint and disgust are usually written by poets in positions of comfort and privilege.

Osip Mandelstam wrote joyous poetry in utter destitution, knowing the state would soon destroy him.

✸ Still I have not died, and still am not alone,
while with my beggarwoman friend

I take my pleasure from the grandeur of the plain
and from its gloom, its hunger and its hurricanes.

In splendid poverty, luxurious beggardom
I live alone—both peaceful and resigned—
blessed are those days and nights
and blameless is the sweetly sounding work.

Unhappy the man who like his shadow
quivers at a bark, is scythed down by the wind,
and poor the man who, half alive himself,
from a shadow begs for charity.

Osip Mandelstam, Russian, 1891–1938, tr. David McDuff

Boethius argued (from prison and under sentence of death) that no amount of good fortune can slake human greed.

Rapid blowing stirs up in the sea
How many grains of sand?
Clear and starry nights allow
How many stars to shine?
Should in such numbers goods be given
From fortune's plenteous horn,
Not for a second would humankind
Stop its miserable moans.
However freely God meets desires—
Showering spendthrifts in gold,
Adorning the greedy with eminent honors—
It all seems soon as nothing;

Raging greed devours the gains,
    And opens fresh jaws for more.
What can rein in headlong greed
    And keep it in reasonable bounds?
Do floods of gifts, more upon more,
    Just parch the thirst for possession?
People aren't rich who anxiously sigh
    And think they're in need of more.

Boethius, Roman, circa 480–524, tr. from Latin by I. M.

If we never feel intense need, we never feel intense satisfaction. But the option of comfort is hard to resist. Who would voluntarily undergo the hunger of the children in the next poem—or wish the experience on their own children?

✸ *The Transfixed*

Black in the snow and in the fog
Against a vent all glowing and warm
Their backsides in a circle

Five little urchins squat—pitiful!—
Watching the baker as he makes
His bread, heavy and white.

They watch the strong white arm knead
The gray dough, then put it in to bake
In the bright hole.

They listen as the good bread cooks.
The baker, with his fat smile,
Hums an old tune.

Huddled together, none of them budge
In the air from the glowing red vent
Hot like a breast.

When, for some midnight breakfast,
Round and bulging like a brioche
The bread comes out

When, under black and smoky beams,
The fragrant crusts hiss, singing
Along with the house-crickets,

How the warm hole breathes life!
Their soul is in such delight
Underneath the rags

That suddenly they're feeling life is good,
Poor little Jesuses, full of frost,
And there they stay

Pressing small and pink noses
Against the trellis, mumbling things
Through the holes,

Stupefied, and saying their prayer,
Bent over toward the lights of
Heaven reopened before them,

Straining so much their trousers rip
And their shirttails flutter free
In the winter wind.

Arthur Rimbaud, French, 1854–91, tr. I. M.

Understanding our desire to avoid pain, political parties promise to provide greater comforts, an easier life. The influence of government is more and more pervasive in our lives. Tragedies that once were seen as part of the fabric of life— to be blamed on God or fate, if on anyone—are now blamed on governments.

In the following poem-within-a-story, written long before governments offered social welfare, Basho looks with pity and terror on an abandoned child. Monkeys' cries (in the first line of the poem) were traditionally a poetic image for sadness.

✹ On the road by the Fuji River we came across an abandoned child, about two years old and crying pathetically. It seems its parents, finding life as unmanageable as the turbulent rapids of the river, had abandoned the child to its fate, which now seemed as evanescent as the dew, as vulnerable as bush-clover flowers in the autumn wind. I gave him food from my sleeve.

> Poets who feel sad at monkeys' cries—
> How about this child,
> Abandoned to the autumn wind?

How did this happen? Did your mother shun you? Did your father cast you out? No, neither father nor mother hated you—this is the will of heaven; you have only an evil fate to blame.

Basho, Japanese, 1644–94, version by I. M.

With so many advances in technology at our disposal, we should be able to build a civilization that would benefit and be shared by all. But we are still in thrall to the laws of nature—human nature included—and it's a tough job to work out what can and what can't be achieved by civilization.

Are we experiencing the growing pains of a new phase in human progress, or are we engaged in a final orgy of unrestrained feasting and violence at the expense of a dying earth? Time alone will give us the answer.

We should proceed with caution. Reckless and cynical arrogance will only lead to our own destruction. The poet Ma'arri wrote, almost a thousand years ago:

> We laughed; our laughing betrayed scorn.
> People on this earth should live in fear.
> When men shake hands with time, time crushes
> Them like tumblers; little pieces of glass.

Ma'arri, Syrian, 973–1057,
tr. George Wightman and Abdullah al-Udhari

Once on the bandwagon, it's hard to get off. Human nature must take the blame for squandering the potential that technology has lain before us. Restraint and sacrifice are out; glimmers of hope are few in the prevailing darkness.

> God help us, we have sold our souls, all that was best,
> To an enterprise in the hands of the Receiver.
> We've no dividends, or rights, for the price we paid.
> Yet should our wills choose between this corrupt business
> And a paradise to come, rest assured they'd want
>
> The world we have now.

Ma'arri, Syrian, 973–1057,
tr. George Wightman and Abdullah al-Udhari

Friedrich Hölderlin provides a more optimistic view of human life. This is a poem written in his madness, which may explain the date and signature attached—and perhaps also the optimism.

 People find themselves on this world to live
As the years are, as the times strive higher;
So, as change rolls on, a lot of truth is left.
Permanence enters into the different years;
Perfection joins to life in such a way
That life accommodates people's high-aimed striving.

Humbly, Scardanelli. May 17, 1748.

Friedrich Hölderlin, German, 1770–1843, tr. I. M.

CHAPTER 6

Old Worlds, New Nations

The worst is true.
Everything you did not want to know.

TOI DERRICOTE

During the twentieth century, we have come to realize that there is no limit imaginable to how badly, stupidly, and cruelly human beings can behave. Perhaps that knowledge is not a bad base on which to build the future.

Nature is full of cruelty and glory, of beauty and of tenderness. But with the emergence of Homo sapiens millions of years ago, a creature was born with vastly increased potential for both creativity and destruction.

❀ *Before Making Love*

I move my hands over your face,
closing my eyes, as if blind;
the cheek bones, broadly spaced,
the wide thick nostrils of the African,
the forehead whose bones push
at both sides as if the horns
of fallen angels lie just under,
the chin that juts forward with pride.
I think of the delicate skull of the Taung child—[1]
earliest of human beings
emerged from darkness—whose geometry
brings word of a small town of dignity
that all the bloody kingdoms rest on.

Toi Derricote, American, born 1941

The great new nations of the earth have been created by the migrations of many peoples from many different cultures. Without civilization, such mixtures of peoples degenerate into a swamp of hates. The next poem describes such a swamp. The poet is writing of the West Indies. He speaks from personal bitterness that his nation has not risen above ethnic hatred to a condition of civilization.

�֎ *At Sangre Grande*

> *Here the Negro, the Chinee,*
> *the white man, the Indian*
> *walk together hand in hand*
> *in this wonderland of calypso,*
> *this wonderland of steelband.*

CALYPSO CHORUS BY LORD BAKER

The jungle presses
we hold a clearing only,
like the late Arawak
that poor mushroom man,
peering at sneering skies.

No distance challenges
our myopic eye;
we hate, lust, fornicate,
cluster and vegetate
like the rain forest around us.

All night the Hindu drums
and chants his baroque East
communicating home,
shaming the creole man's
shabby masquerade.

Fo Chin, in sleeveless vest,
keeps shop, grinning his pidgin,
strumming his cash register,
his eyes slant to the score,
humming a dollar aria in his head.

Dr. Geneticist Lust
experiments with us,
crisscrossing seed,
splitting each breed
to quaint improbable mutations.

But stocks hold true
guarding their pith;
Hindu and Muslim snarl, Chinese
and whites stand off—blacks
seethe and rage in contempt of themselves.

The sun's displeasure
glares on man and mosque;
the moon despises
these rank simian hatreds
of customs, skins and creeds;
the swamps stink with our shames.

Eric Roach, Trinidadian, 1915–74

Societies composed of many cultures must try to avoid wars for ethnic power. No one can expect to emerge unscathed from such a war. Instead, these societies must seek a higher ideal—that of multicultural and multiracial cooperation, the basis of civilization.[2]

The official aims of Western civilization are tolerance, justice, and wealth for all. In the next poem, Anselm Hollo attacks the mentality that would keep all the wealth in the hands of one class.

manifest destiny

to arrive in front of large video screen,
in pleasantly air-conditioned home with big duck-pond in
    back
some nice soft drinks by elbow, some good american snacks
    as well,
at least four hundred grand in the bank, & that's for
    checking,
an undisclosed amount in investments, & a copacetic
    evening
watching the latest military *techné*
wipe out poverty everywhere in the world
in its most obvious form, the poor

Anselm Hollo, Finnish American, born 1934

Civilizations have always contained many peoples and many cultures.

The word *culture* represents a most profound and creative response by people to the world around them; through culture, life has meaning. Though cultures may adapt over time to changes in technology and environment, when the change is abrupt and swift they (and their peoples) experience disruption and trauma.

American Indians underwent terrible attrition in the face of a more diverse and more technologically powerful invading culture. The fight to preserve a way of life seemed lost, and despair set in.

The Man from Washington

The end came easy for most of us.
Packed away in our crude beginnings

in some far corner of a flat world,
we didn't expect much more
than firewood and buffalo robes
to keep us warm. The man came down,
a slouching dwarf with rainwater eyes,
and spoke to us. He promised
that life would go on as usual,
that treaties would be signed, and everyone—
man, woman, and child—would be inoculated
against a world in which we had no part,
a world of money, promise and fabulous disease.

James Welch, American Indian, born 1940

The despair of the last poem is barely mitigated in the next by a sense of community and a sense of humor.

 ## *Anchorage*

This city is made of stone, of blood, and fish.
There are Chugatch Mountains to the east
and whale and seal to the west.
It hasn't always been this way, because glaciers
who are ice ghosts create oceans, carve earth
and shape this city here, by the sound.
They swim backwards in time.

Once a storm of boiling earth cracked open
the streets, threw open the town.
It's quiet now, but underneath the concrete

is the cooking earth,
          and above that, air
which is another ocean, where spirits we can't see
are dancing   joking   getting full
on roasted caribou, and the praying
goes on, extends out.

Nora and I go walking down 4th Avenue
and know it is all happening.
On a park bench we see someone's Athabascan
grandmother, folded up, smelling like 200 years
of blood and piss, her eyes closed against some
unimagined darkness, where she is buried in an ache
in which nothing makes
          sense.

We keep on breathing, walking, but softer now,
the clouds whirling in the air above us.
What can we say that would make us understand
better than we do already?
Except to speak of her home and claim her
as our own history, and know that our dreams
don't end here, two blocks away from the ocean
where our hearts still batter away at the muddy shore.

And I think of the 6th Avenue jail, of mostly Native
and Black men, where Henry told about being shot at
eight times outside a liquor store in L.A., but when
the car sped away he was surprised he was alive,
no bullet holes, man, and eight cartridges strewn

on the sidewalk
        all around him.

Everyone laughed at the impossibility of it,
but also the truth. Because who would believe
the fantastic and terrible story of all of our survival
those who were never meant
        to survive?

Joy Harjo, American Indian, born 1951

Many features of traditional Native American culture—closeness to nature, a sense of community, having no debts—increasingly appeal in our impersonal world, where democracy itself is an irrelevance for the growing number of truly disadvantaged.[3]

Being out of tune with the culture around us can make us feel isolated and even insane. The poet Linda Hogan tells a story about a friend: "She had thought she was crazy and one day she was visiting with her mother out in the chicken coop and suddenly realized she was very sane, except that she was Osage Indian and would never think like the others."[4]

After the slaughter of native peoples, colonial nations imported slaves and bonded laborers to do their dirty work. But the whites wanted to keep the wealth and comforts for themselves.

✸ The Ballad of Rudolph Reed

Rudolph Reed was oaken.
His wife was oaken too.
And his two good girls and his good little man
Oakened as they grew.

"I am not hungry for berries.
I am not hungry for bread.
But hungry for a house
Where at night a man in bed

"May never hear the plaster
Stir as if in pain.
May never hear the roaches
Falling like fat rain.

"Where never wife and children need
Go blinking through the gloom.
Where every room of many rooms
Will be full of room.

"Oh my home may have its east or west
Or north or south behind it.
All I know is I shall know it,
And fight for it when I find it."

It was in a street of bitter white
That he made his application.
For Rudolph Reed was oakener
Than others in the nation.

The agent's steep and steady stare
Corroded to a grin.
Why, you black old, tough old hell of a man,
Move your family in!

Nary a grin grinned Rudolph Reed,
Nary a curse cursed he,

But moved in his House. With his dark little wife,
And his dark little children three.

A neighbor would *look,* with a yawning eye
That squeezed into a slit.
But the Rudolph Reeds and the children three
Were too joyous to notice it.

For were they not firm in a home of their own
With windows everywhere
And a beautiful banistered stair
And a front yard for flowers and a back yard for grass?

The first night, a rock, big as two fists.
The second, a rock big as three.
But nary a curse cursed Rudolph Reed.
(Though oaken as man could be.)

The third night, a slivery ring of glass.
Patience ached to endure.
But he looked, and lo! small Mabel's blood
Was staining her gaze so pure.

Then up did rise our Rudolph Reed
And pressed the hand of his wife,
And went to the door with a thirty-four
And a beastly butcher knife.

He ran like a mad thing into the night.
And the words in his mouth were stinking.
By the time he had hurt his first white man
He was no longer thinking.

By the time he had hurt his fourth white man
Rudolph Reed was dead.
His neighbors gathered and kicked his corpse.
"Nigger—" his neighbors said.

Small Mabel whimpered all night long,
For calling herself the cause.
Her oak-eyed mother did no thing
But change the bloody gauze.

Gwendolyn Brooks, American, born 1917

Next, a poet describes his reaction at having to live with the humiliation of racial oppression.

❋ *The White City*

I will not toy with it nor bend an inch.
Deep in the secret chambers of my heart
I muse my life-long hate, and without flinch
I bear it nobly as I live my part.
My being would be a skeleton, a shell,
If this dark passion that fills every mood,
And makes my heaven in the white world's hell,
Did not forever feed me vital blood.
I see the mighty city through a mist—
The strident trains that speed the goaded mass,
The poles and spires and towers vapor-kissed,
The fortress port through which the great ships pass,

The tides, the wharves, the dens I contemplate,
Are sweet like wanton loves because I hate.

Claude McKay, Jamaican American, 1890–1948

In the next poem, the poet attempts to understand across the racial divide.

 ## *On the Subway*

The boy and I face each other.
His feet are huge, in black sneakers
laced with white in a complex pattern like a
set of intentional scars. We are stuck on
opposite sides of the car, a couple of
molecules stuck in a rod of light
rapidly moving through darkness. He has the
casual cold look of a mugger,
alert under hooded lids. He is wearing
red, like the inside of the body
exposed. I am wearing old fur, the
whole skin of an animal taken and
used. I look at his raw face,
he looks at my dark coat, and I don't
know if I am in his power—
he could take my coat so easily, my
briefcase, my life—
or if he is in my power, the way I am
living off his life, eating the steak
he does not eat, as if I am taking

the food from his mouth. And he is black
and I am white, and without meaning or
trying to I must profit from his darkness,
the way he absorbs the murderous beams of the
nation's heart, as black cotton
absorbs the heat of the sun and holds it. There is
no way to know how easy this
white skin makes my life, this
life he could take so easily and
break across his knee like a stick the way his
own back is being broken, the
rod of his soul that at birth was dark and
fluid, rich as the heart of a seedling
ready to thrust up into any available light.

Sharon Olds, American, born 1942

Amid all the tension, ordinary life must go on. As always, some ordinary people
concern themselves with trying to live decently.

 ## *Dialog Outside the Lakeside Grocery*

The grocery had provided him with
boxes of rotten lettuce
He was loading them onto a
yellow pick-up truck
He was frail white man and
wore a plaid woolen shirt and
frayed dungarees
I was sitting in a gray chevrolet

"I have eight adult geese and
twenty-six ducks," he said
and I said
"I'll bet you have a big management
problem," and he said
"They're no trouble at all. My
wife raised two of them in the house.
When she goes near their pen
the geese waddle towards her
and nibble the lettuce out of her
hand"
"I'd never think of killing them"
he said
"They keep me out of the bars"

Ishmael Reed, American, born 1938

Much of our prosperity depends on the successful harnessing of new sources of energy. The machines that have been put to work on this cheap energy demand a new kind of worker to assist them.

The next poem mourns both the city and the fate of individuals in a world where what's valued is willingness to "put a piece of another piece in a certain place."

✸ *Whitman, Come Again to the Cities*

Burn high your fires, foundry chimneys!
Cast black shadows at nightfall!
Cast red and yellow light over the tops of the houses!

WALT WHITMAN

Father who found this vibrant light
rising out of the fired stomach of the city, rising out of
the fecund genitals,
come with me
to the new and sad cities
laid out on the earth like a tortured soldier,
the skin pulled off his back,
his eyes empty, but alive.
Come with me down the abandoned streets—
vacant lots of weeds, tin cans and blown garbage,
black and blue eyes of the windows,
thin dogs walking stealthily, a new breed neither wild nor
        tame,
but like those young boys walking with a starved eye
that deciphers quickly what can be eaten and what will eat.
What do they celebrate entering through metal doors to
        buy whiskey?
Mutilated seeds of the workers
through whose loins passes rusty blood,
and women who carry dead white ingots in their bellies.
Young men standing on street corners,
their clothes expensive, their cars impractical, wildly
colored; and they will do anything but
put a piece
of another piece
in a certain place.

Toi Derricote, American, born 1941

In the next poem, a black American woman watches a tribal African woman and sees advantages on both sides of the divide.

✸ *African Village Women*

They carry firewood on their heads
in the wet heat.
Their footprints go deep into dust roads
and their breasts are full of milk.
For a few years their skin
is smooth as banana leaves;
their names are heard in the huts
of young men. But they grow old fast
and young friends become second wives
to their husbands.

Yet there is warmth from a baby
strapped to your back,
and something to be said
for sleeping at night
under the blanket with your children.
You learn to balance things—
to walk with your back straight.
The weight of the firewood
carried on your head
flows through your body.
It is left on the road
in your footprint.

Lucinda Roy, American, contemporary

Another divide, this time between the two halves of one life:

✺ *A Bottomlands Farmer Suffers a Sea Change*

A man fits a key into the door of an office in Chicago.
Suddenly he remembers a plowed field.
He remembers the farm
before they took it.
He remembers walking its ditches,
flushing birds.

In a park across the street
pigeons scatter.
He hurries into the office
where a phone is ringing.

Jo McDougall, American, contemporary

A community based on a shared culture accepts individuals regardless of their success in life. In a meritocracy, poverty brings not just discomfort but also exclusion.

Attempts to mitigate, with public money, some of the harsh effects of our civilization are met with howls of indignation by those who don't see the benefit for themselves. They also result in a culture of victimology, in which everyone wishes to appear a victim—even the most unlikely and privileged.

While this parade of privileged victims may appear comic to an outsider, for the truly underprivileged it is insult added to injury. The next poem is by a Japanese American who spent her childhood in an American internment camp.

✺ *Ms.*

I got into a thing
with someone

because I called her
miss ann/kennedy/rockerfeller/hughes
instead of ms.

I said
it was a waste of time
worrying about it.

her cool blue eyes
iced me—a victim of sexism.

I wanted to accommodate her
and call her what
she deserved.
but knowing that would please her
instead
I said,

>   white lace and satin was never soiled by
>   sexism
>   sheltered as you are by mansions
>   built on Indian land
>
>   your diamonds shipped with slaves from Africa
>   your underwear washed by Chinese laundries
>   your house cleaned by my grandmother

so do not push me any further.

>   and when you quit
>   killing us for democracy
>   and stop calling ME *gook*

I will call you
whatever you like.

Janice Mirikitani, Japanese American, born 1942

People arriving in the New World with their old cultures found on offer a new set of beliefs and a developing culture under which they could, perhaps, unite. But a new culture cannot be manufactured overnight. A culture has to support individuals through the difficult periods of life; through courtship, marriage, and bringing up children; through struggles to make a living and feel pride in one's work; through mourning loved ones and all the troubles that life can throw up.

The new culture derives from Anglo-Saxon Protestantism. But it is a very different beast from its parent. It emphasizes self-indulgence rather than self-denial in areas such as sex and material enjoyments. It pays little attention to religion. It sees education as a tool to make people employable, not as a route to self-knowledge. It has dispensed with ideas of public duty and public service. Its idea of freedom is pursuit of whim and appetite, rather than service of a higher good.

The next poem is by a white Christian poet distressed by what is being done in the name of his culture, his religion. It's the fourth part of a seven-section poem about a "corpse that will not stop burning."

from The Dead Shall Be Raised Incorruptible

In the Twentieth Century of my trespass on earth,
having exterminated one billion heathens,
heretics, Jews, Moslems, witches, mystical seekers,
black men, Asians, and Christian brothers,
every one of them for his own good,

a whole continent of red men for living in unnatural
   community
and at the same time having relations with the land,

one billion species of animals for being subhuman,
and ready to take on the bloodthirsty creatures from the
    other planets,
I, Christian man, groan out this testament of my last will.

I give my blood fifty parts polystyrene,
twenty-five parts benzene, twenty-five parts good old
    gasoline,
to the last bomber pilot aloft, that there shall be one acre
in the dull world where the kissing flower may bloom,
which kisses you so long your bones explode under its lips.

My tongue goes to the Secretary of the Dead
to tell the corpses, "I'm sorry, fellows,
the killing was just one of those things
difficult to previsualize—like a cow,
say, getting hit by lightning."

My stomach, which has digested
four hundred treaties giving the Indians
eternal right to their land, I give to the Indians,
I throw in my lungs which have spent four hundred years
sucking in good faith on peace pipes.

My soul I leave to the bee
that he may sting it and die, my brain
to the fly, his back the hysterical green color of slime,
that he may suck on it and die, my flesh to the advertising
    man,
the antiprostitute, who loathes human flesh for money.

I assign my crooked backbone
to the dice maker, to chop up into dice,
for casting lots as to who shall see his own blood
on his shirt front and who his brother's,
for the race isn't to the swift but to the crooked.

To the last man surviving on earth
I give my eyelids worn out by fear, to wear
in his long nights of radiation and silence,
so that his eyes can't close, for regret
is like tears seeping through closed eyelids.

I give the emptiness my hand: the pinkie picks no more
    noses,
slag clings to the black stick of the ring finger,
a bit of flame jets from the tip of the fuck-you finger,
the first finger accuses the heart, which has vanished,
on the thumb stump wisps of smoke ask a ride into the
    emptiness.

In the Twentieth Century of my nightmare
on earth, I swear on my chromium testicles
to this testament
and last will
of my iron will, my fear of love, my itch for money, and my
    madness.

Galway Kinnell, American, born 1927

To truly own the earth means leaving nothing untouched, none of creation unaltered. The rest of us stand impotently by.

❀ The Idiot Speaks

I stood right here,
inert as ever.
Three men arrived
in darkish suits.

"Hey you!" one said.
I went to him.
"We're told, somewhere here
is a vestige of God."

"In man, or woman,
or child?" I asked him.
"No, nothing so awfully
dangerous," he said.

"But, somewhere here
is a quiet place,
where ivy grows
and flourishing trees;

"where dragonflies flit
on the surface of water;
where brown fish lie
in wait among stones."

"I know the place
you speak of," I said,

"though no one goes there
anymore."

"We can't take chances,"
the third man said.
He motioned to
his great machine—

a yellow digger.
It started its engine.
It followed us into
that strange old place,

moved back and forth
its mighty arm,
till all the scene
was destroyed.

The three men looked and saw that it was good.
"We'll put a block of flats up here," one said,
"in case God thinks of coming back."

Ivo Mosley, English, born 1951

The greatest contribution to a more sustaining culture comes from the one element of the population whose ancestors arrived through no choice of their own. Musician Lester Bowie says:

> In my travels, I've had the pleasure to observe a group of people consisting of all races, sexes, religious and sexual persuasions, working, . . . playing, . . . and enjoying life together. There is much to be learned from observing the behavior of this multihued group of world citizens. Who are

these people??? Jazz Fans!! Consequently my answer to the solution of
the world's many problems is MORE JAZZ.[5]

There's not much money to be made in jazz or poetry, but huge fortunes are to be made searching for the worst in us. "No one ever lost money underestimating public taste," to paraphrase H. L. Mencken. Fantasies of liberation by sex, violence, and superhuman heroics are churned out by the entertainment industries, and an army of critics are paid well to mistake them for culture or even art.

High on the list of complaints against our civilization is that it commercializes everything; nothing is sacred. Commercialization produces some odd situations, as in the poem that follows.

✸ The Feet Man

The worst job I ever had was nailing
Jesus' feet to the cross on the
assembly line at the crucifix factory.
Jesus! I'd never thought of myself
as religious before that, but when
I had to strike those nails—I figured
it up once—more than two thousand times
a day, my mind began seeing things:
little tremors along the skin, jerks of
those legs that were bonier than
models' legs, his eyes imploring,
forgiving. I swear, if a tiny drop of blood
had oozed out of that wood at my pounding,
I wouldn't have been surprised at all.
I was ripe for a miracle, or a vacation.
All I got was worse: with each blow
of the hammer, I flinched, as if I
were the one getting pierced. Doing

that job day after day was bad enough,
but doing it to myself—my arms
spread out from one end of my paycheck
to the other—was crazy. I began
to sweat constantly, though the place
was air-conditioned. It wasn't long before
the foreman took me aside and told me
I was taking my job too seriously, that
if I wanted to keep it I had better calm down.
He was right. I pulled myself together
like a man and put all pointless thoughts
out of my head. Or tried to. It wasn't easy:
imagine Jesus after Jesus coming down
at you along that line, and you with
your hammer poised, you knowing
what you have to do to make a living.

Philip Dacey, American, contemporary

There is a certain grotesqueness when living creatures—like the salmon in the next poem—are subject to exploitation and death by machine.

❂ *Progeny of Air*

The propellers undress the sea;
the pattern of foam like a broken zip
opening where the bow cuts the wave

and closing in its wake. The seals bark.
Gulls call and dive, then soar loaded with catch.
The smell of rotting salmon lingers over the Bay

of Fundy, like a mortuary's disinfected air;
fish farms litter the coastline;
metal islands cultivating with scientific

precision these gray-black, pink-fleshed fish.
In the old days, salmon would leap up the river to spawn,
journeying against the current. They are

travelers: When tucked too low searching for
undertows to rest upon, they often scrape
their bellies on the sharp adze and bleed.

Now watch them turn and turn
in the cages waiting for the feed of
colorized herring to spit from the silver

computer bins over the islands of sea farms,
and General, the hugest of the salmon,
has a square nose where a seal chewed

on a superfreeze winter night when
her blood panicked and almost froze.
Jean Pierre, the technician and sea-cage guard,

thinks they should roast the General in onions
and fresh sea water. It is hard to read mercy
in his stare and matter-of-factly way.

He wears layers, fisherman's uniform,
passed from generation to generation:
the plaid shirt, the stained yellow jacket,

the ripped olive-green boots, the black
slack trousers with holes, the whiskers
and eye of sparkle, as if salt-sea has crystallized

on his sharp cornea. He guides the boat in;
spills us out after our visit with a grunt and grin,
willing us to wet our sneakers at the water's

edge. The sun blazes through the chill
The motor stutters, the sea parts, and
then zips shut and still.

Stunned by their own intake of poison,
the salmon turn belly up on the surface;
then sucked up by the plastic piscalator,

they plop limp and gasping in the sunlight.
One by one the gloved technicians
press with their thumbs the underside of the fish

spilling the eggs into tiny cups
destined for the hatchery, anesthetized eyes
glazed shock on the steel deck.

They know the males from the females:
always keep them apart, never let seed touch egg,
never let the wind carry the smell of birthing

through the June air. Unburdened now the fish
are flung back in—they twitch, then tentative
as hungover denizens of nightmares, they swim

the old Sisyphean orbit of their tiny cosmos.
The fish try to spawn at night
but only fart bubbles and herring.

On the beach the rank saltiness of murdered salmon
is thick in the air. Brown seaweed sucks up the blood.
The beach is a construction site of huge cement blocks

which moor the sea-cages when tossed eighty feet down.
They sink into the muddy floor of the bay and stick.
There is no way out of this prison for the salmon,

they spin and spin in the algae-green netting,
perpetually caught in limbo, waiting for years before
being drawn up and slaughtered, steaked and stewed.

And in the morning's silence,
the sun is turning over for a last doze,
and silver startles the placid ocean.

Against the gray green of Deer Island
a salmon leaps in a magical arc,
slaps the metal walkway in a bounce,

and then dives, cutting the chilled water on the other side.
Swimming, swimming is General (this is my fantasy)
with the square nose and skin gone pink with seal bites,

escaping from this wall of nets and weed.
General swims upriver alone,
leaping the current with her empty womb,

leaping, still instinct, still traveling
to the edge of Lake Utopia, where
after so many journeyings, after abandoning

this secure world of spawning and living
at the delicate hands of technicians,
after denying herself social security and

the predictability of a steady feeding
and the safety from predator seal and osprey;
after enacting the Sisyphean patterns of all fish,

here, in the shadow of the Connors Sardine Factory
she spawns her progeny of air and dies.

Kwame Dawes, born Ghana, 1962

The mechanization of farming means that if the return is high enough, then the depreciation of land and of capital is little cause for concern.

Chemical fertilizers utilize the cheap energy of oil to produce food. In doing so, they degrade the land. People who farm with concern for the land and for the quality of their product can't compete in the price wars with chemical farmers, and they tend to go out of business.

✺ My Father's Song

Wanting to say things,
I miss my father tonight.
His voice, the slight catch,
the depth from his thin chest,
the tremble of emotion

in something he has just said
to his son, his song:

We planted corn one spring at Acu—
we planted several times
but this one particular time
I remember the soft damp sand
in my hand.

My father had stopped at one point
to show me an overturned furrow;
the plowshare had unearthed
the burrow nest of a mouse
in the soft moist sand.

Very gently, he scooped tiny pink animals
into the palm of his hand
and told me to touch them.
We took them to the edge
of the field and put them in the shade
of a sand-moist clod.

I remember the very softness
of cool and warm sand and tiny alive mice
and my father saying things.

Simon J. Ortiz, American Indian, born 1942

We must all eat and compete in order to survive. So is it meaningful to talk disparagingly of violence and exploitation, when such are the terms of our existence?

The answer is yes. We need morality and cooperation, as well as competition, in order to flourish. Morality and cooperation are the secret weapons of sociable species. "When each follows the way of the fox, collective wits are thin as air." These words belong to Solon, who created a democracy in ancient Athens similar to the one we have today.

There is a boundary between legitimate and immoral wealth. Where this boundary lies is the subject of aesthetics, instinct, and morality. All our futures rest on being able to draw it and respect it—as Solon argues in the following poem.

> Wealth I desire, but not to hold unrighteously,
>   for surely sometime retribution comes.
> The riches that the gods give are dependable
>   from top to bottom of the storage jar,
> but those that mortals cultivate with violence
>   come awkward and unwilling at the call
> of crime, and soon are tangled in calamity,
>   which from a small beginning grows like fire,
> a trifling thing at first, but grievous in the end,
>   for mortal violence does not live long.

Solon, Greek, 630–560 B.C., tr. M. L. West

Political parties clamor, *"We'll* give you prosperity! Give *us* power!" When they do not meet their promises, they say, "Tomorrow!"

Tribal culture evidently has its liars, too, as we see from the next poem. It is a "hainteny," a traditional poem from the Merina tribe of Madagascar.

> Little grass, soft grass,
> should a liar be respected?
> "Yes," says the liar.

Little grass, soft grass,
should the liar speak?
—But why should he not speak?
Then he who asked the question said:
"Tell me what you do."
"I excite them with whistling, I trip them with talk.
I cover them with lies,
and so the people are pleased with me.
I tell them, 'Tomorrow,'
and they are delighted."

Anonymous, traditional, tr. from Malagasy by Leonard Fox

In reality, prosperity is hard-won and cannot be guaranteed for long by any one formula.

In 1705 Bernard de Mandeville, a Dutchman living in England, published a poem whose cynical pragmatism outraged educated people. He said vice was indispensable to civilization. Without vices like greed, envy, lust, and vanity, we should all be content with very little, and there would be neither consumption nor employment enough for civilization.

But vice by itself is not enough, he said. Civilization bears fruit when vice, which by itself "chokes other plants and runs to wood" is "lopt and bound" by justice.

In the poem, human society is compared to a hive of bees. The following lines are the "Moral" attached to the end of the poem, which is itself much longer.

Then leave complaints: fools only strive
To make a great *and* honest hive.
To enjoy the world's conveniences,
Be fam'd in war, yet live in ease

Without great vices, is a vain
Utopia seated in the brain.
Fraud, luxury and pride must live,
Whilst we the benefits receive:
Hunger's a dreadful plague, no doubt,
Yet who digests or thrives without?
Do we not owe the growth of wine
To the dry, shabby, crooked vine?
Which, whilst its shoots neglected stood,
Chok'd other plants and ran to wood;
But blest us with its noble fruit,
As soon as it was ty'd and cut:
So vice is beneficial found,
When it's by Justice lopt and bound;
Nay, where the people would be great,
As necessary to the State,
As hunger is to make 'em eat.
Bare virtue can't make nations live
In splendor, they that would revive
A Golden Age, must be as free,
For acorns, as for honesty.[6]

Bernard de Mandeville, Dutch English, 1670–1733

In his time, Bernard de Mandeville was considered outrageous, but we have out-done him. We have given what Shakespeare called our "pleasant vices" full rein. If these "pleasant vices" are not to become "instruments to plague us,"[7] we must rein in our headstrong habits as well as our governments and corporations, whose joint efforts have stitched up the world in a straitjacket that may prove to be its shroud.

Let us remember that though the West feeds the world technology and arms, danger and destruction, it also feeds the world hope. In parts of the Muslim world—at the time of this writing—women who have questioned whether the world sits on top of a mountain are being hunted down to be killed.[8] In Africa and in the heart of Old Europe, races are busy trying to exterminate each other in old-fashioned wars for ethnic domination. What used to be the Soviet Empire groans under poverty, corruption, debt, pollution, crime, and multiple dangers of nuclear devastation. In China, people are still being shot for expressing thoughts against the government.

At the moment, the West offers the best possibility that time, understanding, and persuasion may influence the flow of events away from catastrophe. Perhaps we can then—to balance the chapter's opening quotation—recover the best, which is also true and which we're beginning to believe never existed.

CHAPTER 7

Birds, Beasts, Blossoms, Bugs, Trees, . . . and People

A Song

A widow bird sat mourning for her love
    Upon a wintry bough;
The frozen wind crept on above,
    The freezing stream below.

There was no leaf upon the forest bare,
    No flower upon the ground,
And little motion in the air
    Except the mill-wheel's sound.

Percy Bysshe Shelley, English, 1792–1822

Sparrows

Snow in hair, winter in my bones,
The eyes weary, loyal, I greet
The sparrows like friends, this gang
That, in March, is already in my yard.
In a wide band, chirping, clamorous
They come and (hop!) are scattered
Like grain on the thawing snow:
Then call—and they are gone.
Longingly, the eyes follow. My heart wakens.
I recall my friends: my crowd
So noisy, like the sparrows in their dance.

They could not reach the joy of winter.
In summer, they left—before harvest,
The joy of their summer unable to sustain them.

Mani Leib, Yiddish, 1883–1953, tr. Nathan Helper

 ## *To a Goldfinch*

O crimson zither who, at break of day,
Trilling laments for your beloved spouse,
And pasturing on the amber of the rose,
Tints with coral the tip of your golden beak:

Sweet golden linnet, sad small bird,
As soon as you looked out on lovely dawn,
At the first improvised note of your song
Death entered your domain and stilled your voice.

There is in life no certainty of dying;
Your own voice led the hunter to you,
Making sure his shot released was good.

O Fortune most desired, and yet most feared!
Who would think, accomplice in your dying
Would be your own life, not keeping silence?

Juana de Asbaje, Mexican, 1651–95, tr. I. M.

Ode to Salted Mutton Birds

Mutton birds! I like 'em, I'll eat 'em any way.
Skin 'em 'n braise 'em and serve 'em on a tray.
Stuff 'em 'n bake 'em, and serve 'em with sauce.
Or put 'em over the coals, on a spit of course.
I like 'em grilled, I like 'em fried.
And there's plenty of other ways I've tried.
But salted birds, just scar and boil.
With carrots, spuds and swedes as well.
It's the best way known to man or beast
To eat mutton birds and have a feast.

Jim Everett, Aboriginal Australian, born 1942

 The Caged Bird

This bird was happy once in the high trees.
You cage it in your cellar, bring it seed,
Honey to sip, all that its heart can need
Or human love can think of: till it sees,
Leaping too high within its narrow room
The old familiar shadow of the leaves,
And spurns the seed with tiny desperate claws.
Naught but the woods despairing pleads,
The woods, the woods again, it grieves, it grieves.

Boethius, Roman, circa 480–524, tr. from Latin by Helen Waddell

A Bird, Just a Bird

"What fragrance," the bird said, "what sunlight, oh
Spring's come
and I'll go find my mate."

Off the porch sill flew
the bird, flitting like some messenger, and was gone

A little bird
a thoughtless bird
a bird who never reads the news
a bird free from debt
a bird unacquainted with us

The bird flew through the air
above the red lights
unaware in the heights
and deliriously living
moments of blue

The bird was oh, just a bird

> *Forugh Farrokhzad, Persian, 1934–67,*
> *tr. Jascha Kessler and Amin Banani*

 On Seeing a Wounded Hare Limp by Me,
Which a Fellow Had Just Shot At

Inhuman man! curse on thy barb'rous art,
And blasted be thy murder-aiming eye;

May pity never soothe thee with a sigh,
Nor pleasure glad thy cruel heart!

Go live, poor wanderer of the wood and field,
The bitter little that of life remains!
No more the thickening brakes and verdant plains
To thee shall home, or food, or pasture yield.

Seek, mangled wretch, some place of wonted rest,
No more of rest, but now thy dying bed!
The sheltering rushes whistling o'er thy head,
The cold earth with thy bloody bosom pressed.

Oft as by winding Nith I, musing, wait
The sober eve, or hail the cheerful dawn,
I'll miss thee sporting o'er the dewy lawn,
And curse the ruffian's aim, and mourn thy hapless fate.

Robert Burns, Scottish, 1759–96

 ## *Putu*

It was a long-drawn Chaitra noon;
the earth was thirsty, burned by the day.
Suddenly I heard someone calling
somewhere outside, "Puturani,[1] come!"
The riverbank's deserted in the midday,
so the voice of affection made me curious.
Closing my book, I slowly got up,
opened the door a little and looked outside.

A huge buffalo, covered in mud,
tender-eyed, was standing on the bank.
A young man was in the water, calling her
to give her a bath, "Puturani, come!"
When I saw the young man and his Puturani,
gentle tears mingled with my smiles.

Rabindranath Tagore, Bengali, 1861–1941, tr. Ketaki Kushari Dyson

 ## *The Man Who Encountered a Bear*

Rumbling down the slope
something blackly black came sliding along,
poised on its haunches, front paws raised . . .
A bear! The moment I realized it,
he tumbled sideways into the cover of some bamboo
    bushes.
—I'd no sooner thought he was gone than I saw him again,
scurrying away from me up the mountain trail

I had set out walking again,
Resolved not to look back.
I moved deliberately
but told myself I didn't need to walk so calculatedly slow.
I took a cigarette from my pocket,
finally found a match and lit up.
Half a kilometer down the mountain I met a woodcutter
He badgered me about my pale face.
"A bear!" I told him.

"Frightening?" After consideration I replied,
"It was certainly uncanny."
Indeed no deception there.
Quite an eerie sensation.
When the beast looked at me with those eyes,
innocent yet burning brightly deep within,
I immediately sensed reality fade.
No no not exactly—I sensed rather that
Time from an entirely other dimension
had crossed the Time where I'd existed,
in which I continue to exist,
an unknown time breathing and pulsing wildly like
    the wind.
Unexpectedly absolutely unexpectedly
I stood at their intersection.

Instantly the mountain stream stood still.
In response to the hush, the forest, the grass, the earth,
    the rocks
briefly echoed a shriek
resounding even now within my head.

Maruyama Kaoru, Japanese, 1899–1974, tr. Robert Epp

Untitled

Today I feel bearish
I've just climbed out of
A stream with a jerking
Trout in my paw

Anyone who messes with
Me today will be hugged
And dispatched

Ishmael Reed, American, born 1938

 Song of the Lemming

(On a cold winter's day, a little lemming came out of his
warm hole. He looked about him, shivered, shook
himself, and sang:)
The sky,
like a vast belly,
arches itself
around my burrow.
The air is clear,
no clouds in sight:
icy weather! Aiee!
I'm freezing! freezing!

Anonymous, Eskimo, written down 1920s,
tr. Knud Rasmussen and Tom Lowenstein

 Pangur Ban

I and Pangur Ban, my cat,
'Tis a like task we are at;

Hunting mice is his delight,
Hunting words I sit all night.

Better far than praise of men
'Tis to sit with book and pen;
Pangur bears me no ill will,
He too plies his simple skill.

'Tis a merry thing to see
At our tasks how glad are we,
When at home we sit and find
Entertainment to our mind.

Oftentimes a mouse will stray
In the hero Pangur's way;
Oftentimes my keen thought set
Takes a meaning in its net.

'Gainst the wall he sets his eye
Full and fierce and sharp and sly;
'Gainst the wall of knowledge I
All my little wisdom try.

When a mouse darts from its den,
O how glad is Pangur then!
O what gladness do I prove
When I solve the doubts I love!

So in peace our tasks we ply,
Pangur Ban, my cat and I;
In our hearts we find our bliss,
I have mine and he has his.

Practice every day has made
Pangur perfect in his trade;
I get wisdom day and night
Turning darkness into light.

Anonymous, Irish, eighth century, tr. Robin Flower

 ## *The Sick Rose*

O rose thou art sick.
The invisible worm,
That flies in the night
In the howling storm:

Has found out thy bed
Of crimson joy:
And his dark secret love
Does thy life destroy.

William Blake, English, 1757–1827

 ## *The Rain at Night*

The good rain knows when to fall,
Coming in this spring to help the seeds,
Choosing to fall by night with a friendly wind,
Silently moistening the whole earth.

Over this silent wilderness the clouds are dark.
The only light shines from a riverboat.
Tomorrow morning everything will be red and wet,
And all Chengtu will be covered with blossoming flowers.

Tu Fu, Chinese, 713–70, tr. Nee Wen-yei

 ### *1921*

Everything has been plundered, betrayed, sold out,
The wing of black death has flashed,
Everything has been devoured by starving anguish,
Why, then, is it so bright?

From fantastic woods near the town
Wafts the scent of cherry blossoms by day,
At night new constellations shine
In the transparent depths of the skies of July—

And how near the miraculous draws
To the dirty, tumbledown huts . . .
No one, no one knows what it is,
But for centuries we have longed for it.

Anna Akhmatova, Russian, 1889–1966,
tr. Judith Hemschemeyer

The following poem was written at a mountain temple:

 Such stillness!
Into the rocks sink
Cicadas' cries.

Basho, Japanese, 1644–94, tr. I. M.

 The Fly

She sat on a willow-trunk
watching
part of the battle of Crécy,
the shouts,
the gasps, the groans,
the tramping and the tumbling.

During the fourteenth charge
of the French cavalry
she mated
with a brown-eyed male fly
from Vadincourt.

She rubbed her legs together
as she sat on a disemboweled horse
meditating
on the immortality of flies.

With relief she alighted
on the blue tongue
of the Duke of Clervaux.

When silence settled
and only the whisper of decay
softly circled the bodies

and only
a few arms and legs
still twitched jerkily under the trees,

she began to lay her eggs
on the single eye
of Johann Uhr,
the Royal Armorer.

And thus it was
that she was eaten by a swift
fleeing
from the fires of Estrees.

Miroslab Holub, Czech, born 1923, tr. George Theiner

 Encounter

Knowing too much altogether about beetles:
Latin names, classifications, numbers—six legs, four wings,
thorax, antennae, eyes, segmented abdomen,
I stoop, cut off his light like a thunderstorm
or bird of prey. My interfering finger
chases this hurrying black-clad person,
turns him over. Earthquake. This beetle can scream!
Heaving and bellowing, world turned upside-down,

he begs and curses. Given a stick to fasten
on, he clasps it, click, like a pocket-knife,
a mechanical clown.

After that mutual surprise
suddenly his whole shape turns to blur and buzz,
he's off, wholly at home in air, in life.

I've no idea what beetle is.
Beetle never recognized me. Nevertheless,
it was a double event, a wild encounter.

Judith Wright, Australian, born 1915

 Earwig

Maligned, the earwig. Unlikely he'd take shelter
Within the labyrinth of your ear, still more improbable
He'd penetrate the brain and start to eat it.
He's safer refuges—dry hedgerow kexes[2]
More appetizing fare than that gray soggy blob
Inside your skull, that's stuffed with indigestible
And useless information. He'll devour
The pink and overblown hearts of dahlias,
The golden mop-heads of chrysanthemums,
And the last roses that the summer leaves.

John Heath-Stubbs, English, born 1918

Willow

To understand
A little of how a shaken love
May be sustained

Consider
The giant stillness
Of a willow

After a storm.
This morning it is more than peaceful
But last night that great form

Was tossed and hit
By what seemed to me
A kind of cosmic hate,

An infernal desire
To harass and confuse,
Mangle and bewilder

Each leaf and limb
With every vicious
Stratagem

So that now I cannot grasp
The death of nightmare,
How it has passed away

Or changed to this
Stillness,
This clean peace

That seems unshakable.
A branch beyond my reach says
"It is well

"For me to feel
The transfiguring breath
Of evil

"Because yesterday
The roots by which I live
Lodged in apathetic clay.

"But for that fury
How should I be rid of the slow death?
How should I know

"That what a storm can do
Is to terrify my roots
And make me new?"

Brendan Kennelly, Irish, born 1936

 ## Trees

When the soul, incensed,
Has drunk its fill of insult,
When it has seven times vowed to cease
Battle with the demons—

Not with those who are cast down into the abyss
By showers of fire:

With the earthly lowliness of days,
With human stagnation—

Trees! I come to you! To save myself
From the roar of the marketplace.
How my heart breathes out
Through your flights upward!

Theomachist[3] oak! Striding into battles
With all your roots!
My willow-prophetesses!
Virginal birches!

Elm—fierce Absalom,
Pine—racked
In torture—thou, psalm of my lips:
Bitter taste of rowan.

To you! To the alive-plashing mercury
Of the leaves—what if they are falling!
For the first time to throw open my arms!
To abandon my manuscripts!

A swarm of green reflections
As into applauding hands . . .
My bareheaded ones,
My trembling ones!

Marina Tsvetayeva, Russian, 1892–1941,
tr. Jane A. Taubmann

Domus Caedet Arborem[4]

Ever since the great planes were murdered at the end of
    the gardens
The city, to me, at night has the look of a Spirit brooding
    crime;
As if the dark houses watching the trees from dark
    windows
Were simply biding their time.

Charlotte Mew, English, 1869–1928

 The Poplar-Field

The poplars are fell'd, farewell to the shade
And the whispering sound of the cool colonnade,
The winds play no longer, and sing in the leaves,
Nor Ouse on his bosom their image receives.

Twelve years have elapsed since I last took a view
Of my favorite field and the bank where they grew,
And now in the grass behold they are laid,
And the tree is my seat that once lent me a shade.

The blackbird has fled to another retreat
Where the hazels afford him a screen from the heat,
And the scene where his melody charm'd me before,
Resounds with his sweet-flowing ditty no more.

My fugitive years are all hasting away,
And I must ere long lie as lowly as they,
With a turf on my breast, and a stone at my head,
Ere another such grove shall arise in its stead.

'Tis a sight to engage me, if anything can,
To muse on the perishing pleasures of man;
Though his life be a dream, his enjoyments, I see,
Have a being less durable even than he.

William Cowper, English, 1731–1800

Binsey Poplars

felled 1879

My aspens dear, whose airy cages quelled,
  Quelled or quenched in leaves the leaping sun,
All felled, felled, are all felled;
    Of a fresh and following folded rank
           Not spared, not one
           That dandled a sandaled
      Shadow that swam or sank
On meadow and river and wind-wandering weed-winding
  bank.

O if we but knew what we do
      When we delve or hew—
    Hack and rack the growing green!
      Since country is so tender

To touch, her being so slender,
That, like this sleek and seeing ball
But a prick will make no eye at all,
Where we, even where we mean
      To mend her we end her,
  When we hew or delve:
After-comers cannot guess the beauty been.
  Ten or twelve, only ten or twelve
    Strokes of havoc unselve
      The sweet especial scene,
  Rural scene, a rural scene,
  Sweet especial rural scene.

Gerard Manley Hopkins, English, 1844–89

 ## *Trees*

Hag hand
Scratch sky

Devil foot
Grub earth

Outlive your babies
Eat dog shit
And buried birds

Toi Derricote, American, born 1941

On the river shallows too
Rain is falling.
From within the palace
I hear plovers crying,
Never a place to settle.

Across spring fields
Mist is trailing.
Sad and lonely
In the evening shadows
A bush-warbler sings.

Close to my house,
Small clusters of bamboo
Blown in the wind
Rustle indistinctly
This spring evening.

Soft and gentle
Shines the spring sun.
A lark rises,
My heart is sad,
I'm alone with my thoughts.

Otomo Yakamochi, Japanese, 718–85, tr. I. M.

My clothes are silent as I walk the earth
Or stir the waters. Sometimes that which
Makes me beautiful raises me high
Above men's heads, and powerful clouds
Hold me, carry me far and wide.
The loveliness spread on my back rustles
And sings, bright, clear songs,
And loud, whenever I leave lakes
And earth, floating in the air like a spirit.[5]

    A worm ate words. I thought that wonderfully
Strange—a miracle—when they told me a crawling
Insect had swallowed noble songs,
A nighttime thief had stolen writing
So famous, so weighty. But the bug was foolish
Still, though its belly was full of thought.[6]

Anonymous, Old English, eleventh century, tr. Burton Raffel

    from Song of Myself

I think I could turn and live with animals, they are so
placid and self-contain'd,
I stand and look at them long and long.
They do not sweat and whine about their condition,
They do not lie awake in the dark and weep for their sins,

They do not make me sick discussing their duty to God, 279
Not one is dissatisfied, not one is demented with the mania
    of owning things,
Not one kneels to another, nor to his kind that lived
    thousands of years ago,
Not one is respectable or unhappy over the whole earth.

Walt Whitman, American, 1819–92

 from The Romance of the Rose

Without fail, all dumb beasts
Naked and empty of understanding
By nature have no knowledge of themselves.
For if they had communication,
And reason enough to understand,
They could learn from one another,
And no good would come to us from it!
Never would fine battle-chargers
Allow themselves to be tamed by men
Or knights to ride astride them!
Never the ox his horn-crowned head
Would submit to be put to yoke and plow!
Asses, mules, and camels all
Would deny their help as beasts of burden—
Indeed, they'd give not a damn for man!
To carry a castle on his back
An elephant would never agree,

Who's used to trumpeting out of his nose,
And who eats through it too, night and morning,
Just as a man does with his hands.
Dogs or cats wouldn't serve man,
For they can get on fine without him.
Bears, wolves, lions, leopards, and boars
Would all like to bite man to death;
Even rats would bite him to death
As he lies small, in his cradle.
Never would birds, however instructed,
Put their skins in peril for man;
Indeed, they could do him much harm
By pecking open his eyes as he sleeps.
And if man's reply to all this
Is that he could confound them all
By making such things for himself as armor,
And helmets, and halberds, and sharp swords;
By making bows, and crossbows too;
Why then, so too could the beasts!
Haven't they monkeys, and marmosets,
Who'd make strong coats for them
Of leather, of iron—and jackets too?
Nor would they be at a loss over stitching,
They're perfectly able to use their hands,
They'd be as good at it as man;
And monkeys could also be their scribes.
Truly, they wouldn't be such fools
As to overlook gathering skills

With which to fight off armed attack;
Some kind of engine they'd probably make
By which to hurt man grievously.
Even fleas, and earwigs too,
Once they manage to worm their way in—
Through the ear, while he's asleep—
Could do wondrous damage to man.
Lice also, and crabs, and nits
Often pay man such close attention
That he has to leave off work
And bend over, grovel down,
Writhe, twist, jump, and leap,
Scratch himself and rub his clothes—
Finally tearing off clothes and shoes
So badly they harass him.
Even flies, while man is eating,
Often bring him great peril
And attack him in the face
Not bothering if he's king or page.
Ants and other nasty pests
Could trouble man far too much
If they realized their powers;
But, you see, their ignorance
Comes to them from their own natures.
But for creatures possessed of reason—
Be they mortal men or angels
All of whom owe praise to God—
If they fail to know themselves,

The fault in their case comes from vice
Which troubles and makes drunk their sense.
Because they're able to understand reason
And exercise freedom of choice,
Nothing can excuse their failure.

Jean de Meung, French, died 1305(?), tr. I. M.

CHAPTER 8

Men and Women

The questions explored in this chapter are these: does the domination of society by men promote our destruction of the planet, and would more female influence make things any better?

The first poem, by a woman, clearly implies that female influence would and will make things better.

The Pan, the Pot, the Burning Fire
I Have in Front of Me

For a long time
these things have always been placed
in front of us women:

a pan of reasonable size
suited to one's strength,
a pot in which it's convenient for rice
to begin to swell and shine, grain by grain,
the heat of the fire inherited since the very beginning—
in front of them there have always been mothers,
    grandmothers, and their mothers.

What measures of love and sincerity
they must have poured
into these utensils—
sometimes red carrots,
sometimes black seaweed,
sometimes crushed fish

in the kitchen, always accurately
for morning, noon, and evening, preparations have been
    made

and in front of the preparations, in a row, there have always
   been
some pairs of warm knees and hands.

Ah without those persons waiting
how could women have gone on
cooking so happily,
their unflagging care
so daily a service they became unconscious of it?

Cooking was assigned oddly
as the woman's role,
but I don't think that was unfortunate;
because of that, her knowledge and position in society
may have lagged behind the times
but it isn't too late:
the things we have in front of us,
the pan and the pot and the burning fire,

in front of these familiar utensils
let us also study government, economy, literature
as sincerely
as we cook potatoes and meat,

not for vanity and promotion
but so everyone
may be served for mankind
so everyone may work for love.

Ishigaki Rin, Japanese, born 1920, tr. Hiroaki Sato

The next poem is the despairing cry of a young man looking at the work in progress of his own sex's domination. He committed suicide shortly after the poem was written.

 ## *Untitled Poem (him to her)*

I'll show you
I'll give you
a ruined world
I'll give you lonely people
I'll give you
dark streets
where thin dogs walk
and steal the bread from beggars
I'll give you
old and sooty buildings
where families live
without a father
without a decent mother
I'll give you
thieves aged 14
and murderers aged 18

And you, girl, give me your body
and your hair
give me your breath
close, close to my face
give me your eyes
and the smell of your skin

I'll give you
plundered continents
exterminated nations
burned bodies
and beheaded children
I'll give you
hunger and wanderings
fear and sufferings
I'll give you
wars, exterminations,
genocides,
and concentration camps.

And you, give me . . .

I'll give you
garbage heaps in city streets
rivers of sewage streaming to the sea
cats, hungry and ferreting,
mice carrying diseases
and black plagues
which spread mercilessly,
taking their victims
from all of woman born
I'll give you madmen
who lead nations
to destruction

And you, give me . . .

I'll give you a God
who's cruel and cold
I'll give you
suffering prophets
and crucified apostles
I'll give you Jobs
and Abrahams and Moses
I'll give you promises
written on tablets of stone

And you, give me . . .

I'll give you
obelisks and pyramids
built on the bodies of thousands of slaves
I'll give you flourishing gardens
and green groves
which have sprouted over vales of slaughter
I'll give you charred earth
green earth
I'll give you snows
which one day will melt
and will flood our land
and your people.
I'll give you black clouds
carrying terror and fear
I'll give you Inquisitors
I'll give you creatures of Satan

And you, give me . . .

I'll give you oil wells
which sprouted in place of tepees
I'll give you blocks of houses
which sprouted in the place of sloping vineyards
I'll give you fenced-in camps
which sprang up in the wilderness of ice
I'll give you crematoriums
which were born out of the young green grass
I'll give you tanks and planes
fire machines and bombs
created to glorify the names of
leaders and victors
at the expense of the pure souls
who are no more

And you, give me . . .

I'll give you
the polished offices
where are buried alive
your parents, your acquaintances, and your friends
I'll give you
the murderous mechanism
which leads us all
to a future that's frozen,
mechanical, inconsiderate,
of computers and machines
sophisticated bombs
and pilotless planes

But you, keep for me your body
and your hair
keep for me your breath
close, close to my face
keep for me your eyes
and the smell of your skin.
Keep for me this pure corner,
the last in the world:
give me
give me your smile

That is all I can give you now

And you won't want me this way.
Will you want me?

Ron Adler, Israeli, 1957–76, tr. Richard Flantz

Anthropologists male and female write that nowhere on earth is a society where women hold more power than men. In the history of human societies, women have historically had the most influence when hunter-gatherers have settled down to cultivate crops and live in larger communities. Marija Gimbutas argues that a golden age existed in Old Europe at just such a time, between 6500 and 3500 B.C., when peaceful cities flourished where women had public influence and the Mother Goddess was chief deity.[1] Their written records are not deciphered.

Later on, when populations began to come into conflict over living space, communities dominated by warrior men could (and did) overwhelm communities attuned to peace. Human evolution thus favored male-dominated warlike tribes that bred with no restraint.

After five thousand years or more, these two characteristics—unrestrained population growth and the mentality of conquest—have ceased to be useful for the human species; on the contrary, they threaten our survival.

Restraint is obviously the key to living in harmony, no matter how big or small the community. It has been said, "The supreme achievement of civilization is the domestication of the human male." Our civilization has rather channeled the aggression of the human male into corporations where it can plunder whole countries.

The first of the two poems that follow praises an object of natural beauty. The second describes the reaction to it of the kind of small-minded inadequate man whose exercise of power is ruining our planet.

 ## *The Wattle-Tree*

The tree knows four truths—
earth, water, air and the fire of the sun.
The tree holds four truths in one.
Root, limb and leaf unfold
out of the seed, and these rejoice
till the tree dreams it has a voice
to join four truths in one great word of gold.

—Oh, that I knew that word!
I should cry loud, louder than any bird.
O let me live forever, I would cry.
For that word makes immortal what would wordless die;
and perfectly, and passionately,
welds love and time into the seed,
till tree renews itself and is forever tree—

Then upward from the earth
    and from the water
then inward from the air
    and the cascading light
poured gold, till the tree trembled with its flood.

Now from the world's four elements I make
my immortality; it shapes within the bud.
Yes, now I bud, and now at last I break
into the truth I had no voice to speak:
into a million images of the Sun, my God.

✳ . . . *and Mr. Ferritt*

But now Mr. Ferritt
with his troublesome nose,
with his shaven chin
and his voice like a grief
that grates in dark corners,
moves in his house
and scrapes his dry skin
and sees it is morning.

O day, you sly thief,
now what have you taken
of all the small things
I tie on my life?
The radio serial
whines in the kitchen,
caught in a box,
and cannot get out.
The finch in his cage,
the border of phlox

as straight as a string
drawn up in my garden,

the potted geranium,
all are there.
But day from his cranium
twitches one hair;
and never again
will a hair grow there.
—O day, you sly thief,
how you pluck at my life,
frets Mr. Ferritt;
but there, he must bear it.

Outside the fence
the wattle-tree grows.
It tosses; it shines;
it speaks its one word.
Beware! beware!
Mr. Ferritt has heard.
—What are axes for?
What are fences for?
Who planted the wattle-tree
right at my door?
God only knows.
All over the garden
its dust is shaken.
No wonder I sneeze
as soon as I waken.

O world, you sly thief;
my youth you have taken,
and what have you given

who promised me heaven,
but a nagging wife
and a chronic catarrh,
and a blonde on the pictures
as far as a star?

And wild and gold
as a film-star's hair
that tree stands there,
blocking the view
from my twenty-perch block.
What are axes for,
what are fences for
but to keep this tree
away from my door?

And down came the tree.
But poor Mr. Ferritt
still has hay fever.
Nothing will cure it.

Judith Wright, Australian, born 1915

The difference between men and women is argued about more in ideological terms than in terms of what we know. Ideologies are systems of ideas designed to get power for their holders; they are akin to superstition, not wisdom. When truth is ignored in favor of fanaticism, there's normally a high price to pay. In this case, pretending that men and women are the same except in a few physical details means that any special contribution women are able to make is abolished. In effect, women are encouraged to join in the rape of the earth that corporate competitive capitalism has become.

When Genghis Khan had conquered almost half the earth, he was told, "You cannot rule from the horse what you have conquered from the horse." The success of his conquest had made his conqueror's role redundant; what was needed then was able and just administration. We can say something similar about competitive capitalism: what we need now is careful and loving concern for nature, not more rape and pillage from the seats of machines.

The geneticist C. D. Darlington wrote that the two sexes are "genetically as different as two species; sometimes two very remote species."[2] These genetic differences are mirrored in the different values held by men and women. Values are the priorities we give to qualities; for instance, men seem to give a higher priority to their aggressive side while women favor their protective side.

The next six poems offer some examples of the values held more often by women than by men—values that could restrain humans from destroying the world.

In the first, Anna Akhmatova takes the familiar tale of Lot's wife—in which God the Father punishes her for looking back on his destruction of Sodom—and makes it into a defense of woman's love of place and home.

✸ *Lot's Wife*

And the righteous man followed the envoy of God,
Huge and bright, over the black mountain.
But anguish spoke loudly to his wife:
It is not too late, you can still gaze

At the red towers of your native Sodom,
At the square where you sang, at the courtyard where you
    spun,
At the empty windows of the tall house
Where you bore children to your beloved husband.

She glanced and, paralyzed by deadly pain,
Her eyes no longer saw anything;

And her body became transparent salt
And her quick feet were rooted to the spot.

Who will weep for this woman?
Isn't her death the least significant?
But my heart will never forget the one
Who gave her life for a single glance.

Anna Akhmatova, Russian, 1889–1966, tr. Judith Hemschemeyer

The next poem defends the sanctity of the family and of sexual fidelity. And in the last few lines, it seems to call for legislation against sexual harassment.

 ## An Answer to a Love-Letter in Verse

Is it to me, this sad lamenting strain?
Are heaven's choicest gifts bestowed in vain?
A plenteous fortune, and a beauteous bride,
Your love rewarded, and content your pride:
Yet leaving her—'tis me that you pursue,
Without one single charm but being new.
How vile is man! how I detest the ways
Of artful falsehood, and designing praise!
Tasteless, an easy happiness you slight,
Ruin your joy, and mischief your delight.
Why should poor pug[3] (the mimic of your kind)
Wear a rough chain, and be to box confined?
Some cup, perhaps, he breaks, or tears a fan,
While moves unpunished the destroyer, man.

Not bound by vows, and unrestrained by shame,
In sport you break the heart, and rend the fame.
Not that your art can be successful here,
Th'already plundered need no robber fear:
Nor sighs, nor charms, nor flattery can move,
Too well secured against a second love.
Once, and but once, that devil charmed my mind;
To reason deaf, to observation blind,
I idly hoped (what cannot love persuade?)
My fondness equaled, and my troth repaid:
Slow to distrust, and willing to believe,
Long hushed my doubts, and would myself deceive;
But oh! too soon—this tale would ever last;
Sleep, sleep my wrongs, and let me think 'em past.
But you, who mourn with counterfeited grief,
And ask so boldly like a begging thief,
May soon on other nymph inflict the pain
You know so well with cruel art to feign.
Though long you've sported with Don Cupid's dart,
You may see eyes, and you may feel a heart.
So the brisk wits, who stop the evening coach,
Laugh at the fear which follows their approach;
With idle mirth, and haughty scorn, despise
The passenger's pale cheek and staring eyes:
But, seized by Justice, find a fright no jest,
And all the terror doubled in their breast.

Lady Mary Wortley Montagu, English, 1689–1762

The often-commented-on difficulty that men have in expressing emotion is the subject of the next poem.

 Ancestral Burden

You told me: My father did not weep;
You told me: My grandfather did not weep;
They have never wept, the men of my race;
They were of steel.

Speaking thus, a tear welled from you
And fell upon my mouth. . . . More venom
Have I never drunk from any other glass
As small as that.

Weak woman, poor woman who understands,
Sorrow of centuries I knew in the drinking of it:
Ah, this soul of mine cannot support
All of its weight!

Alfonsina Storni, Argentinian, 1892–1938, tr. Richard O'Connell

The next poem looks at boys and girls; the boys take after their fathers.

 The Secret Life of Frogs

Mr. Gabriel Fur, my Siamese,
brings to the hearth a Common Toadlet,
Crinia tasmaniensis.
Mice are permitted, frogs forbidden.
It will live. I carry it outside.

Its heartbeat troubles my warm hand
and as I set it down I see
two small girls in a warmer land.

My friend Alice and I would sit
cradling our frogs behind the tankstand.
Our fathers would talk about
the Great War. Mine would only say,
"I used to be a stretcher-bearer."
Not seen, not heard, in childhood's earshot
of the women on the back verandah,
we knew about atrocities.
Some syllables we used as charms;
Passchendaele   Mons   Gallipoli.
We knew about Poor George, who cried
if any woman touched her hair.
He'd been inside a brothel when
the Jerries came and started shooting.
(We thought a brothel was a French
hotel that served hot broth to diggers.)
The girl that he'd been with was scalped.
Every Frog in the house was killed.

Well, that was life for frogs. At school
the big boys blew them up and spiked them.
One bully had the very knife
with which his father killed ten Germans—
twenty—a hundred—numbers blossomed.
Dad the Impaler! making work
for the more humble stretcher-bearers.

In safety by the dripping tankstand
our frogs with matchstick hands as pale
as the violet stems they lived among
cuddled their vulnerable bellies
in hands that would not do them wrong.

Gwen Harwood, Australian, born 1920

In 1731 women in the Bishnoi community of northwest India hugged trees that were to be axed for timber; 360 were killed by axmen before the felling was stopped. Now, the Bishnoi area is a green oasis in a barren landscape.

In the next poem, Charlotte Mew watches men cutting down trees.

✸ *The Trees Are Down*

> *—and he cried with a loud voice:*
> *Hurt not the earth, neither the sea, nor the trees—*

They are cutting down the great plane-trees at the end of
    the gardens.
For days there has been the grate of the saw, the swish of
    the branches as they fall,
The crash of the trunks, the rustle of trodden leaves,
With the "Whoops" and the "Whoas," the loud common
    talk, the loud common laughs of the men, above it all.

I remember one evening of a long past Spring
Turning in at a gate, getting out of a cart, and finding a
    large dead rat in the mud of a drive.

I remember thinking: alive or dead, a rat was a god-
    forsaken thing,
But at least, in May, that even a rat should be alive.

The week's work here is as good as done. There is just one
    bough
        On the roped bole, in the fine gray rain,
            Green and high
            And lonely against the sky.
                (Down now!—)
            And but for that,
            If an old dead rat
Did once, for a moment, unmake the Spring, I might never
    have thought of him again.

It is not for a moment the Spring is unmade today;
These were great trees, it was in them from root to stem:
When the men with the "Whoops" and the "Whoas" have
    carted the whole of the whispering loveliness away
Half the Spring, for me, will have gone with them.

It is going now, and my heart has been struck with the
    hearts of the planes;
Half my life it has beat with these, in the sun, in the rains,
    In the March wind, the May breeze,
In the great gales that came over to them across the roofs
    from the great seas.
    There was only a quiet rain when they were dying;
    They must have heard the sparrows flying,

And the small creeping creatures in the earth where they
were lying—
But I, all day, I heard an angel crying:
"Hurt not the trees."

Charlotte Mew, English, 1869–1928

The next poem is almost the only fragment by its (woman) author to survive. It
survived in textbooks written by men as an example of how not to write poetry. In
its love of simple objects, it must have undermined the male value of creating
very important things—like armies, philosophy, and progress.

Loveliest of what I leave
is the sun himself
Next to that the bright stars
and the face of mother moon
Oh yes, and cucumbers in season,
and apples, and pears.

Praxilla, Greek, circa 450 B.C.,
tr. John Dillon

The next poem appeals more generally, perhaps, to men than to women. African
American "toasts" are recited among groups of men. A version of the most fa-
mous one follows. Its humor resembles that of Homer's lost epic, *The Margites*,
whose few surviving lines describe a man getting his penis stuck in a pot.

Down in the jungle 'bout treetop deep
A signifying Monkey was wantin' some sleep.
Now he'd been tryin' a week or more;
Every time he got to sleep some damn Lion would roar.
So the Monkey says to the Lion one day,
"There's a bad motherfucker over the way
Called your mother a bitch and a whore,
An' if I hadn't have left, he'd have called her some more.
Say he screwed your sister and he screwed your niece,
Next time he see your granma, he ask her for a piece.
An' I'd rather be deaf, be dumb, and be blind,
Than hear talk like that 'bout my kind."
The Lion jumped up with a hell of a roar,
His tail stuck out like a forty-four.
He goes through the jungle in such a breeze
He knocks all the nuts off the coconut trees.
He saw Mr. Elephant layin' by the tree
Said, "Get up, big rusty motherfucker, it's either you or me!"
The Elephant looked out the corner of his eye,
Said, "Go find someone your own size!"
The Lion jumped to make his pass,
The Elephant kicked him dead in the ass.
They fought all night and they fought all day,
Lord only knows how that Lion got away.
He come back through the jungle more dead than alive,
And that's when Monkey started his jive:
Said, "Oh, Mr. Lion, you say you so fast

How come you got no hair to cover your ass?"
Said, "Now, you sonofabitch, don't you roar,
Or I'll get down off this tree and kick your ass some more."
Said, "Every time me an' my missus try to get a little bit
You come around with this 'hi ho' shit."
Said, "Now get yourself out from under my tree
'Fore I swing on your chickenshit head and pee."
The Lion looked up with his one good eye,
Said, "Lord, let that skinny bastard fall out of that tree 'fore
    I die."
The monkey got frantic, jumped up and down,
His left foot missed, he fell on the ground.
Like a streak of lightning and a wave of heat
The Lion hit him with all four feet.
Mr. Monkey look up with tears in his eyes
Said, "Mr. Lion, please, I want to apologize."
"Apologize, hell!" said the Lion.
"This is the end of your signifyin'!"
"Brother Lion, people saw I fell from the tree,
They know you takin' advantage of me.
But let me get my nuts up outa this sand,
I'll fight your ass all over this land!"
The Lion jumps back, says, "Count to three!"
Monkey tear his ass right back up that tree.
Said, "On your way, Lion, you hairy slut,
'Fore I split your head open with a coconut!"

Anonymous, African American, traditional

The next poem is about intimacy between women.

The Female of the Species

Sometimes you want to talk
about love and despair
and the ungratefulness of children.
A man is no use whatever then.
You want then your mother
or sister
or the girl with whom you went through school,
and your first love, and her
first child—a girl—
and your second.
You sit with them and talk.
She sews and you sit and sip
and speak of the rate of rice
and the price of tea
and the scarcity of cheese.
You know both that you've spoken
of love and despair and ungrateful children.

Gauri Deshpande, Indian, born 1942

In endurance tests, women beat men—a thousand generations of necessity have taught them how, some would say.

the old wicker chair unraveling
& him snoring, asleep on my right.

& too early we have to wake & get the children
& bring them home now & any day now
i'll be happy.
i mean really. really happy.

Alta, American, born 1942

One of the earliest philosophical works to come down to us, the Tao Te Ching, concerns itself with the dualities of endurance and violence, of female and male, and of passivity and activity. It asks, "What is good government?" in relation to these.

The Tao Te Ching takes the form of a sage addressing a ruler who would rule wisely. Some extracts from it follow.

The spirit of the Fountain never dies:
It is called the Mysterious Female.
The entrance to the Mysterious Female
Is the root of all Heaven and Earth.
Frail, frail it is, hardly existing,
But touch it; it will never run dry.

In the world there is nothing more submissive and weak than water. Yet for attacking that which is hard and strong, nothing can surpass it. This is because there is nothing that can take its place.

That the weak overcomes the strong,
And the submissive overcomes the hard,
Everyone in the world knows yet no one can put into
    practice.

Straightforward words
Seem paradoxical.

Would a man lay siege to the whole world and make it his
    own?
I have seen that he will not succeed.
All beneath heaven is a sacred vessel.
Do not tamper with it,
Do not make it your own.
Tampering with it you will spoil it,
Making it your own you will lose it.

The more prohibitions there are,
The poorer the people will be.
The more sharp weapons there are,
The more benighted the state.
The more cunning skills there are
The more pernicious contrivances will be invented.
The more laws are promulgated,
The more thieves and bandits there will be.

Therefore the sage says:
> Do nothing; the people will transform themselves.
> Prefer stillness; the people will rectify themselves.
> Do not meddle; the people will of themselves
>   become prosperous.
> Have no wants; the people will be simple like the
>   Uncarved Block.[4]

Lao Tzu, Chinese, fourth to third century B.C.,
from the Tao Te Ching, compiled from various translations

For most of recorded history, women have been denied a substantial public role in society. The next poem expresses the frustration of a poet denied public office because of her sex.

On a Visit to Ch'ung Chen Temple I See the List of Successful Candidates in the Imperial Examinations

Cloud-capped peaks fill the eyes
In the spring sunshine.
Their names are written in beautiful characters
And posted in order of merit.
How I hate this silk dress
That conceals a poet.
I lift my head and read their names
In powerless envy.

Yu Hsuan-Chi, Chinese, mid ninth century,
tr. Kenneth Rexroth and Ling Chung

Some women undertake the task of revenge.

Siren Song

This is the one song everyone
would like to learn: the song
that is irresistible:

the song that forces men
to leap overboard in squadrons
even though they see the beached skulls

the song nobody knows
because anyone who has heard it
is dead, and the others can't remember.

Shall I tell you the secret
and if I do, will you get me
out of this bird suit?

I don't enjoy it here
squatting on this island
looking picturesque and mythical

with these two feathery maniacs,
I don't enjoy singing
this trio, fatal and valuable.

I will tell the secret to you,
to you, only to you.
Come closer. This song

is a cry for help: Help me!
Only you, only you can,
you are unique

at last. Alas
it is a boring song
but it works every time.

Margaret Atwood,
Canadian, born 1939

The principle of sexual selection (as important in evolution as natural selection) is that over the generations, one sex is responsible for how the other sex develops. Men are stronger because for thousands of years women have found strong men sexy. Looked at the other way, Darlington writes, "We know how Adam complained of Eve's enticing and deceptive arts. Yet it is now clear that these arts are themselves the effect of man's preference over the last ten thousand years for those women who enticed and deceived him most successfully."[5] The Mexican (woman) poet Juana Asbaje made the same point three hundred years earlier:

 from Verses Against the Inconsistency of Men[6]

Foolish men, who accuse
Women without reason
Not seeing you're the cause
Of the very thing you blame!

If your unequaled craving
Is inspired by her disdain,
Why demand good behavior
While inciting her to wrong?

You combat her resistance
Then later gravely blame
Her fickleness in giving
What your persistence won.

You resemble, in the bravery
Of your insane behavior,
A child inventing a monster
Then holding it in fear!

Could anything be odder than
Such lack of common sense,
Which breathes upon a mirror,
Then fumes when it's not clear?

No woman's well reputed,
Even the most discreet;
If she won't let you in she's cold,
And if she does she's loose.

Of what should she be made,
She who would win your love,
When if she's cold she offends you,
And if she's easy she's boring?

Between the boredom and pain
You throw in our direction,
Good luck to her who rejects you—
And welcome your complaints!

Why are you so appalled
By a blame of your own making?
Either like her as you've made her,
Or make her as you'd like her!

Juana Asbaje, Mexican, 1651–95, tr. I. M.

As for men, their strength and capacity for aggression has for thousands of years
been a valuable asset to women needing protection, as well as meat and other
toiled-for food, for their families.

The next poem is a woman's lament for her brother slain in battle. Al-Khansa wrote many laments for her brother Sahr; this one witnesses yet another day of slaughter, as she watches other sisters and mothers mourning their dead. Al-Khansa was a pre-Islamic Arab poet. Islam united the various Arab tribes and turned their warlike habits against the outside world.

Evening brings memories, which banish sleep from my eyes;
Morning breaks me with a fresh assault of anguish.
I weep for Sahr; what warrior is equal to Sahr,
When the time comes to fight a valiant chief,
To hold the head high in face of unjust aggressors,
To vindicate by arms the rights of the oppressed?
No, never before has misery struck like this,
Not in the realm of the angels, nor of humankind.
Unflinching, he fought the onslaughts of the age;
Without equivocation, he solved insoluble problems.
If at night a guest knocked on the door,
Heart trembling, alarmed at the slightest noise,
Sahr would welcome him and give him safety
Banishing from his heart all thought of fear.
The rising sun brings Sahr before my eyes;
The setting sun leaves Sahr still in my heart.
Were not a crowd of mourners at my side
Lamenting their brothers, too, grief would have killed me.
How many mothers I see, lamenting their sons!
How many eyes cry for the day to turn back!
A sister weeps for her brother taken this day,
Weeps for the day that brought misery to her life.
The dead they mourn are not my brother Sahr,

314

And I command in my soul the strength of patience.
God be my witness! No, I will not forget you!
Not when my blood is dry and my grave is dug!
The day I lost Sahr Abu Hassan,
I said farewell to joy and lightness of heart.
I weep for him, my mother weeps with me—
How else, when morning and evening he sleeps in the tomb!

Al-Khansa, Arab, seventh century,
version by I. M. from 1889 French tr. by
Le Père de Coppier

The next poem, a thousand years old, compares men's relations with the world to the relations between men and women.

If the intellect is unstable
It is overwhelmed by the world,
A weak man embraced by a whore.

If the mind becomes disciplined,
The world is a distinguished woman
Who rejects her lover's advances.

Ma'arri, Syrian, 973–1057,
tr. George Wightman and Abdullah al-Udhari

In the Book of Genesis, Eve—Woman—is blamed for the expulsion of Adam and her from the garden of Eden. Judith Wright takes up the story from Eve's point of view.

Eve to Her Daughters

It was not I who began it.
Turned out into draughty caves,
hungry so often, having to work for our bread,
hearing the children whining,
I was nevertheless not unhappy.
Where Adam went I was fairly contented to go.
I adapted myself to the punishment; it was my life.

But Adam, you know . . . !
He kept on brooding over the insult,
over the trick They had played on us, over the scolding.
He had discovered a flaw in himself
and he had to make up for it.

Outside Eden the earth was imperfect,
the seasons changed, the game was fleet-footed,
he had to work for our living, and he didn't like it.
He even complained of my cooking
(it was hard to compete with Heaven).

So he set to work.
The earth must be made a new Eden
with central heating, domesticated animals,
mechanical harvesters, combustion engines,
escalators, refrigerators,
and modern means of communication
and multiplied opportunities for safe investment
and higher education for Abel and Cain
and the rest of the family.
You can see how his pride had been hurt.

In the process he had to unravel everything,
because he believed that mechanism
was the whole secret—he was always mechanical-minded.
He got to the very inside of the whole machine
exclaiming as he went, So this is how it works!
And now that I know how it works, why, I must have
        invented it.
As for God and the Other, they cannot be demonstrated,
and what cannot be demonstrated
doesn't exist.
You see, he had always been jealous.

Yes, he got to the center
where nothing at all can be demonstrated
And clearly he doesn't exist; but he refuses
to accept the conclusion.
You see, he was always an egotist.

It was warmer than this in the cave;
there was none of this fallout.
I would suggest, for the sake of the children,
that it's time you took over.

But you are my daughters, you inherit my own faults of
        character;
you are submissive, following Adam
even beyond existence.
Faults of character have their own logic
and it always works out.
I observed this with Cain and Abel.

Perhaps the whole elaborate fable
right from the beginning
is meant to demonstrate this; perhaps it's the whole secret.
Perhaps nothing exists but our faults?
At least they can be demonstrated.

But it's useless to make
such a suggestion to Adam.
He has turned himself into God,
who is faultless, and doesn't exist.

Judith Wright, Australian, born 1915

Conflict and cooperation between the sexes are part of our struggle to flourish. The aggression of men has helped our species become dominant all over the earth; perhaps a restoration of female power and influence will help us survive the attrition that has followed.

The last poem in this section is reconciliatory. Eric Roach pays tribute to the women of his people, who generation after generation have "taught faith and love and hope" under some of the most dreadful of circumstances. Roach was disillusioned at the end of his life by the failure of Caribbean countries, after slavery had ended, to give birth to a new and vital culture. But in this poem he finds hope in the power of women to shape a new destiny, and he calls on men not to deny women their voice.

I Say It Was the Women

FOR ALL THE TALL UPSTANDING
SISTERS OF THE GENERATION

Hard poems bruise my mind
(you're one of them)

but I can't write them.
My slave age knees give way;
new tides of old ideas
shake my crumbling rock:
I fall asleep at the wrong moments
but I dream of your grave faces,
your dark earnest faces,
your daring voices hard in argument,
and in the dream I listen, I approve,
but in the bitter day I turn aside.
The long hard years confound me like a curse.

It's not been easy.
Since the Trade began
you perished; you gave birth in coffles[7]
and slave ships; the children died;
they flung each stillborn fetus
to the sharks; you spawned on slave
plantations; some of your young
were you; some were a splinter tribe;
white was the seed but black the soil
and brown the issue of that raving age.
You worked and spawned and wept
and nurtured and endured
throughout the mad Slave Trade, the mad slave system.

A black cock's rhetoric,
but I say again
it's not been easy.
In the first freedom time

in wattle mud-straw huts
you cradled a new age with bare hands,
shaping civilization
from cow dung and marl and sweat,
working provision grounds,
tending black cooking pots on stones
in dooryards while mosquitoes and flies
raged round from bush and filth
like Tartar horsemen.
I affirm it here,
I touched that generation and I know
that you gave suck and succor,
taught faith and love and hope
to your rock-clinging season
to lumbering men who else
had plunged into the precipice of chaos.
You raked the embers of the race
out of its ashes. Your breasts alone bridged eras.

In time, my time,
(don't doubt a poet's witness)
you cooked and washed and scrubbed,
planted and prayed and taught
in those harsh clapboard schools
that nurtured villages.
You fought too,
marching long barefoot marches
sweating, singing psalms
with the white captain and that Tubal Butler,

killing the great beast that stood
between us and a brighter sun,
breaking hard barricades of history,
bursting an Empire's walls,
draining its fetid swamps.

Always some hide in terror
from the sweating seasons:
some turn to harlotry
and some disperse among the alien,
some under Jesu's robes;
and some go mad, staring in nightmare,
dreaming in the sun,
wailing like ghosts in alien cultures
from the broken ramparts of the race.
But still you turn and turn
to take the gown of honor,
the mud-stained shift, the purple of the race:
you kiss tradition, fate, and circumstance.

Our gospel truth
is harder than we know it.
Written in the ink of blood,
molasses and spent sweat,
it reads:
Centuries of slavery
left the nigger naked,
stripped bare of human attributes
cropped back to the ape stock.
At one cold cutlass stroke religion went;

down fell another and the language went
and pride and names and cultures
all drained out like blood from mortal wounds—
Africa dismembered, disemboweled.

I die maintaining this:
It was the women who restored us.
I've known them in my time—
mother, sister, teacher, wife,
a green corn row of lovers—
and in my last dry season, going blind,
I look on you who would not yield
to night nor nothing.
I know the end's not chaos,
that you have shaped an end, a destiny,
and we shall grow
though we ourselves,
ashamed of our own shames,
shamed of our need to fight
those last and hardest battles with ourselves,
our waste, our worthlessness,
would silence you.

Eric Roach, Trinidadian, 1915–74

CHAPTER 9

Poetry Itself

The word *poet* comes from the Greek for "maker, creator." A sense of mystery surrounds the making of creative art, suggesting a sacred communion with a muse or patron god. There is a sense that truth—"inspiration"—comes to the poet from somewhere more exalted.

This section looks at the way in which poetry has influenced our lives. All forms of art can bring to our attention ways of being and behaving of which we were previously unaware. Poetry is credited with the birth of romanticism in Europe, which profoundly changed peoples' values and expectations. Social order, personal sacrifice, conventional morality, and authority were out; individual experience, liberty, wild nature, and social progress were in. Blame for life's inadequacies was taken away from God and the natural order and placed on the shoulders of human beings.

Today, we are reaping both the benefits and the banes of this shift. An awareness that our whims can be satisfied has become an expectation that they will be. Two centuries of slaking human appetites has left the planet badly bruised.

Poetry's credentials as guardian spirit of nature are well established. Basho's feeling was that poetry was born out of our relationship with nature:

Poetry's source—
In the far north,
Rice-planting songs.

Basho, Japanese, 1644–94, tr. I. M.

According to Sanskrit tradition, poetry began as a way for humans to converse with gods. Secular poetry had its origins later, about 2,500 years ago, when Valmiki, author of *The Ramayana,* was out walking in the forest. He heard the anguished cry of a bird whose mate, while in the act of love, had been shot by a hunter. Valmiki was moved to compose a poem as an elegy for the bird and a rebuke to the hunter.

Prologue to The Ramayana

Once, not far from the river Tamasa,
The ascetic Valmiki was wandering in a forest,
Meditating on the beauty of nature.
Nearby, unafraid,
Two sweet-voiced krauncha[1] birds were mating
Savoring the delights of spontaneous love.
An ill-minded fowler of the Nishada tribe,
With deliberate malice,
In Valmiki's presence,
Killed the male bird.
Pierced by an arrow in the act of love,
The pink-tufted crane, wings outspread,
Toppled.
Wrenched from under her lover,
The female, seeing blood gush out,
Screamed.
She screamed piteously.
Compassion stirred in Valmiki's heart
When he saw the bird die.
More compassion stirred in him
When he heard the screams of the female.
Horrified by the act of transgression
He cursed the fowler:

"Fowler! Listen to my words.
May peace of mind never be yours!
For you have killed this innocent bird
In his act of innocent love."

Even as the words issued from his mouth,
He felt uneasy, and he thought:
What is this that I have said
In the intensity of my grief?
For some time wise Valmiki brooded;
Then, turning to his disciple Bharadvaja,
He said:

> "Four lines of eight syllables each!
> From my sorrow came this song!
> From grief comes the making of verse:
> There is no poetry without compassion."

*Valmiki, Sanskrit, between the eighth and
second centuries B.C., tr. P. Lal*

Nature's need of protection increased dramatically with the Industrial Revolu-
tion. The gray alienation of the next poem has spread a long way since 1865, when
it was written.

 ## In a London Drawingroom

The sky is cloudy, yellowed by the smoke.
For view there are the houses opposite
Cutting the sky with one long line of wall
Like solid fog: far as the eye can stretch
Monotony of surface and of form
Without a break to hang a guess upon.
No bird can make a shadow as it flies,
For all is shadow, as in ways o'erhung

By thickest canvas, where the golden rays
Are clothed in hemp. No figure lingering
Pauses to feed the hunger of the eye
Or rest a little on the lap of life.
All hurry on and look upon the ground,
Or glance unmarking at the passersby.
The wheels are hurrying too, cabs, carriages
All closed, in multiplied identity.
The world seems one huge prison-house and court
Where men are punished at the slightest cost,
With lowest rate of color, warmth and joy.

George Eliot (Mary Ann Evans), English, 1819–80

Alfonsina Storni could not have read Eliot's poem, but her "Street" is like a twentieth-century version of it, complete with the image of "multiplied identity" —only this time such identity takes a psychological, nightmarish guise.

 ## Street

An alley open
between high gray walls.
At any moment: the dark mouth of the doors,
the tunnels of the entries,
traps that lead
to human catacombs.
Isn't there a shudder
in the entrance halls?
A bit of terror

in the rising whiteness
of a stairway?
I pass by hastily.
Every eye that looks at me
doubles me and scatters me
through the city.

A forest of legs,
a whirlwind
of rolling circles,
a cloud of shouts and sounds,
separate my head from my body,
my hands from my arms,
my heart from my chest,
my feet from my legs,
my will from its source.
Up above
the blue sky
calms its transparent water:
cities of gold
sail across it.

Alfonsina Storni, Argentinian, 1892–1938, tr. Marion Freeman

A poem by Judith Wright brings the theme of poetry as nature's guardian angel up to date. Passenger pigeons were once so numerous that flocks of them blackened the sky. This lament for them becomes a protest against our human besmirching of the natural world as we turn it exclusively to our use. And it reaffirms the role of poetry, which by singing celebrates and recreates the value and meaning of life.

Lament for Passenger Pigeons

Don't ask for the meaning, ask for the use.
WITTGENSTEIN

The voice of water as it flows and falls,
the noise air makes against earth-surfaces
have changed; are changing to the tunes we choose.

What wooed and echoed in the pigeon's voice?
We have not heard the bird. How reinvent
that passenger, its million wings and hues,

when we have lost the bird, the thing itself,
the sheen of life on flashing long migrations?
Might human musics hold it, could we hear?

Trapped in the fouling nests of time and space,
we turn the music on; but it is man,
and it is man who lends a deafening ear.

And it is man we eat and man we drink
and man who thickens round us like a stain.
Ice at the polar axis smells of men.

A word, a class, a formula, a use:
that is the rhythm, the cycle we impose.
The sirens sang us to the ends of sea,

and changed to us; their voices were our own,
jug-jug to dirty ears in dirtied brine.
Pigeons and angels sang us to the sky

and turned to metal and a dirty need.
The height of sky, the depth of sea we are,
sick with a yellow stain, a fouling dye.

Whatever Being is, that formula,
it dies as we pursue it past the word.
We have not asked the meaning, but the use.

What is the use of water when it dims?
The use of air that whines in emptiness?
The use of glass-eyed pigeons caged in glass?

We listen to the sea, that old machine,
to air that hoarsens on earth-surfaces
and has no angel, no migrating cry.

What is the being and the end of man?
Blank surfaces reverb a human voice
whose echo tells us that we choose to die:

or else, against the blank of everything,
to reinvent that passenger, that bird-
siren-and-angel image we contain
essential in a constellating word.
To sing of Being, its escaping wing,
to utter absence in a human chord
and recreate the meaning as we sing.

Judith Wright, Australian, born 1915

Many poets have suffered for following their art with conviction. Poverty, persecution, even torture and death have awaited them. Today, in the democratic West, being ignored is the widespread fate of poets (particularly the good ones), as poetry seems irrelevant in the struggle for wealth.

During times when poets *are* widely read, there's always the danger that they will annoy those in power. The fourteenth-century Persian poet Hafiz wrote that he would gladly give two great cities for a mole on his beloved's cheek. The psychopathic conqueror Timur, to whom the cities in question belonged, summoned Hafiz to account for his impudence. Hafiz explained, "Because I can't help giving things away, that's why I'm as poor as you see me now." He survived.

Poets have wandered far and wide in search of audiences and remuneration. The following lines describe a poet's life in Anglo-Saxon times.

  Thus wandering, they who shape songs for men
Pass over many lands, and tell their need,
And speak their thanks, and ever, south or north,
Meet someone skilled in songs and free in gifts,
Who would be raised among his friends to fame,
And do brave deeds till light and life are gone;
He who has thus wrought himself praise shall have
A settled glory underneath the stars.

Anonymous, Anglo-Saxon, seventh century,
final lines of Widsith, *tr. H. Morley*

The poet as wanderer appears in many traditions.

  ## *Light Rain on the Road to Sword Gate*

Wine stains and mud mottle my coat.
As I travel on, my heart breaks with every scene.

It looks as if I'm a poet at last,
Riding my donkey through Sword Gate in the drizzling rain.

Lu Yu, Chinese, 1125–1209,
tr. Jonathan Chaves

What calls poets to a life of uncertainty and the risk of being a permanent outsider?

 Peace

And sometimes I am sorry when the grass
Is growing over the stones in quiet hollows
And the cocksfoot leans across the rutted cart-pass
That I am not the voice of country fellows
Who now are standing by some headland talking
Of turnips and potatoes or young corn
Or turf banks stripped for victory.
Here Peace is still hawking
His colored combs and scarves and beads of horn.

Upon a headland by a whiny hedge
A hare sits looking down a leaf-lapped furrow
There's an old plow upside down on a weedy ridge
And someone is shouldering home a saddle-harrow.
Out of that childhood country what fools climb
To fight with tyrants Love and Life and Time?

Patrick Kavanagh, Irish, 1904–67

Poverty is a common condition for poets—especially in the twentieth century.

  he sees me
as nothing
but a useless poet—
I owe the man money

Takuboku, Japanese, 1885–1912, tr. Carl Sesar

The Chinese poet Chu Yuan became a wanderer because he would not compromise his integrity. He was a statesman whose advice was ignored by his sovereign. Leaving court, he wrote a long poem called "Encountering Sorrow," then drowned himself in a river. In this excerpt, he laments the takeover of his country by greedy and unscrupulous men.

  They go stampeding in search of money and grain.
Surfeited, they are not afraid to come for more.
Alas, they forgive themselves and blame only others.
They fret their hearts away, swayed by envy and greed.

They ride roughshod in pursuit of their ends.
My heart does not hunger after such things.
Gradually old age will fall about me;
Perhaps I shall never establish my good fame.

At dawn I drink the dropping dews of magnolias,
At dusk I eat fallen chrysanthemum petals.
If I respect only the good and the virtuous,
Why should I grieve over their interminably hungry jaws?

Chu Yuan, Chinese, 340–278 B.C., tr. Robert Payne

When a monarch wished to rule justly, poets and philosophers would find themselves welcome at court. The poet Sa'di, at the end of his long life (he is supposed to have lived to 108), wrote books of poetry and prose describing the principles of good government, from which the following extract is taken.

There is a story that while some game was being roasted for Nushirvan the Just during a hunting party, no salt could be found. A boy was sent to a nearby village to get some. Nushirvan said, "Pay for the salt lest it should become a custom and the village be ruined." When asked what harm could come from such a trifling demand, Nushirvan replied, "The foundation of oppression was small in the world; but those coming later have added to it, so it reached its present size."

> If a king eats an apple from the garden of a subject,
> His slaves will uproot the whole tree for him.

> Should a king allow the theft of five eggs,
> His soldiers will steal and roast a thousand fowls.

> A tyrant does not stay long in this world,
> But the curse on his name remains forever!

Sa'di, Persian, story 19 from The Gulistan,
version derived by I. M. from nineteenth-century translations

When government is less benevolent, poets find themselves voicing the discontents of the people. Popular poets keep the spirit of the people alive.

While Russia was under totalitarian rule, there was a hunger for poetry, which was in scarce supply because most of what was good was banned. The poet Anna

Akhmatova describes an event that happened while she waited day after day outside the prison gates for news of her son, who had been taken away by the secret police.

 In the terrible years of the Yezhov terror, I spent seventeen months in the prison lines of Leningrad. Once, someone recognized me. Then a woman with bluish lips standing behind me, who, of course, had never heard me called by name before, woke up from the stupor to which everyone had succumbed and whispered in my ear (everyone spoke in whispers there):

"Can you describe this?"

And I answered: "Yes, I can."

Then something that looked like a smile passed over what had once been her face.

The long poem "Requiem," which this story prefaces, describes the Yezhov terror. It ends as follows.

 Epilogue 1

I learned how faces fall,
How terror darts from under eyelids,
How suffering traces lines
Of stiff cuneiform on cheeks,
How locks of ashen-blonde or black
Turn silver suddenly,
Smiles fade on submissive lips
And fear trembles in a dry laugh.

And I pray not for myself alone,
But for all those who stood there with me
In cruel cold, and in July's heat,
At that blind, red wall.

 Epilogue 2

Once more the day of remembrance draws near.
I see, I hear, I feel you:

The one they almost had to drag at the end,
And the one who tramps her native land no more,

And the one who, tossing her beautiful head,
Said: "Coming here's like coming home."

I'd like to name them all by name,
But the list is confiscated and nowhere to be found.

I have woven a wide mantle for them
From their meager, overheard words.

I will remember them always and everywhere
I will never forget them no matter what comes.

And if they gag my exhausted mouth
Through which a hundred million scream,

Then may the people remember me
On the eve of my remembrance day.

And if ever in this country
They decide to erect a monument to me,

I consent to that honor
Under these conditions—that it stand

Neither by the sea, where I was born:
My last tie with the sea is broken,

Nor in the czar's garden near the cherished pine stump,
Where an inconsolable shade looks for me

But here, where I stood for three hundred hours,
And where they never unbolted the door for me.

This, lest in blissful death
I forget the rumbling of the Black Marias,

Forget how that detested door slammed shut
And an old woman howled like a wounded animal.

And may the melting snow stream like tears
From my motionless lids of bronze,

And a prison dove coo in the distance,
And the ships of the Neva sail calmly on.

Anna Akhmatova, Russian, 1889–1966, tr. Judith Hemschemeyer

The American prose writer and humorist Mark Twain resorted to poetry to express his bad conscience. In the interests of keeping his popularity, he let himself be persuaded (by his publishers) not to publish work critical of the direction his country had taken.

Twain felt that the U.S. government had abandoned its role as "defender of the weak" and become instead an "extinguisher of struggling liberties." The poem that follows was written in secret in 1901 and not published until 1966. The poem is written in the voice of an imaginary American president, who has overseen the betrayal of values and is now filled with remorse.

✸ *My Last Thought*

      I meant my country well—
God is my witness, this is true. In the beginning
I did not waver in my trust, but gave her loyal service—
The fair and just, when they reflect, will grant me this.
They know I was not bad at heart,
Though now they think my heart has changed . . .
And so it has—but not as *they* conceive! They think
It black and hard—whereas it only bleeds! Bleeds
For the widows it has made, the orphans it has starved,
The freedom it has crushed, the humble friends
It turned against, the faiths it broke,
The treacheries it devised, the freed slaves
It chained again,
The land it took by fraud and keeps by force,
The praise it won from sceptered thieves
For stooping to their ways,
The dirt it put upon our flag and name!

      Lord God, forgive! For I was only weak,
Not bad. And I was out of place—
A lost and wandering atom in that vast Seat
Which only Lincolns and their like compactly fill.
I loved my country, and I meant it well:
I say it with my dying breath. . . .
      Pearl of the Antilles, speak!

I broke your chains, I set you free; I raised
My country's honor to the skies; I won
The Old World's scorn and hate, the New World's
"Well done, thou faithful son!"

O *then* I was myself! Grant me that!
Remember only that, dear land of my nativity,
Which I have brought to shame—forget the rest!
I erred through weakness, not intent. For I
Was overborne by sordid counsels,
Base ambitions, and from my head I took
The precious laurel I had earned, and in its place
I set this poor tin glory, now my wear,
Of World-Power, Conqueror of helpless tribes,
Extinguisher of struggling liberties!

Forget? Thou? No—that is a dream.
Thou canst not. The memory of treasons such as mine
Remains. They make a bartered nation blush;
And the wise know that only deeds
That lift a people's pride, and deeds
That make it hang its head,
Abide forever in its heart.

Arnold![2] How they crimson at his name! And yet—
Why, his meditated treason but concerned a garrison—
Mine—accomplished—peddled out a Nation and its honor:
And sold them for a song!

Upon my fading sight a holy vision rises:
Our flag of snow and flame far-flashing in the sky!

And toward it the oppressed of every clime
Uplifting their poor fettered hands
In hope and trust and worship. . . .

     It is gone. . . . How blest am I
That the last office of my dying eyes should be
To show it me as once it was: protector of the wronged,
Defender of the weak, friend of the homeless and forlorn!
     . . . But there!—is not this the Flag again?
The dimness grows. It is the Flag, I think, but changed. . . .
The twilight mellows. . . .
Now the picture clears. . . . It is the Flag, but—
Oh, not as it was in its great old days!
The Stars are gone, a Skull and Bones
Are in their place; the Red Bars are there,
But soaked with guiltless blood;
The White Bars are Black—
Hide it from my sight!

     The night of Death is come:
Its shadows deepen—let me sleep. . . .
Sleep and forget, sleep and be forgotten—
If that dear boon might but be mine!
     Farewell, my country—
So beloved by me, and so betrayed! I have sinned,
And I repent—have charity!
     Teach the flowers that spring where I am hid,
And wandering summer airs that blow above my grave,
To speak for my dumb lips
And say to any that would search me out, "Pass on—

Naught can ye learn of him:
Give him of your peace, forgive him and forget—
Pass on!"[3]

Mark Twain (Samuel Langhorne Clemens),
American, 1835–1910

Poetry is the guardian angel of words. The ancient sanctity of words is recalled by the Russian poet Nicolai Gumilev, who was Akhmatova's husband. He argues that when words are only used about worldly things, they die.

It is written that the Word is God.
But we have limited Its range
To the paltry boundaries of this world,
And like dead bees in an empty hive
Dead words emit a foul odor.

Nicolai Gumilev, Russian, 1886–1921,
tr. Jane G. Harris and Constance Link

Brendan Kennelly describes the same process eighty years later. His character Ozzie wonders what use words are.

 Words

what's words ozzie assed me
sounds dat kum outa peepul's mouths i said
where dey kum from first sez ozzie
dunno i replied

fukken fish have no words ozzie went on
but dey enjoy de fukken sea
and fukken tigers have no words
but dey enjoy eatin you and me

only peepul has words ozzie said
an luk at de shit dey talk
if i kud reed i'd say buks are shit as well

words are to kummynikate sez i
like shit sez ozzie won good bomm
blow de whole fukken world ta hell

Brendan Kennelly, Irish, born 1936, from The Book of Judas

Ozzie never thought about words making pleasure and beauty. Eskimos used to expect each other to be poets—some good, some bad. For them, words were part of the magic of the world, reflecting its harshness and its beauty.

❋ Delight in Singing

It's wonderful
to make up songs:
but all too many of them fail.

It's wonderful
to have your wishes granted:
but all too often
they slip by.

It's wonderful
to hunt reindeer:

but all too seldom
you succeed,
standing like a bright fire
on the plain.

Anonymous, Eskimo, 1920s, tr. Knud Rasmussen and Tom Lowenstein

A similar poem from another culture:

It's a pleasure
When, after a hundred days
Of twisting my words
Without success,
Suddenly
A poem turns out nicely.

Tachibana Akemi, Japanese, 1812–68, tr. Donald Keene

Using words, poets fashion visions to entrance us. The next three poems concern visions of harmony and peace. Humans have a deep-rooted and haunting conception, almost like a memory, of what it's like to live in peace. The myth of the garden of Eden is just one of many stories recording a memory that became a vision—or is it the other way around? High expectations lead to bitter disappointment when they are not fulfilled.

If only I could live
In the shade of spring leaves
Instead of in a world
Of disillusion and despair.

Higuchi Ichiyo, Japanese, 1872–96, tr. Robert Danley

A vision of happiness and harmony is the subject of the next poem, which is prefaced by a story. The story became known to all educated Chinese.

During the T'ai-yuan period of the Chin dynasty a fisherman of Wu-ling once rowed upstream, unmindful of the distance he had gone, when he suddenly came to a grove of peach trees in bloom. For several hundred paces on both banks of the stream there was no other kind of tree. The wildflowers growing under the peach trees were fresh and lovely, and fallen petals covered the ground—it made a great impression on the fisherman. He went on for a while with the idea of finding out how far the grove extended. It came to an end at the foot of a mountain from which issued the spring that supplied the stream. There was a small opening in the mountain, and it seemed as though light were coming through it. The fisherman left his boat and entered the cave, which at first was extremely narrow, barely admitting his body; after a few dozen steps it suddenly opened out onto a broad and level plain on which well-built houses were surrounded by rich fields and pretty ponds. Mulberry, bamboo, and other trees and plants grew there, and crisscross paths skirted the fields. The sounds of cocks crowing and dogs barking could be heard from one courtyard to the next. Men and women were coming and going about their work in the fields. The clothes they wore were like those of ordinary people. Old men and boys were carefree and happy.

When these people caught sight of the fisherman, they asked in surprise how he had got there. The fisherman told the whole story and was invited to go to one of their houses, where he was served wine while they killed a chicken for a feast. When the other villagers heard about the fisherman's arrival they all came to pay him a visit. They told him that their ancestors had fled the disorders of Ch'in times and, having taken refuge there with wives and children and neighbors, had never ventured out again; consequently they had lost all contact with the outside world. They asked what the present ruling dynasty was, for they had never heard of the Han, let alone the Wei and the Chin. They sighed unhappily as the fisherman enumerated the dynasties one by one and recounted the vicissitudes of each. The visitors all asked him to come to their houses in turn, and at every house he had wine and food. He stayed several days. As he was about to go away, the people said, "There's no need to mention our existence to outsiders."

After the fisherman had gone out and recovered his boat, he carefully marked the route. On reaching the city, he reported what he had found to the magistrate, who at once sent a man to follow him back to the place. They proceeded according to the marks he had made, but went astray and were unable to find the cave again.

A high-minded gentleman of Nan-yang named Liu Tzu-chi heard the story and happily made preparations to go there, but before he could leave, he fell sick and died. Since then there has been no one interested in trying to find such a place.

The Ying clan disrupted heaven's ordinance
And good men withdrew from such a world.
Huang and Ch'i went off to Shang Mountain
And these people too fled into hiding.
Little by little their tracks were obliterated,
The paths they followed overgrown at last.
By agreement they set about farming the land;
When the sun went down each rested from his toil.
Bamboo and mulberry provided shade enough,
They planted beans and millet, each in season.
From spring silkworms came the long silk thread,
On the fall harvest no king's tax was paid.
No sign of traffic on overgrown roads,
Cocks crowed and dogs barked within each other's
    earshot.
Their ritual vessels were of old design,
And no new fashions in the clothes they wore.
Children wandered about singing songs,
Graybeards went paying one another calls.
When grass grew thick they saw the time was mild,
As trees went bare they knew the wind was sharp.
Although they had no calendar to tell,
The four seasons still filled out a year.
Joyous in their ample happiness
They had no need of clever contrivance.
Five hundred years this rare event stayed hid,
Then one day the fay retreat was found.
The pure and the shallow belong to separate worlds:
In a little while they were hidden again.

Let me ask you who are convention-bound,
Can you fathom those outside the dirt and noise?
I want to tread on the thin thin air
And rise up high to find my own kind.

Tao Yuan Ming (T'ao Ch'ien), Chinese, 372–427, tr. J. R. Hightower

Gwen Harwood presents a modern-day vision of harmony in which people, sailing boats, and engines are not incompatible with peace on earth.

 ## *Threshold*

Know that a peaceful harbor
framed by low hills, a refuge
that might be glimpsed one moment
in a happy dream, exists:
a marina spiky with masts;
salt glitter, boat-brightness rocking
in gray-green shallows, and gulls
reading in deeper sea-gleam
the text of wind and tide.

Some genius of earth
devised this generous place,
this charm of light compacting
sea, sky, the hills of Bruny,
the birds with airfilled bones,
the clouds like ghosts of sails,
into one form, one presence
whose guests we are, and welcome.
The ferry's engines throb

among water's ancient voices.
Children's and seabirds' cries
fade at the fringe of language
as the road leads gently upwards
to a gate where casuarinas
crosshatch the shining water.
The road leads on. But pause:
lift clear from time's refractions,
from the mind's reflective tricks,

this day; see its true shape.
Look how a lizard skims
from leaf-shade, and is basking
stone-still on stone, a finger-length
creature absorbing sunlight.
A crow with steel-bright eye
testing the pitch of silence
flaps to a neighboring pine,
settles his dark voice down;

pause for a moment here.
These gums that fracture light
are home to the intricate compound
eyes of the insect kingdom,
and birds, whose eyes can read
the to-us invisible pattern
of the polarized sky, are singing
what is real but still unnamed.
Our words and thoughts are polished

like pebbles ground in the stream
of time, but here's an enclave,
land held in arms of water,
where the plover and their young
are safe in feathery grasses
stirred by the seawind breathing
a prayer of peace and healing
in the pure, authentic speech
that earth alone can teach.

Gwen Harwood, Australian, born 1920

By holding out these visions, poets remind us of what life can be like and what is worth striving for. But the yearning for harmony and order can also lead us into dangerous territory. The poet Gabriele D'Annunzio invented fascism,[4] and Yeats flirted with it. Mao Tse-tung loved poetry and wrote it while devising the deaths of millions. Heaven on earth is a fine ideal, but life is cruel, and we should not use cruelty of our own in trying to outwit it. Jean Ingelow wrote of the difference between the afflictions of providence and the inflictions of our fellow human beings:

 When troubles come of God,
When men are frozen out of work, when wives
Are sick, when working fathers fail and die,
When boats go down at sea—then naught behooves
Like patience; but for troubles wrought of men
Patience is hard—I tell you it is hard.

Jean Ingelow, English, 1820–97

From visions of harmony we move to dissent. The voice of dissent is strong in Islamic poetry, which was given much freedom by Muhammad's statement that all poets are liars. This gave poets protection from criticism—for who pays serious attention to liars?—and many of them devoted themselves to celebrating drunkenness, a sin in Islam. Furthermore, because simple belief in God protects an individual from persecution under Islamic law, poets were free to be critical of religious hypocrisy. The poet Ma'arri freely criticized the orthodox religious thinking of his time:

You said we've a wise creator
And I replied you're right, but look,
You claim he's timeless and nowhere.
Such terms, for all we know, could be
A secret language: which amounts
To saying we cannot think straight.

Ma'arri, Syrian, 973–1057, tr. George Wightman and Abdullah al-Udhari

Poets can be like pipers, playing a tune for the world to dance to, and they can lead us to new ideas of how life can be lived. In 1955, the Persian poet Forugh Farrokhzad shocked readers by writing of female sexual desire.

I sinned a sin full of pleasure,
in an embrace that was warm and fiery,
I sinned surrounded by arms
that were hot and avenging and iron.

In that dark and silent seclusion,
I looked into his secret-full eyes.

My heart impatiently shook in my breast
in response to the request of his needful eyes.

In that dark and silent seclusion,
I sat disheveled at his side.
His lips poured passion on my lips,
I escaped from the sorrow of my crazed heart.

I whispered in his ear the tale of love:
I want you, O life of mine,
I want you, O life-giving embrace,
O crazed lover of mine, you.

Desire sparked a flame in his eyes;
the red wine danced in the cup.
In the soft bed, my body
drunkenly quivered on his chest.

I sinned a sin full of pleasure,
next to a shaking, stupefied form.
O god, who knows what I did,
In that dark and quiet seclusion.

Forugh Farrokhzad, Persian, 1934–67, tr. Michael Hillman

Aleksandr Pushkin was in trouble with the authorities throughout most of his short life. In the next poem, he defends the poet's instinct to follow what he knows is right and not what others tell him. The lines about Desdemona and the Moor have a personal relevance: Pushkin was the great-grandson of a Moor employed by Peter the Great, and he was proud of the black element in his ancestry.

Eyes open wide, the poet weaves,
Blind as a bat, his urgent way;
But feels a tug upon his sleeve,
And hears a passing stranger say:
"Why do you betray the Muse
By wandering aimlessly, my friend?
Before you reach the heights, you choose
To gaze beneath you, and descend.
Blind to the great harmonious scheme
Of creation, you become possessed,
Too often, by some trivial theme,
And sterile fevers rack your breast.
A genius should look up—the duty
Of a true poet is to rise;
His dwelling place should be the skies;
His theme and inspiration, beauty."
—Why does a wind swirl through a dusty
Ravine and shake its stunted trees,
And yet a ship spread out its thirsty
Canvas in vain for a light breeze?
Why does an eagle leave the peak,
And, gliding past the church spire, seek
The miserable tree stump? Why
Did youthful Desdemona swoon
In the Moor's spasm, as the moon
In the night's shadow loves to lie?
Because for wind, and eagle's claws,
And a girl's heart, there are no laws.
The poet too, like Aquilon,[5]

Lifts what he wants, and bears it on—
Flies like an eagle, heeds no voice
Directing him, spurns all control,
And clasps the idol of his choice,
Like Desdemona, to his soul.

Aleksandr Pushkin, Russian, 1799–1837, tr. D. M. Thomas

Pushkin suffered censorship under the autocratic government of the czar, which by the standards of nineteenth-century Europe was most unenlightened. But twentieth-century governments, defying notions of steady progress in human affairs, have far outstripped past dictators in the scale of their brutality.

Modern armaments make it possible for gangsters to take over whole countries and subject them to rule by terror. Even governments that were moderate to begin with, once they escape democratic accountability and gain the aid of modern weapons, may shift toward military dictatorship.

In the next poem, not only is the outspoken poet imprisoned but the traditional protection accorded to women in his society is violated.

 They Came Looking for You

One day
they came looking for you
for you too
They couldn't forgive you
for being the companion
of a rebel poet
for loving an outcast
and for sustaining him with your own
resistance

You knew
the night of the blindfold
the underworld of the Question
you heard those voices
beyond humanity
shouting words of menace and sarcasm
you felt before you
those tatty men (so little like men)
whom you knew were torturers and assassins
you felt near you
other men (a little more than ordinary men)
scarred by electrodes and whips
but with unwavering hearts
And so
there is nothing left to hide from you

Abdellatif Laabi, Moroccan, born 1952, tr. Ariel Daigre

What can be done against such governments?

In the next poem, a concerned liberal is humbled by the person he is trying to help.

❁ *Little Girl*

Her body reminded me of
areca palm in quiet country
tall and thin
in heavy storms
broken branches fall around

but the palm stands erect
awaiting the morning sun.

So it was with this little girl
thin as areca palm
year after year meeting her father
across the barbed wire of a prison
imprisoned these many years
courageously fighting oppression
steady and faithful.

This little girl surprised me
calm and smiling broadly
politely turning down my help
"I don't need money, Uncle,
just paper and books."

Young in age
her soul matured by experience
not everyone grows strong this way
a unique steadiness that charms.

When I expressed sympathy and sadness,
feeling sorry for her,
once again she smiled and said:
"Don't be sad, uncle, steady your heart,
there are many children like me in the world."

I became quite still,
she calmed me, this little girl

pacifying waves of emotion
forbidding pity for her bitter experiences.
Is it not shameful for a grown man,
wanting to help suffering prisoners,
to receive counsel from the child of one in prison
to be brave and steady?

Ten children like this
will destroy the purpose of a thousand prisons.

Usman Awang, Malaysian, born 1929, tr. Adibah Amin

Some poets escape persecution by going into exile. But exile can be painful; deprived of an audience, their work banned at home, living in an uncaring host country, these poets often lead bleak lives.

The author of the next poem spent twenty-six years in exile before returning to Guatemala to visit her mother. There she was abducted, and (it is presumed) killed, by soldiers.

Poets always speak to someone.
With sword or wheat sheaf
They address the people
or sing softly
to a loved one,
revealing unexpected
dazzling scenes.
Their path is strewn with flowers.
But in my dark retreat
I bear poetry
like a secret disease,

a hidden
illicit fruit.

Alaide Foppa, Guatemalan, born 1914, disappeared December 19, 1980,
tr. Rozenn Frère and Dennis Wurkse

The list of twentieth-century poets who have suffered terrible fates is long. Some poets, however, betray their humanity and devote their talents to praising the government; such poets may be rewarded with wealth, prestigious jobs, and literary honor.

In the next poem, George Faludy complains to a friend who has won Hungary's chief literary award.

 They'll never give me such a medal,
Not in a thousand years they won't!
Not me, because of what I write;
But you, because of what you don't.

George Faludy, Hungarian, born 1910, tr. Eric Johnson

Praise, adulation, and wealth can corrupt even when they are justly earned. After Wordsworth became respectable and successful, he was accused of trading in his "storm cloud's thunderous melody" for the bleat of "an old half-witted sheep."[6]

Truth can be uncomfortable and fantasies are soothing. In the West, a pervasive admiration for what is commercially successful banishes thoughtful voices to the fringe. The shock of the new takes on the role and even the name of art, and it must grow more and more bizarre in order to satisfy more and more jaded appetites.

Purveyors of popular culture, however, fall back on the more traditional fascinations of gossip, sex, and violent death. The next poem describes the kind of stuff a modern "professional" writer is expected to churn out. A scriptwriter is being told by a film producer to get down to basics, forget his love of islands, and give people "what they want."

🏵 The Man Who Loved Islands

A Two-Page Outline

A man is leaning on a cold iron rail
watching an islet from an island and so on,
say, Charlotte Amalie facing Saint John,
which begins the concept of infinity
uninterrupted by any mortal sail,
only the thin ghost of a tanker drawing the horizon
behind it with the silvery slick of a snail,
and that's the first shot of this forthcoming film
starring James Coburn and his tanned, leathery, frail
resilience and his now-whitening hair,
and his white, vicious grin. Now, we were where?
On this island, one of the Virgins, the prota-
gonist established. Now comes the second shot,
and chaos of artifice still called the plot,
which has to get the hero off somewhere
else, 'cause there's no kick in contemplation
of silvery light upon wind-worried water
between here and the islet of Saint John,
and how they are linked like any silver chain
glinting against the hero's leather chest,
sold in the free gift ports, like noon-bright water.
The hero's momentary rest on the high rail

can be a good beginning. To start with rest
is good—the tanker can come later.
But we can't call it "The Man Who Loved Islands"
any more than some Zen-Karate film
would draw them with "The Hero Who Loves Water."
No soap. There must be something with diamonds,
emeralds, emeralds the color of the shallows there,
or sapphires, like blue unambiguous air,
sapphires for Sophia, but we'll come to that.
Coburn looks great with or without a hat,
and there must be some minimum of slaughter
that brings in rubies, but you cannot hover
over that first shot like a painting. Action
is all of art, the thoughtless pace
of lying with style, so that when it's over,
that first great shot of Coburn's leathery face,
crinkled like the water which he contemplates,
could be superfluous, in the first place,
since that tired artifice called history,
which in its motion is as false as fiction,
requires an outline, a summary. I can think of none,
quite honestly. I'm no photographer; this
could be a movie. I mean things are moving,
the water for example, the light on the man's hair
that has gone white, even those crescent sands
are just as moving as his love of islands;
the tanker that seems still is moving, even
the clouds like galleons anchored in heaven,
and what is moving most of all of course

is the violent man lulled into this inaction
by the wide sea. Let's hold it on the sea
as we establish their ancient interaction,
a hint of the Homeric, a little poetry
before the whole mess hits the bloody fan.
All these islands that you love, I guaran-
tee we'll work them in as background, with
generous establishing shots from Jim's car and
even a few harbors and villages, *if*
we blow the tanker up and get the flames
blazing with oil, and Sophia, if she's free,
daintily smudged, with her slip daintily torn,
is climbing down this rope ladder, and we shoot up
from Coburn's P.O.V.—he's got the gems—
that's where we throw in Charlotte Amalie
and the waterfront bars, and this Danish alley
with the heavies chasing, and we can keep all the
business of Jim on the rail; that lyric stuff
goes with the credits if you insist on keeping it tend-
er; I can see it, but things must get rough
pretty damn fast, or else you lose them, pally,
or tell you what, let's save it for THE END.

Derek Walcott, Saint Lucian, born 1930

The next poem presents a very different idea of what society wants from its
writers.

The wisdom of the scribe depends on the opportunity of
    leisure;
only the one who has little business can become wise.
How can one become wise who handles the plow,
and who glories in the shaft of a goad,
who drives oxen and is occupied with their work,
and whose talk is about bulls?
He sets his heart on plowing furrows,
and he is careful about fodder for the heifers.
So too is every artisan and master artisan
who labors by night as well as by day;
those who cut the signets of seals,
each is diligent in making a great variety;
they set their heart on painting a lifelike image,
and they are careful to finish their work.
So too is the smith, sitting by the anvil,
intent on his ironwork;
the breath of fire melts his flesh,
and he struggles with the heat of the furnace;
the sound of the hammer deafens his ears,
and his eyes are on the pattern of the object.
He sets his heart on finishing his handiwork,
and he is careful to complete its decoration.
So too is the potter sitting at his work
and turning the wheel with his feet;
he is always deeply concerned over his products,
and he produces them in quantity.
He molds the clay with his arm
and makes it pliable with his feet;

he sets his heart to finish the glazing,
and he takes care in firing the kiln.

All these rely on their hands,
and all are skillful in their own work.
Without them no city is inhabited,
and wherever they live, they will not go hungry.
Yet they are not sought out for the council of the people,
nor do they attain eminence in the public assembly.
They do not sit in the judge's seat,
nor do they understand the decisions of the courts;
they cannot expound discipline or judgment,
and they are not found among the rulers.
But they maintain the fabric of the world,
and their concern is for the exercise of their trade.

How different the one who devotes himself
to the study of the law of the Most High!
He seeks out the wisdom of all the ancients,
and is concerned with prophecies;
he preserves the sayings of the famous
and penetrates the subtleties of parables;
he seeks out the hidden meanings of proverbs
and is at home with the obscurities of parables.
He serves among the great
and appears before rulers;
he travels in foreign lands
and learns what is good and evil in the human lot.
He sets his heart to rise early
to seek the Lord who made him,

and to petition the Most High;
he opens his mouth in prayer
and asks pardon for his sins.

Jesus Ben Sira, Jewish Egyptian, circa 180 B.C., Sirach 38:24–39:5,
Bible, New Revised Standard Version

The next poem tells of a thirteenth-century poet's attitude toward her own poems, which have now been handed down orally for six hundred years. Though she never expected such a thing, the "wine" of Lalla's poetry enabled her to destroy her inner darkness.

 I didn't put my hope in it,
not even for a moment.
I didn't trust it,
not even by a hair.
Still I, Lalla, drank the wine of my own sayings.
Yet, then I seized an inner darkness,
I brought it down,
I tore it and cut it to pieces.

Lalla, Kashmiri, fourteenth century, version by I. M. from
tr. by Lionel Burnett and Sir George Grierson

The next poem celebrates the power of poetry to keep hope alive.

 Testament

To the youngest prostitute
In the oldest and darkest barrio

I leave my earrings
Cut in crystal, limpid and pure . . .

And to that forgotten virgin
Girl without tenderness
Dreaming somewhere of a happy story
I leave my white dress
My wedding dress
Trimmed with lace. . . .

I offer my old rosary
To that old friend of mine
Who does not believe in God . . .

And my books—rosaries
That tell of a different suffering—
Are for humble folk
Who never learned to read.

As for my crazy poems
Those that echo sincerely
The confusion and sadness in my heart
Those that sing of hope
Where none can be found
Those I give to you my love . . .

So that in a moment of peace
When my soul comes from afar
To kiss your eyes

You will go into the night
Accompanied by the moon

To read them to children
That you meet along each street. . . .

Alda Lara, Angolan, 1930–62, tr. Don Burness

Poetry springs from our experience of living, its intense joys and sorrows. "Who knows what horrors go to make a song?" writes Brendan Kennelly. In the next poem, Oswald Mtshali describes beautiful singing coming from the hearts of degraded mine workers. Those who are degrading them lose such beauty as surely as they gain luxury.

 Amagoduka[7] at Glencoe Station

> We traveled a long journey
> through the wattle forests of Vryheid,
> crossed the low-leveled Blood River
> whose water flowed languidly
> as if dispirited for the
> shattered glory of my ancestors.
>
> We passed the coalfields of Dundee—
> blackheads in the wrinkled face
> of Northern Zululand—
> until our train ultimately came
> to a hissing stop at Glencoe.
>
> Many people got off,
> leaving the enraged train
> to snort and charge at the night
> on its way to Durban.

The time was 8 P.M.

I picked up my suitcase,
sagging under the weight of a heavy overcoat,
I shambled to the "Non-European Males" waiting room.

The room was crowded,
the air hung, a pall of choking odor,
rotten meat, tobacco and sour beer.

Windows were shut tight
against the sharp bite of winter.

Amagoduka sat on bare floor
their faces sucking the warmth
of the coal fire crackling in the corner.

They chewed dried bread
scooped corned beef with rusty knives,
and drank *mqombothi* from the plastic can
which they passed from mouth to mouth.

They spoke animatedly
and laughed in thunderous peals.

A girl peeped through the door,
they shuddered at the sudden cold blast,
jumped up to fondle and leer at her
"Hau! ngena Sisi!—Oh! come in sister!"

She shied like a frightened filly
banged the door and bolted.
They broke into tumultuous laughter.

One of them picked up a guitar
plucked it with broken fingernails
caressed its strings with a castor oil bottle—

it sighed like a jilted girl.
"You play down! *Phansi!* Play D," he whispered.

Another joined in with concertina,
its sound fluttered in flowery notes
like a butterfly picking pollen from flower to flower.

The two began to sing,
their voices crying for the mountains
and the hills of Msinga, stripped naked of
their green garment.

They crossed rivers and streams,
gouged dry by the sun rays,
where lowing cattle genuflected
for a blade of grass and a drop of water
on riverbeds littered with carcasses and bones.

They spoke of hollow-cheeked maidens
heaving drums of brackish water
from a faraway fountain.

They told of big-bellied babies
sucking festering fingers
instead of their mothers' shriveled breasts.

Two cockroaches
as big as my overcoat buttons
jived across the floor

snatched meat and bread crumbs
and scurried back to their hideout.

The whole group joined in unison:
curious eyes peered through frosted windows
"Ekhaya bafowethu!—Home, brothers!"

We come from across the Tugela river,
we are going to EGoli! EGoli! EGoli![8]
where they'll turn us into moles
that eat the gold dust
and spit out blood.

We'll live in compounds
where young men are pampered
into partners for older men.

We'll visit shebeens
where a whore waits for a fee
to leave your balls burning
with syphilitic fire.

If the gods are with us—
Oh! beloved black gods of our forefathers
What have we done to you
Why have you forsaken us—
We'll return home
to find our wives nursing babies—
unknown to us
but only to their mothers and loafers.

Oswald Mbuyiseni Mtshali, South African, born 1940

Simone Weil comments on a life without poetry: "Slavery is work without any light from eternity, without poetry, without religion."[9] The more poetry of all sorts is ignored by society, the grimmer people's lives become. In the next poem, the poet says that however unhappy her life has been, at least she has "lived" in the fullest sense of the word.

❀ Life

When I have watched the people crawling by
So haggard-visaged, and so wrinkled-browed,
With eyes that see naught save the greedy ground,
With ears that hear naught save their toiling feet,
To whom there can exist no other world
Besides the one of Commonplace and Real,
Where Fancy's idle beams ne'er fleck the gloom
With dancing, changing lights of flitted dreams,
I do rejoice, for I, with all my woes
May see the sights and hear the sounds they miss,
For I may see the beauty in a cloud
Or tiny flower or slender blade of grass,
May watch the tree tops whispering with the winds,
The slanting rain drops grayed by solemn skies,
And find insistent joyousness in all;
May speechless stand before some landscape grand,
Where mountains lift their regal heads in peace,
Enwrapped at morn in frail, sheer robes of mist,
Enwrapped at even in voluptuous garb,
For I may hear the songs of little things,
The cricket, locust, tree-toad, and the bird
That sings within the woods at summer dawns

And twitters sleepily at summer dusks;
For I may hear the yearnings of the soul
Within the voice or throbbing violin
Until the ear so wrung by chords of joy
Comes nigh to bursting in delicious pain;
For I may feel the fierceness of great love
With all its agony and rare delights,
Its dire despair and lightning heights of joy.
What though I die mid racking pain,
And heart seared through and through by grief,
I still rejoice for I, at least, have lived.

Angelina Weld Grimke, American, 1880–1958

In the following poem, Osip Mandelstam, surrounded by the carnage of the Stalin era, prophesies the survival of the values by which he lives.

 Into the distance go the mounds of people's heads.
I am growing smaller here—no one notices me anymore,
but in caressing books and children's games
I will rise from the dead to say the sun is shining.

Osip Mandelstam, Russian, 1891–1938, tr. David McDuff

CHAPTER 10

The End?

The twentieth century isn't the first historical age to be racked by anxiety and despair about the future. The first poem of this chapter was written in Germany during the Thirty Years' War, when Christians were tearing each other to pieces (literally) over points of doctrine. It's comforting to look back on another time when hope seemed to be the exclusive property of idiots.

✸ *All Is Vanity*

Whichever way we look, only vanity on earth.
What one man builds today, another destroys tomorrow.
The land where cities stand will soon again be meadows;
On them, peasant children, playing among the flocks.
Blooms, luxurious now, are soon trodden down;
What boasts defiantly now is just tomorrow's ashes.
Nothing on earth can last; not of stone or bronze.
Should fortune shine today, hardships soon will thunder.
The fame of lofty deeds vanishes like a dream,
Can Time's plaything, Man, be expected then to last?
Ah! What is everything dear to us, everything we value
But wretched triviality; like shadow, dust, and wind,
Like a flower in a meadow found once but nevermore.
Yet—not a single person wants to think on the eternal.

Andreas Gryphius, German, 1616–64, tr. I. M.

Petronius saw the greedy decadence of Rome from the inside. Helen Waddell, the translator of the next poem, notes, "He was an aristocrat who had been an admirable provincial governor in the old tradition, and then came back to Rome, recording the civilization that he relished and sickened at." Despite the decadence of the time he observed, it was another four centuries before Rome finally collapsed.

The Roman was the victor of the world.
All seas, all lands, the journeys of the sun,
Aye, and the moon,
He owned them all and was not satisfied.
The fretted seas he sent this way and that
With his great-bellied keels: if round yon headland
A little bay hid, or distant land
That cropped with gold, she was the enemy;
The obedient oracles for war stood ready,
The hunt for wealth was up.
He had no pleasure in familiar things
That please the common folk: the well-worn joys
That poor men's hands have handled. Out at sea
Soldiers would prate about the bronze of Corinth;
The purple that was once got from the shellfish
Is dull stuff now beside their chemicals.
The men of Africa have cause to curse them.
China's despoiled of silk, Arabia
Hath stripped her incense fields.
Always fresh killing and new wounds of peace . . .
They hew the citron tree in Africa
And make their tables of its gold-flecked surface,
And round that barren and ignoble wood
Gather a crowd of men sodden with drink,
And yon mercenary swills the wealth of the world,
Rust on his idle sword.

Your gluttony is an ingenious rascal.
Seawater keeps your wrasse[1] alive,

Come all the way to your plate from Sicily.
The Lucrine oysters are extravagance,
But most reviving to a dulled appetite.
Silent, O Phasis, are thy waters now,
Silent the shore.
A solitary wind sighs through the boughs,
Where the birds nest no more.
The selfsame madness is in politics:
Easy to buy a Roman citizen:
He'll sell you his vote any day for a bucket-shop share
Or a spot of cash. The man in the street's for sale,
And so is the man in the House: they all have their price.
The pristine liberal virtue of the old men
Has dropped away, the power they had they lost
Scrambling for gold, their ancient dignity
Rotted by money, trodden underfoot.
They set the mob on Cato, drove him out,
And now they are more sick at heart than he.
The man's abashed that took his office from him.
Here is the symbol of a people's shame,
The ruin of their standards:
When they beat the old man up, sent him to exile,
It was no man they banished,
It was the honor and the power of Rome.

Lost, lost is Rome, her own self her own prey.
She hath made herself a spoil and there is none
That will avenge her.
This flooding sewer of money out at interest

Has caught the common folk in a double whirlpool,
Their usury has choked them.
Not a house but is mortgaged, not a man but in pawn.
Like a disease hatched in the silent cells
This madness rages through their harried bodies,
Baying them down.
Men ruined think of robbery in arms:
The good things luxury has spent and spoiled
They'll win again by wounds.
Your beggar dare be bold: he has naught to lose.
There's Rome asleep in the gutter, snoring fast.
And what's to wake her?
Sound reason or the arts?
Or naught but war and madness and the lust
That's wakened by the sword?

Petronius, Roman, died 66 A.D.; tr. Helen Waddell

After the Roman Empire's final collapse, its provinces were left at the mercy of marauders who reestablished a more primitive order. A poem survives from Britain telling of these times. Appropriately, it is partly lost; the two pages on which it was written are damaged by fire.

 Fate has smashed these wonderful walls,
This broken city, has crumbled the work
Of giants. The roofs are gutted, the towers
Fallen, the gates ripped off, frost
In the mortar, everything molded, gaping,
Collapsed. The earth has clutched at rulers

And builders, a hundred generations rotting
In its rigid hands. These red-stained stones,
Streaked with gray, stood while governors
And kingdoms dissolved into dust, and storms
Crashed over them; they were broad and high, and they fell.
. . . .
. . . .
. . . . strong-hearted men hung
The walls together with beaten wire.
It was a shining city, filled with bathhouses,
With towering gables, with the shouts of soldiers,
With dozens of rousing drinking halls,
Until Fate's strength was swung against it.
The riches died away, pestilence
Came, the crowds of soldiers were dead;
Their forts and camps crumbled to the ground,
And the city, with all its idols and temples,
Decayed to these ruins, its buildings rotted,
Its red-stoned arches splitting brick
From brick. And the ruined site sank
To a heap of tumbled stones, where once
Cheerful, strutting warriors flocked,
Golden armor gleaming, giddy
With wine; here was wealth, silver,
Gems, cattle, land, in the crowning
City of a far-flung kingdom. There were buildings
Of stone, where steaming currents threw up
Surging heat; a wall encircled
That brightness, with the baths inside at the glowing

Heart. Life was easy and lush.
They'd make the warm streams pour over
Old gray stones . . . .
. . . . until
The rounded pools grew hot . . . .
. . . .
. . . . a kingly thing,
A house . . . . a city . . . . . .

Anonymous, Anglo-Saxon, before 940 A.D.(?), tr. Burton Raffel

Since our destiny is physical extinction, it's often argued that we should eat, drink, and be merry while we are able. However, many poets respond to the fact of our mortality in a different way. For them, death makes a mockery of our constructions of wealth and glory, so we should take life seriously while we are able.

In the next poem, Luis de Gongora uses images of imminent mortality to urge his friend Licio to change his foolish ways.

 On Life's Deceptive Brevity

Solicitous, the swift arrow speeds
Toward its destined mark, in which it bites;
Silent in the mute sand, the chariot
Turns in victory round the winning post;
Yet swifter, and more secretly, our life
Hurries us to our end. For those that doubt—
Beasts bereft of reason though they be—
Day by day the sun is a warning comet.
Has Carthage[2] learned this, Licio, yet you doubt?
You live dangerously, Licio, persisting

In chasing shadows and holding to deceptions.
The hours will hardly forgive you your folly;
The hours, which are filing away at the days,
The days, which are gnawing away at the years.

Gongora, Spanish, 1561–1625, tr. I. M.

Primo Levi expresses frustration that our lack of sense will hasten our end unnecessarily.

✸ *Almanac*

They'll continue their flow to the sea, the indifferent rivers,
Overwhelming ancient dikes of tenacious men.
The glaciers will continue their grinding and smoothing,
Or crashing down to shorten the lives of firs.
The sea must continue to batter the lands that contain it,
More and more a skinflint with its riches.
Stars and comets continue on their courses;
Earth, too, obeys creation's immutable laws.
But we, rebellious offshoots, ingenious fools,
Destroy and corrupt, always in more of a hurry;
Spreading the desert to the forests of Amazon;
To the living hearts of our cities; to our very own hearts.

Primo Levi, Italian, 1919–87, version by I. M.

Baudelaire relishes mortality, since it mocks the pretensions of humanity that disgust him.

The Lid

Wherever he may go, on land or sea,
Under a climate of flame or a white sky,
Be he a servant of Jesus, or courtier of Venus,
A beggar lost in darkness or glittering Croesus,

City or country dweller, vagrant or in a chair,
Whether his little brain is active or slow—
Everywhere man submits to the terror of mystery,
And looks above him only with trembling eye.

Above him, the Heavens!—the wall of his stifling tomb,
A ceiling lit by a comic opera's glare
Where each buffoon stomps the blood-soaked earth;

Terror of the libertine, hope of the mad hermit;
The Sky! Blackened lid of the great stew-pot
Where humanity boils, imperceptible and vast!

Baudelaire, French, 1821–67, tr. I. M.

Wallowing in despair can make our own human destructiveness seem less bad; after all, if life in general is so terrible, how can we be otherwise? The reasonable voice of Goethe speaks out against this attitude.

 "It alarms me, the insidiousness
Of all this worthless talk
In which nothing lasts, all is fugitive
And what one sees is already gone;
And it entangles me, the fearsome

Gray-knit ensnaring net."—
Take comfort! What perishes not
Is the everlasting law, by which
Flourish and bloom the lily and the rose.

Goethe, German, 1749–1832, tr. I. M.

Macbeth, in Shakespeare's play, having ruined his personal prospects of survival, utters one of the great speeches of despair. It expresses an attitude fashionable in contemporary art and literature (as our own culture moves us close to self-destruction)—that life signifies nothing.

To-morrow, and to-morrow, and to-morrow,
Creeps in this petty pace from day to day,
To the last syllable of recorded time;
And all our yesterdays have lighted fools
The way to dusty death. Out, out, brief candle!
Life's but a walking shadow, a poor player,
That struts and frets his hour upon the stage,
And then is heard no more; it is a tale
Told by an idiot, full of sound and fury,
Signifying nothing.

William Shakespeare, English, 1564–1616, from Macbeth *5.5.19–28*

The next poem was written in the shadow of war. As civilized values collapse, a mythical beast, "vexed to nightmare" by the image of the gentle Christ child, makes its "second coming" in the town where Jesus was born.

✸ *The Second Coming*

Turning and turning in the widening gyre
The falcon cannot hear the falconer;
Things fall apart; the center cannot hold;
Mere anarchy is loosed upon the world,
The blood-dimmed tide is loosed, and everywhere
The ceremony of innocence is drowned;
The best lack all conviction, while the worst
Are full of passionate intensity.

Surely some revelation is at hand;
Surely the Second Coming is at hand.
The Second Coming! Hardly are those words out
When a vast image out of *Spiritus Mundi*[3]
Troubles my sight: somewhere in sands of the desert
A shape with lion body and the head of a man,
A gaze blank and pitiless as the sun,
Is moving its slow thighs, while all about it
Reel shadows of the indignant desert birds.
The darkness drops again; but now I know
That twenty centuries of stony sleep
Were vexed to nightmare by a rocking cradle,
And what rough beast, its hour come round at last,
Slouches towards Bethlehem to be born?

W. B. Yeats, Irish, 1865–1939

The beast in Yeats's poem can only be identified, in retrospect, with totalitarianism—which is ironic since Yeats himself was strongly attracted to the fascist version of total state control.

Edwin Muir, writing forty years later, identifies a different kind of beast, composed of the masters of commerce and their machines, whose betrayal of peace transforms "stout everyman" into an "ignorant clown."

✸ *Ballad of Everyman*

I.

Stout Everyman set out to meet
His brothers gathered from every land,
And make a peace for all the earth
And link the nations hand to hand.

He came into a splendid hall
And there he saw a motionless dove
Swung from the roof, but for the rest
Found little sign of peace or love.

Two days he listened patiently,
But on the third got up and swore:
"Nothing but slaves and masters here:
Your dove's a liar and a whore.

"Disguised police on the high seats,
In every corner pimps and spies.
Good-bye to you; I'd rather be
With friends in Hell or Paradise."

The great room turned to watch him go,
But oh the deadly silence then.

From that day brave Everyman
Was never seen by friend again.

2.
Night after night I dream a dream
That I am flying through the air
On some contraption old and lame
As Icarus' unlucky chair.

And first I see the empty fields—
No sign of Everyman anywhere—
And then I see a playing field
And two great sides in combat there.

And then they change into a beast
With iron hoofs and scourging tail
That treads a bloody harvest down
In readiness for the murdering flail.

And then a rash of staring eyes
Covers the beast, back, sides and head,
And stare as if remembering
Something that long ago was said.

And the beast is gone, and nothing's there
But murderers standing in a ring,
And at the center Everyman.
I never saw so poor a thing.

Curses upon the traitorous men
Who brought our good friend Everyman down,

And murder peace to bring their peace,
And flatter and rob the ignorant clown.

Edwin Muir, Scottish, 1887–1959

Though nature is "red in tooth and claw," there is nevertheless an innocent joy in most of nature's proceedings. To Wordsworth, our human species looks bad in comparison.

Lines Written in Early Spring

I heard a thousand blended notes
While in a grove I sat reclined
In that sweet mood when pleasant thoughts
Bring sad thoughts to the mind.

To her fair works did Nature link
The human soul that through me ran;
And much it grieved my heart to think
What man has made of man.

Through primrose tufts, in that green bower,
The periwinkle trailed its wreaths;
And 'tis my faith that every flower
Enjoys the air it breathes.

The birds around me hopped and played,
Their thoughts I cannot measure:—
But the least motion that they made,
It seemed a thrill of pleasure.

The budding twigs spread out their fan,
To catch the breezy air;
And I must think, do all I can,
That there was pleasure there.

If this belief from heaven be sent,
If such be Nature's holy plan,
Have I not reason to lament
What man has made of man?

William Wordsworth, English, 1770–1850

Tagore was nearly eighty when the Second World War began. Reading of the slaughter in the West, he despaired, almost wishing that his own species would suffer extinction for its crimes.

 When the god of death gave the command for annihilation,
men took on themselves the task of self-destruction.
Depressed, I've thought: why doesn't a sudden disaster
hit this errant planet which has veered from its course,
so we all die together, in one big blazing pyre?
But then I reflect: if through suffering on suffering
sin hasn't rotted, its seed will surely sleep
in the ashes of the holocaust, and on the breast
of a new creation
once more raise its thorns.

Tagore, Bengali, 1861–1941,
tr. Ketaki Kushari Dyson

Despair at the behavior of human toward human is an old subject for poetry. The poem that follows was written four thousand years ago. It is from "A Dispute over Suicide." A man is talking to his soul, arguing that it's right for him to end his own life.

To whom shall I speak today?
Brothers are evil,
The companions of yesterday do not love.
To whom shall I speak today?
Hearts are rapacious,
Every man seizes the goods of his neighbor.
To whom shall I speak today?
Men are contented with evil,
Goodness is neglected everywhere.
To whom shall I speak today?
One who should make a man enraged by his evil behavior
Makes everyone laugh, though his iniquity is grievous.
To whom shall I speak today?
The wrongdoer is an intimate,
The brother with whom one should act is become an enemy.
To whom shall I speak today?
Yesterday is not remembered,
No one now helps him that hath done good.
To whom shall I speak today?
Faces are averted,
Every man has his face downcast toward his brethren.
To whom shall I speak today?
Hearts are rapacious,
No man has a heart upon which one can rely.
To whom shall I speak today?

There are no righteous men.
The land is given over to workers of iniquity.
To whom shall I speak today?
I am laden with misery
Through lack of an intimate.
To whom shall I speak today?
The sin that roams the land,
It has no end.
Death is in my sight today,
Like the recovery of a sick man,
Like going abroad after detention.
Death is in my sight today
Like the smell of myrrh,
Like sitting under an awning on a windy day.
Death is in my sight today
Like the scent of lotus flowers,
Like sitting on the bank of drunkenness.
Death is in my sight today
Like a well-trodden path,
As when a man returns home from an expedition.
Death is in my sight today
Like the clearing of the sky,
Like a man attracted thereby to what he knows not.
Death is in my sight today
Like the longing of a man to see home,
When he has spent many years held in captivity.
Surely he who is yonder shall
Be a living god,
Punishing the sin of him who commits it.

Surely he who is yonder shall
Stand in the barque of the sun,
Causing the choicest things to be given therefrom to the
    temples.
Surely he who is yonder shall
Be a man of knowledge,
Who cannot be prevented from petitioning Re when he
    speaks.
(*The Soul replies*)
Put care aside, my comrade and brother. Make an offering
    on the brazier and cling to life. Desire me here and
    reject the West,[4] but desire to reach the West when
    the body goes into the earth, that I may alight when
    you grow weary. Then let us make an abode together.

Anonymous, Old Egyptian, circa 2000 B.C., tr. T. W. Thacker

The soul at the end of the last poem seems to be saying, Don't hurry things, death will come to you soon enough.

Despair at humanity's treatment of nature is a newer phenomenon than despair at "what man has made of man." In the next poem, Judith Wright praises the justice that if we kill nature, we ourselves must die.

✸ *Australia 1970*

Die, wild country, like the eaglehawk,
dangerous till the last breath's gone,
clawing and striking. Die
cursing your captor through a raging eye.

Die like the tigersnake
that hisses such pure hatred from its pain
as fills the killer's dreams
with fear like suicide's invading stain.

Suffer, wild country, like the ironwood
that gaps the 'dozer-blade.
I see your living soil ebb with the tree
to naked poverty.

Die like the soldier-ant
mindless and faithful to your million years.
Though we corrupt you with our torturing mind,
stay obstinate; stay blind.

For we are conquerors and self-poisoners
more than scorpion or snake
and dying of the venoms that we make
even while you die of us.

I praise the scoring drought, the flying dust,
the drying creek, the furious animal,
that they oppose us still;
that we are ruined by the thing we kill.

Judith Wright, Australian, born 1915

A recent theory suggested that dinosaurs became extinct as a result of their flatulence, which created massive global warming. Our mechanical and chemical flatulences are well on the way to doing the same for us.

born like this
into this
as the chalk faces smile
as Mrs. Death laughs
as the elevators break
as political landscapes dissolve
as the supermarket bag boy holds a college degree
as the oily fish spit out their oily prey
as the sun is masked

we are
born like this
into this
into these carefully mad wars
into the sight of broken factory windows of emptiness
into bars where people no longer speak to each other
into fist fights that end as shootings and knifings

born into this
into hospitals which are so expensive that it's cheaper to die
into lawyers who charge so much it's cheaper to plead guilty
into a country where the jails are full and the madhouses
    closed
into a place where the masses elevate fools into rich heroes

born into this
walking and living through this
dying because of this
muted because of this

castrated
debauched
disinherited
because of this
fooled by this
used by this
pissed on by this
made crazy and sick by this
made violent
made inhuman
by this

the heart is blackened
the fingers reach for the throat
the gun
the knife
the bomb
the fingers reach toward an unresponsive god

the fingers reach for the bottle
the pill
the powder

we are born into this sorrowful deadliness
we are born into a government 60 years in debt
that soon will be unable even to pay the interest on that debt
and the banks will burn
money will be useless
there will be open and unpunished murder on the streets
it will be guns and roving mobs
land will be useless

food will become a diminishing return
nuclear power will be taken over by the many
explosions will continually shake the earth
radiated robot men will stalk each other
the rich and the chosen will watch from space platforms
Dante's Inferno will be made to look like a children's
      playground

the sun will not be seen and it will always be night
trees will die
all vegetation will die
radiated men will eat the flesh of radiated men
the sea will be poisoned
the lakes and rivers will vanish
rain will be the new gold

the rotting bodies of men and animals will stink in the dark
      wind
the last few survivors will be overtaken by new and hideous
      diseases
and the space platforms will be destroyed by attrition
the petering out of supplies
the natural effect of general decay

and there will be the most beautiful silence never heard

born out of that.

the sun still hidden there

awaiting the next chapter.

Charles Bukowski, American, born 1920

Most people now live in towns and cities. They need have little awareness of the creeping death that is stifling the planet. In fact, many who live in the country manage to insulate themselves from such knowledge.

 ### *The Fish Are All Sick*

The fish are all sick, the great whales dead,
the villages stranded in stone on the coast,
ornamental, like pearls on the fringe of a coat.
Sea men, who knew what the ocean did,
turned their low houses away from the surf.
But new men, who come to be rural and safe,
add big glass views and begonia beds.

Water keeps to itself.
White lip after lip
curls to a close on the littered beach.
Something is sicker and blacker than fish.
And closing its grip, and closing its grip.

Anne Stevenson, English, born 1933

Western scientists, observing the slowness of some races to pick up and manage the new technology, deem them less intelligent. But this lesser intelligence begins to seem the greater, as our pursuit of mercurial inventiveness brings disaster on the world.

But only disaster seems to focus the mind of Homo sapiens on its limitations. In the next poem, Edwin Muir finds hope in looking beyond catastrophe.

Barely a twelvemonth after
The seven days war that put the world to sleep,
Late in the evening the strange horses came.
By then we had made our covenant with silence,
But in the first few days it was so still
We listened to our breathing and were afraid.
On the second day
The radios failed; we turned the knobs; no answer.
On the third day a warship passed us, heading north,
Dead bodies piled on the deck. On the sixth day
A plane plunged over us into the sea. Thereafter
Nothing. The radios dumb;
And still they stand in corners of our kitchens,
And stand, perhaps, turned on, in a million rooms
All over the world. But now if they should speak,
If on a sudden they should speak again,
If on the stroke of noon a voice should speak,
We would not listen, we would not let it bring
That old bad world that swallowed its children quick
At one great gulp. We would not have it again.
Sometimes we think of the nations lying asleep,
Curled blindly in impenetrable sorrow,
And then the thought confounds us with its strangeness.
The tractors lie about our fields; at evening
They look like dank sea-monsters couched and waiting.
We leave them where they are and let them rust;
"They'll molder away and be like other loam."

We make our oxen drag our rusty plows,
Long laid aside. We have gone back
Far past our fathers' land.
And then, that evening,
Late in the summer the strange horses came.
We heard a distant tapping on the road,
A deepening drumming; it stopped, went on again
And at the corner changed to hollow thunder.
We saw the heads
Like a wild wave charging and were afraid.
We had sold our horses in our fathers' time
To buy new tractors. Now they were strange to us
As fabulous steeds set on an ancient shield
Or illustrations in a book of knights.
We did not dare go near them. Yet they waited,
Stubborn and shy, as if they had been sent
By an old command to find our whereabouts
And that long-lost archaic companionship.
In the first moment we had never a thought
That they were creatures to be owned and used.
Among them were some half a dozen colts
Dropped in some wilderness of the broken world,
Yet new as if they had come from their own Eden.
Since then they have pulled our plows and borne our loads
But that free servitude still can pierce our hearts.
Our life is changed; their coming our beginning.

Edwin Muir, Scottish, 1887–1959

Pao Chao's view is different. Nature's rule is harsh, and we must work hard, in-
telligently, and in an orderly fashion to establish our dominion within it.

✸ *The Ruined City*

The immense plain
runs south to the foamy waves of the sea
and north to the purple passes of the Great Wall.
In it
canals are cut through the valleys;
And rivers and roads
lead to every corner.

In its golden past,
axles of chariots and carts
often rubbed against each other
like men's shoulders.
Shops and houses stood row upon row
And laughter and songs rose up from them.
Glittering and white were the salt fields;
Gloomy and blue were the copper mines.
Wealth and talents
And cavalry and infantry
Reinforced the strict and elaborate
Regulations and laws.
Winding moats and lofty walls
Were dug and built, to ensure
That prosperity would long endure.
People were busy working
On palaces and battlements

And ships and beacon stations
Up and down, far and wide
At all places.
Magnets[5] were installed at mountain passes;
Red lacquer was applied to doors and gates.
The strongholds and fortresses
would see to it
That for a myriad generations
the family's rule should last.
But after five centuries or three dynasties
The land was divided like a melon
Or shared like beans.

Duckweed flourishes in the wells
And brambles block the roads.
Skunks and snakes dwell on sacred altars
While muskdeer and squirrels quarrel on marble steps.
In rain and wind,
Wood elves, mountain ghosts,
Wild rats, and foxes
yawp and scream from dusk to dawn.
Hungry hawks grind their beaks
As cold owls frighten the chicks in their nests.
Tigers and leopards hide and wait
for a drink of blood
and a feast of flesh.
Fallen tree trunks lie lifelessly across
Those once-busy highways.
Aspens have long ceased to rustle

And grass dies yellow
In this harsh frosty air
Which grows into a cruelly cold wind.
A solitary reed shakes and twists,
And grains of sand, like startled birds,
are looking for a safe place to settle.
Bushes and creepers, confused and tangled,
seem to know no boundaries.
They pull down walls
And fill up moats.
And beyond a thousand miles
Only brown dust flies.
Deep in my thoughts, I sit down and listen
To this awesome silence.

Behind the painted doors and embroidered curtains
There used to be music and dancing.
Hunting and fishing parties were held
In the emerald forests or beside the marble pools.
The melodies from various states
And works of art and rare fish and horses
Are all now dead and buried.
The young girls from east and south
Smooth as silk, fragrant as orchids,
White as jade with their lips red,
Now lie beneath the dreary stones and barren earth.

The greatest displeasure of the largest number
Is the law of nature.
For this ruined city,

I play the lute and sing:
"As the north wind hurries on,
the battlements freeze.
They tower over the plain
where there are neither roads nor field paths.
For a thousand years and a myriad generations,
I shall watch you to the end in silence."

Pao Chao, Chinese, 414–66, tr. Jerome Ch'en and Michael Bullock

An old children's story tells of a goose that lays golden eggs. The greedy owner wants more eggs and disembowels it, ending the supply of eggs forever.

What can we do, as individuals, to avoid feeling overwhelmed by the stupidity of our species? We can strive to understand. We can attempt to put into practice more life-sustaining values. We can use our votes to protest against the slaughter of the goose that lays the golden eggs. Meanwhile, we have to live and create our lives as best we can, in a civilization for which we bear limited responsibility and over which we can have limited influence.

In the next poem, the black poet Gwendolyn Brooks reminds younger blacks, protesters against the evil of racism, that life is not just a battleground; it is also there to be lived.

 ## *Speech to the Young.*
Speech to the Progress-Toward.

Say to them,
say to the down-keepers,
the sun-slappers,
the self-soilers,
the harmony-hushers,

"Even if you are not ready for day
it cannot always be night."
You will be right.
For that is the hard home-run.

And remember:
live not for Battles Won.
Live not for The-End-of-the-Song.
Live in the along.

Gwendolyn Brooks, American, born 1917

Those who "live in the along" are apt to value life. They can be trusted more than those who live for "Battles Won," who are all too ready to sacrifice their fellow human beings for Ends-That-Justify-the-Means.

The poet of the next poem protested against injustice in his own country (Turkey) and took refuge in another country (Russia), where even greater injustice was on the rampage.

Whatever the future holds and whatever mistakes we make, while there is life there is joy to be found.

 A Fable

Resting by the waterside
the plane tree and I.
Our reflections are thrown on the water
the plane tree's and mine.
The sparkle of the water hits us
the plane tree and me.

Resting by the waterside
the plane tree, I, and the cat.
Our reflections are thrown on the water
the plane tree's, mine, and the cat's.
The sparkle of the water hits us
the plane tree, me, and the cat.

Resting by the waterside
the plane tree, I, the cat, and the sun.
Our reflections are thrown on the water
the plane tree's, mine, the cat's, and the sun's.
The sparkle of the water hits us
the plane tree, me, the cat, and the sun.

Resting by the waterside
the plane tree, I, the cat, the sun, and our life.
Our reflections are thrown on the water
the plane tree's, mine, the cat's, the sun's, and our life's.
The sparkle of the water hits us
the plane tree, me, the cat, the sun, and our life.

Resting by the waterside.

First the cat will go
its reflection will be lost on the water.
Then I will go
my reflection will be lost on the water.
Then the plane tree will go
its reflection will be lost on the water.
Then the water will go

the sun will remain
then it will go too.

Resting by the waterside
the plane tree, I, the cat, the sun, and our life.
The water is cool
the plane tree spreading
I am writing a poem
the sun is warm
it's great to be alive.
The sparkle of the water hits us
the plane tree, me, the cat, the sun, and our life.

Nazim Hikmet, Turkish, 1902–1963, tr. Richard McKane

Concerning innocence and the value of a clear conscience, the poet Muriel Rukeyser relates a vision of Saint Fursey, taken up into the sky by angels.[6]

 Saint Fursey on high, and earth far below him a dark valley. Despair, gloom on earth, and around him in the air four streaming flames, fires kindled separate in the four directions.

> One to burn the souls of those forsworn and
>   untruthful.
> Two, to burn those given up to greed.
> Three, those who stir up strife and discord.
> Four, those who find it no crime to deceive the
>   helpless.

Then the fires swept together; they coalesced, and threatened him. Fursey cried out. A voice answered him; the angel said, "That which you did not kindle shall not burn within you." Fursey drew breath, and a great voice could be heard, saying,

> *Respice mundum.*
> RESPECT THE WORLD.

Epilogue

Looking back in time, civilizations seem, like organisms, to have lived their lives and then died. But the longevity of civilizations is not predetermined. Conceivably our own might last till the sun explodes and the planet boils—or even longer, if by then we are colonizers of space. Alternatively, it may collapse soon, as our wasteful habits damage the living world of which we are a part.

The three motors speeding us toward ecological disaster are ever higher expectations of consumption, population growth, and economics driven by waste. Legislation to protect the environment is an inadequate brake against the power of these three motors.

A high tax on energy would change the economic climate in significant ways. Unemployment would be less, for the simple reason that human beings would be more competitive with machines. No longer would we need to increase our consumption relentlessly in order to maintain a demand for jobs. No longer would goods be made to perish in as short a time as the manufacturers can get away with. Waste would become manageable, and recycling more economically viable.

Such a tax would also allow us to share in the bonanza of cheap energy, which is now fought over (by governments and corporations) like the treasure of the Sierra Madre.

Population growth has slowed or stopped in the richer countries. A more shared affluence and a higher status for women are already curtailing population growth in some of the poorer countries where these developments are taking place.

Perhaps when we've forgotten our obligation to get and spend, we will remember the pleasure to be had in what's free and all around us (except where we've destroyed it)—the pleasures of the natural world as celebrated by poets rather than by market makers.

Is it just *human* nature or is it in the nature of life itself to be wise only after the event? Memory of disaster is a source of wisdom, whether for a tree deciding when to flower or for humans learning restraint. Such ecological wisdom as we have now acquired comes only after much destruction. The question is not "Will there be a disaster?" but "How acute and all-embracing will the disaster become?"

To understand the sometimes unpalatable story of how we came to make such a mess, we need a much greater understanding of our own human species—an understanding that is not colored by the illusions that we love to believe and that politicians find it profitable to encourage. We have no divine rights over creation; technology and progress are not our guardian angels; indulgence in society does not create decent behavior in its citizens. Right now, we seem to show greater intelligence and better intentions as individuals than as nations or as a species.

We assume dinosaurs weren't intelligent enough to avoid their fate. We know we are intelligent enough to alter ours; it's a question of when and how we choose to use our intelligence.

Notes

Introduction

1. For the story of how the famous speech was altered through several versions, see *How Can One Sell the Air: Chief Seattle's Vision,* published by The Book Publishing Company, P.O. Box 99, Summertown, TN 38483.

2. C. D. Darlington, *The Little Universe of Man* (London: Allen and Unwin, 1969), 133.

Chapter 1

1. Land was nationalized and turned over to collectives.

Chapter 2

1. *Nightingales* is assumed to be the title of a collection of poems. Only one of Heraclitus's poems is still "awake."

2. "I have had times when girls enough . . ."

3. "I am not as I was, under the reign of the good Cynara."

4. If.

5. Found a set of erect equipment.

6. Know.

7. Own.

8. Self.

9. What if a.

10. Daren't admit.

11. Flame.

12. An earlier Chinese poet.

Chapter 3

1. Wildfowl.

2. Make me bleed.

3. Places holy to the Hindus.

4. "The great extent of time when I shall no longer be alive moves me more than this paltry span."

5. Weeds.

6. The three ages are past, present, and future. The three worlds are desire, form, and formlessness. The last line is a quote from a famous poem of farewell, written when a monk was setting off on the long journey from China back to India where Buddhism began. Chang-an was the capital of China.

Chapter 4

1. W. H. Auden, "Thank You, Fog," in *Complete Poems* (London: Faber and Faber, 1976).

2. "Sweet it is and fitting."

3. "Sweet it is and fitting to die for one's country."

4. "Forget-me-not."

5. "May this omen keep its distance."

Chapter 5

1. The motorcar.

2. Pillage.

3. The god of fire.

4. A sea nymph, Achilles's mother.

5. Priapus was cursed with a permanent erection.

6. The isthmus of Panama, between Central and South America.

7. To bless them.

Chapter 6

1. Poet's note: "The Taung child is a fossil, a juvenile *Australopithecus africanus*, from Taung, South Africa, two million years old."

2. The Greek word for making a city was *synoecism*, meaning the bringing together of different peoples.

3. See, for instance, J. K. Galbraith, *The Culture of Contentment* (New York: Houghton Mifflin, 1992), 150–151.

4. From an interview with Linda Hogan in Joseph Bruchac, *Survival This Way: Interviews with Native American Writers* (Tucson: Sun Tracks and Univ. of Arizona Press, 1987).

5. From the liner notes for *The Fire This Time,* In & Out Records, Freiburg, Germany, 1992.

6. In other words, acorns and honesty both must thrive: acorns grow into mighty oaks; honesty and justice put a check on growth that bears no fruit.

7. *King Lear* 5.3.172–73: "The gods are just, and of our pleasant vices make instruments to plague us."

8. Sara Whyatt, Interview of Taslima Nasreen, *Index on Censorship,* vol. 23, no. 4/5. April 5, 1994, pp. 202ff.

Chapter 7

1. "Little Queenie."

2. The dried-up stems of weeds.

3. One who fights against God.

4. "House kills tree."

5. A swan.
6. A bookworm.

Chapter 8

1. Marija Gimbutas, *Goddesses and Gods of Old Europe* (London: Thames and Hudson, 1982); *The Civilization of the Goddess* (San Francisco: HarperSanFrancisco, 1991).
2. C. D. Darlington, *The Evolution of Man and Society* (London: Allen and Unwin, 1969), 56.
3. Pet ape.
4. A metaphor for the Way, the order of spontaneous change that governs the universe.
5. Darlington, *Evolution of Man and Society,* 56.
6. Nine verses out of seventeen.
7. A train of slaves chained together.

Chapter 9

1. Translator's note: "A species of curlew or heron, the Ardea Jaculator."
2. Benedict Arnold was an infamous traitor who, during the American War for Independence, attempted to hand over his garrison to the British.
3. Written May 1901.
4. In 1921 Gabriele D'Annunzio invaded the disputed port of Fiume with some Nationalist friends, and he ruled it for sixteen months as fascist leader.
5. The north wind.
6. J. K. Stephen made the accusation in a sonnet titled "Lapsus Calami."
7. Mine labor recruits.
8. Johannesburg.
9. Simone Weil, *Simone Weil: An Anthology,* ed. Sian Miles (London: Virago Press, 1986), 180.

Chapter 10

1. A type of fish.
2. A city destroyed by Rome in 146 A.D.
3. The term means "spirit of the world" and is used by Yeats to represent a kind of corporate imagination, similar to Jung's collective unconscious.
4. In the West is the land of the dead.
5. To attract enemy arrows.
6. Muriel Rukeyser, *The Orgy* (London: Andre Deutsch, 1965), 134.

Index by Title or First Line

Index by Poet

*Denotes woman poet.

Permissions Acknowledgments

The following books were particularly influential in the forming of the ideas contained in the prose linking the poems:

C. D. Darlington, *The Evolution of Man and Society* (London: George Allen & Unwin, 1969).

Nadezhda Mandelstam, *Hope Against Hope* (New York: Atheneum, 1970); *Hope Abandoned* (New York: Atheneum, 1974).

Acknowledgment is due to all the copyright holders of the poems included in this book. In each case, the editor has tried to contact the copyright holder. The publishers and the editor apologize where material has been used without permission and would be glad to hear from copyright holders who have not been consulted.

Translations and versions by Ivo Mosley (I. M.) are copyright 1993 by Ivo Mosley. Translations by I. M. from Hitomaro first appeared in *Dublin Magazine,* 1973, issue 2.

For the reader's easy reference, books are listed by name of poet in alphabetical order.

"Untitled (him to her)" by Ron Adler is reprinted from *Lines Cut: Posthumous Poems of Four Young Israelis,* ed. A. Zehavi. Hakibbutz Hameuchad Publishing House and The Institute for the Translation of Hebrew Literature Ltd., 1981.

"Lament" and "Prayer" by Endre Ady, tr. F. Marnau and M. Hamburger, are reprinted, by kind permission of Michael Hamburger, from *New Road 1944,* ed. Alex Comfort and John Bayliss.

"Solitary Pleasures" by Tachibana Akemi is reprinted from *An Anthology of Japanese Literature,* ed. Donald Keene. Penguin Classics, 1968.

"After the wind and the frost," "Lot's Wife," "Everything has been plundered, betrayed, sold out . . . ," "Instead of a Preface," and Epilogues 1 and 2 from "Requiem" by Anna Akhmatova are translated by Judith Hemschemeyer and are reprinted from *The Complete Poems of Anna Akhmatova* (2nd edition, 1992) with the permission of Zephyr Press. Translations copyright 1990, 1992 by Judith Hemschemeyer.

"A Voiced Lament" by Gulten Akin is reprinted from *The Penguin Book of Turkish Verse,* ed. N. Menemencioglu, 1978.

Five lines from "The Word" by N. Gumilev are quoted from p. 117 of *Osip Mandelstam: The Collected Critical Prose and Letters,* ed. Jane Grey Harris. Collins Harvill, 1991.

"The dawn is breaking . . ." and "I went into the garden . . ." are reprinted from *Hafiz of Shiraz: Thirty Poems,* tr. Peter Avery and John Heath-Stubbs. John Murray (Publishers), 1952.

"In a tangle of cliffs I chose a place" by Han Shan is reprinted from *Riprap and Cold Mountain Poems* by Gary Snyder. Four Seasons Foundation, San Francisco, 1969. Reprinted by permission of Gary Snyder. "Life on Cold Mountain" and "Man, living in the dust . . ." are reprinted from *Cold Mountain: One Hundred Poems by the T'ang Poet Han Shan* by Burton Watson. Published by Jonathan Cape, 1970.

"Anchorage" is reprinted from *She Had Some Horses* by Joy Harjo. Thunder's Mouth Press, 1983.

"Threshold," "Andante," and "The Secret Life of Frogs" are reprinted by permission of Oxford University Press from *Collected Poems* by Gwen Harwood. Copyright Gwen Harwood, 1991.

"Earwig" is reprinted from *Selected Poems* by John Heath-Stubbs. Carcanet Press 1990.

"A Fable" by Nazim Hikmet is reprinted from *The Penguin Book of Turkish Verse,* ed. N. Menemencioglu, 1978.

"manifest destiny" is reprinted from *No Complaints* by Anselm Hollo. Toothpaste Press 1983.

"The Fly" is reprinted by permission of Bloodaxe Books from *The Fly* by Miroslav Holub, tr. Ewald Osers, George Theiner, and Jarmila Milner. Bloodaxe Books, 1987.

The excerpt from *The Iliad* is reprinted from *The Iliad of Homer,* tr. Ennis Rees. Oxford University Press, New York, 1991.

"Harlem" is reprinted from *The Panther and the Lash* by Langston Hughes by permission of Alfred A. Knopf, Inc. Copyright 1951 by Langston Hughes.

"The Sound of Leaves" by Razia Hussain, translated by Chitra Divakarumi, is reprinted from *Blood into Ink,* edited by Miriam Cooke and Roshni Rustomji-Kerns. Westview Press, 1994.

"If only I could live" by Higuchi Ichiyo is reprinted from *In the Shade of Spring Leaves* by Robert Lyons Danly, 1992. W. W. Norton Co., Inc., 1992.

"Father" by Margit Kaffka, tr. Laura Schiff, is reprinted from *The Penguin Book of Women Poets,* ed. Carol Cosman, Joan Keefe, and Kathleen Weaver, 1973. Copyright Artisjus, Budapest.

"The old woman's shoulders" by Kakkaipatiniyar Naccellaiyar is reprinted from *Poems of Love and War,* by A. K. Ramanujan. Copyright Columbia University Press, New York, 1985. Reprinted with the permission of the publisher.

"Shantytown" by Orhan Veli Kanik is reprinted from *The Penguin Book of Turkish Verse,* ed. N. Menemencioglu, 1978.

"Peace" is reprinted from *Patrick Kavanagh: The Complete Poems.* The Goldsmith Press, 1992.

"The Distinct Impression," "Open Your Hearts," "Words," "Whenever That Happened," and "Money in Love" are reprinted by permission of Bloodaxe Books from *The Book of Judas* by Brendan Kennelly (Bloodaxe Books, 1991). "The Pig" and "Willow" are reprinted by permission of Bloodaxe Books from *A Time for Voices* by Brendan Kennelly (Bloodaxe Books, 1990).

"The Dead Shall Be Raised Incorruptible," Part Four, is reprinted from *The Book of Nightmares* by Galway Kinnell, 1971.

Poem no. 1 from the cycle *Destruction* by N. Kluyev is reprinted from *Index on Censorship*, vol. 20, no. 8, 1991.

"Where the Lilies Were in Flower" by Kumattur Kannanar is reprinted from *Poems of Love and War* by A. K. Ramanujan. Copyright Columbia University Press, New York, 1985. Reprinted with the permission of the publisher.

"To a Young Man Driving His Own Car" is reprinted from *Faint Shadows of Love: Poems by Kwang-Kyu Kim,* tr. Brother Anthony of Taize. Forest Books, 20 Forest View, Chingford, London, England.

"They Came Looking for You" by Abdellatif Laabi is reprinted from *Index on Censorship*, vol. 11, no. 1, p. 22, 1982.

"There is a thing confusedly formed" is reprinted from *Tao Te Ching* by Lao Tzu, tr. D. C. Lau. Penguin Books, 1963.

"Testament" by Alda Lara is reprinted from *A Horse of White Clouds: Poems from Lusophone Africa,* tr. Don Burness. Ohio University Press, 1989.

"Sparrows" by Mani Leib is reprinted from *A Treasury of Yiddish Poetry,* ed. Irving Howe and Eliezer Greenberg. Schocken Books, 1976.

"Fighting South of the Ramparts" is reprinted from *The Poetry and Career of Li Po* by Arthur Waley; Allen and Unwin, 1950. "To Tu Fu" by Li Po is reprinted from *The White Pony,* ed. Robert Payne, 1947. "To His Wife" by Li Po is reprinted from *Love and Protest: Chinese Poems from the Sixth Century B.C. to the Seventeenth Century A.D.* by John Scott. Andre Deutsch, 1972.

"Light Rain on the Road to Sword Gate" by Lu Yu is reprinted from *Heaven My Blanket, Earth My Pillow: Poems by Yang Wan-Li,* intr. and tr. Jonathan Chaves. John Weatherhill, Publishers, 1975.

"The Motoka" by Theo Luzuka is reprinted from *Poems of Black Africa,* ed. Wole Soyinka, Heinemann International, 1975, and was first published in the magazine *Dhana.*

"The oddest event in life," "If she believes or wears a cross," "I see mankind under two lights," "They say the soul's ferried," "God help us, we have sold our souls," "We laughed; our laughing betrayed scorn," "You said we've a wise creator," and "If the intellect is unstable" by Ma'arri are reprinted from *Birds Through a Ceiling of Alabaster: Three Abassid Poets,* tr. G. B. H. Wightman and A. Y. al-Udhari. Penguin Books, 1975.

"The Sun Parrots Are Late This Year" is reprinted from *Essequibo* by Ian McDonald. Story Line Press, 1992.

"A Bottomlands Farmer Suffers a Sea Change" is reprinted from *Towns Facing Railroads* by Jo McDougall. The University of Arkansas Press, 1991.

"Other men are thorn" by Mahadevi is reprinted from *Speaking of Siva,* tr. A. K. Ramanujan. Penguin Books, 1973.

"I sing when my throat is wet, my soul is dry . . . ," "Still I have not died . . . ," and "Into the distance go the mounds of people's heads" are reprinted from *Osip Mandel'shtam: Selected Poems,* tr. David McDuff. Writers and Readers Publishing Cooperative Society Ltd., 1983.

"Now I must mend my manners" by Marbod of Rennes is reprinted from *More Latin Lyrics* by Helen Waddell. Victor Gollancz, London, 1980. Copyright Dame Felicitas Corrigan.

"The Man Who Encountered a Bear" and "Snares" are reprinted from *Self-Righting Lamp: Selected Poems by Maruyama Kaoru*, tr. Robert Epp. Copyright Robert Epp and Katydid Books, 1992, 1994.

"Ms." by Janice Mirikitani is reprinted from *The Hawk's Well: A Collection of Japanese American Art and Literature*, ed. Hiura. Asian American Arts Projects, 1986.

"Amagoduka at Glencoe Station" by Oswald Mbuyiseni Mtshali is reprinted from *Poems of Black Africa*, ed. Wole Soyinka. Heinemann International, 1975.

"One Foot in Eden" and "The Horses" are reprinted from *Edwin Muir: Collected Poems*. Faber and Faber, 1960.

"Moving fast, a girl came to me one night" by Mut'azz is reprinted from *Birds Through a Ceiling of Alabaster: Three Abassid Poets*, tr. G. B. H. Wightman and A. Y. al-Udhari. Penguin Books, 1975.

"Panic" by Behcet Necatigil is reprinted from *The Penguin Book of Turkish Verse*, ed. N. Menemencioglu, 1978.

"The Unhappy Race" and "Time Is Running Out" by Oodgeroo Noonuccal are reprinted from *Inside Black Australia*, ed. Kevin Gilbert. Penguin Books Australia Ltd., 1988.

"The Ruined City" by Pao Chao is reprinted from *Poems of Solitude* by Jerome Ch'en and Michael Bullock. Abelard-Schuman, 1960.

"The Roman was the victor of the world" by Petronius is reprinted from *More Latin Lyrics* by Helen Waddell. Victor Gollancz, London, 1980. Copyright Dame Felicitas Corrigan.

"In My Black Book" by Frank Polite is reprinted from *A New Geography of Poets*, compiled and edited by Edward Field, Gerald Locklin, and Charles Stetler. The University of Arkansas Press, Fayetteville, 1992. Reprinted with the permission of City Miner Books, Berkeley, CA.

Praxilla's fragment "Adonis Dying," tr. John Dillon, is reprinted from *The Penguin Book of Women Poets*, ed. Cosman, Keefe, and Weaver, 1973.

"Eyes open wide, the poet weaves . . ." and "No, I don't miss the dissipated nights . . ." are reprinted from *Pushkin: The Bronze Horseman and Other Poems*, tr. D. M. Thomas. Martin Secker and Warburg, 1982.

"O God, whenever . . ." is reprinted from *Doorkeeper of the Heart: Versions of Rabi'a*, tr. Charles Upton. Threshold Books, RD4, Box 600, Putney, VT 05346.

"Untitled (Today I feel bearish . . .)" is reprinted from *A Secretary to the Spirits* by Ishmael Reed. NOK Publishers International, 1978. "Dialog Outside a Lakeside Grocery" by Ishmael Reed is reprinted from *Up Late*, ed. Codrescu. Four Walls Eight Windows, 1989.

"The Pan, the Pot, the Burning Fire I Have in Front of Me" by Ishigaki Rin is reprinted from *From the Country of Eight Islands*, ed. and tr. Hiroaki Sato and Burton Watson. Anchor Press/Doubleday, 1981.

"At Sangre Grande" and "I Say It Was the Women" are reprinted from *The Flowering Rock: Collected Poems 1938–1974* by E. M. Roach. Peepal Tree, 1992.

"African Village Women" by Lucinda Roy is reprinted from *Wailing the Dead to Sleep* by Lucinda Roy. Bogle L'Ouverture Publications, 1988.

"In the month of June the grass grows high," "Drinking Wine 1 and 2" by Tao Ch'ien are reprinted from *Chinese Poems* by Arthur Waley; Allen and Unwin 1961.

My version of Tchernikhovsky's "Behold, O Earth" is an adaptation of Hilda Auerbach's translation in *An Anthology of Modern Hebrew Poetry*, ed. Abraham Birman. Abelard-Schuman, 1968.

"Poem of Sorrow" by Tsai Yen is reprinted by permission of Oxford University Press from *An Anthology of Chinese Verse*, tr. J. D. Frodsham and Ch'eng Hsi (1967). Copyright Oxford University Press.

"Trees" by Marina Tsvetayeva is reprinted from *A Life Through Poetry: Marina Tsvetayeva's Lyric Diary* by Jane A. Taubman. Slavica Publishers, 1989.

"A Little Primer of Tu Fu" by David Hawkes, Oxford University Press, 1967—a wonderful book—was indispensable to me in making English versions of "Dreaming of Li Po" and "Thinking of My Brothers on a Moonlit Night." "The Rain at Night" by Tu Fu is reprinted from *The White Pony*, ed. Robert Payne, 1947.

"Letter from the Bird Community to the Mayor" and "Little Girl" by Usman Awang are reprinted from *The Puppeteer's Wayang*, ed. and intr. Muhammad Haji Salleh. In Print Publishing and Dewan Bahasa dan Pustaka Malaysia, 1992.

The Prologue to the *Ramayana* is from *The Ramayana of Valmiki*, transcreated by P. Lal. Tarang Paperbacks, 1989.

"The Man Who Loved Islands" is reprinted from *Collected Poems 1948–1984* by Derek Walcott. Faber and Faber, 3 Queen Square, London WC1N 3AU. Copyright Derek Walcott.

"Homage to JC" by Maureen Watson is reprinted from *Inside Black Australia*, ed. Kevin Gilbert. Penguin Books Australia Ltd., 1988.

". . . and Mr. Ferritt," "Australia 1970," "Builders," "Encounter," "Eve to Her Daughters," "Lament for Passenger Pigeons," "The Flame-Tree Blooms," "The Wattle-Tree," "To Hafiz of Shiraz," and "Victims" are reprinted from *Collected Poems 1942–1970* by Judith Wright. Angus and Robertson, 1971.

"Third Day of the Third Month, Rain: Written to Dispel My Depression" by Yang Wan-Li is reprinted from *Heaven My Blanket, Earth My Pillow: Poems by Yang Wan-Li*, intr. and tr. Jonathan Chaves. John Weatherhill, Publishers, 1975.

"On a Visit to Ch'ung Chen Temple . . ." by Yu Hsuan-Chi is reprinted from *The Orchid Boat: Women Poets of China*, tr. and ed. Kenneth Rexroth and Ling Chung. The Seabury Press, Inc., 1972.